RACE DIFFERENCES
IN ETHNOCENTRISM

EDWARD DUTTON

RACE DIFFERENCES IN ETHNOCENTRISM

ARKTOS
LONDON 2019

Copyright © 2019 by Arktos Media Ltd.

All rights reserved. No part of this book may be reproduced or utilised in any form or by any means (whether electronic or mechanical), including photocopying, recording or by any information storage and retrieval system, without permission in writing from the publisher.

ISBN	978-1-912975-05-1 (Paperback)
	978-1-912975-25-9 (Hardback)
	978-1-912975-06-8 (Ebook)
EDITOR	Elliot Tardif
COVER & LAYOUT	Tor Westman

Arktos.com   fb.com/Arktos   @arktosmedia   arktosmedia

Contents

About the Author ix

Acknowledgements x

CHAPTER ONE

'At Least They Hear the Things I Hear...' 1

    1. Introduction 1

    2. Previous Studies of Ethnocentrism 5

    3. Historical Observation of Differences in Ethnocentrism. 6

    4. Outline. 10

CHAPTER TWO

What Is 'Race'? 15

    1. Introduction 15

    2. What Is Race?. 16

    3. Taxonomies of Races. 19

    4. Criticisms of the Concept of Race 28

    6. Conclusion 33

CHAPTER THREE

What Is Intelligence? 35

    1. Introduction 35

    2. What Is Intelligence? 35

    3. Race Differences in Intelligence 40

    4. Criticisms of Race and IQ Data 42

    5. Conclusion 46

CHAPTER FOUR

What Are 'Ethnocentrism' and 'Ethnicity'? 47

    1. Introduction 47

    2. What Is Ethnocentrism? 47

3. Lexical Definitions of Ethnicity 49
4. Constructivism 50
5. Primordialism 60
6. The Sociobiological School. 62
7. Criticisms of the Sociobiological School 69
8. What Causes Ethnocentrism? 77
9. Conclusion 81

CHAPTER FIVE
Evidence for Genetic Similarity Theory   83

1. Introduction 83
2. Genetic Similarity Theory. 83
3. Social Assortment Studies 86
4. Twin and Adoption Studies 87
5. Blood Tests, Bereavement, Scent and Faces 89
6. Genetic Similarity, Race and Race Proxies. 90
7. Other Lines of Research. 96
8. Conclusion 101

CHAPTER SIX
Ethnocentrism, Personality Traits and Computer Modelling   103

1. Introduction 103
2. Personality 103
3. Tracking the Spread: Computer Modelling 110
4. Prisoner's Dilemma 111
5. Developments of the Model 115
6. Why Do Ethnocentrics Always Win? 117
7. Limitations to the Computer Modelling of Ethnocentrism . . . 119
8. Bruce Charlton's Model. 120
9. Conclusion 121

CHAPTER SEVEN
The Genetics of Ethnocentrism   123
    1. Introduction 123
    2. Measures of Ethnocentrism 124
    3. Genes for Race Differences in Ethnocentrism 125
    4. Parasite Stress. 129
    5. Problems with the Parasite Stress Model 131
    6. The Life History Theory Model of Ethnocentrism 133
    8. Testing the Life History Theory Hypothesis 140
    9. Conclusion 142

CHAPTER EIGHT
Race Differences, Cousin Marriage and Religion   143
    1. Introduction 143
    2. Race Differences in Ethnocentrism 143
    3. Why Are Northeast Asians More Ethnocentric
    than Europeans?. 148
    4. Arabs and South Asians. 151
    5. Cousin Marriage Among Arabs 153
    6. Testing the Relationship between Cousin Marriage
    and Ethnocentrism 158
    7. Religiousness and Ethnocentrism 159
    8. Genes for Ethnocentrism and Jews 166
    9. Low Ethnocentrism: Europeans and Africans 172
    10. Selection for Low Ethnocentrism in Europeans? 174
    11. The Fleeting Nature of Race Differences in Ethnocentrism . . 178
    12. Conclusion. 180

CHAPTER NINE
Stress, Demographics and Diversity   181
    1. Introduction 181
    2. Risk, Stress and Ethnocentrism. 181
    3. Age Profile and Gender 185

    4. Pregnancy 192
    5. Ethnic Diversity 193
    6. Intelligence and Education 199
    7. Conclusion 204

CHAPTER TEN
Industrialization and the Decline of Ethnocentrism   205

    1. Introduction 205
    2. General Effects of Industrialization: The Decline of Religion . . 205
    3. Dysgenics. 208
    4. Mutational Meltdown in Mouse Utopia 216
    5. Conclusion 226

CHAPTER ELEVEN
Why Did Different Ethnicities React Differently in 2015?   227

    1. Introduction 227
    2. Positive Ethnocentrism 227
    3. Negative Ethnocentrism 229
    4. Group Differences in Ethnocentrism 230
    5. Conclusion 232

References   234
Index of Names   260

About the Author

Edward Dutton is a freelance researcher and writer. Born in London in 1980, he lives in northern Finland. Dutton was educated at the University of Durham, where he graduated in Theology in 2002, and the University of Aberdeen, from which he received his PhD in Religious Studies in 2006.

Dutton has been guest researcher at Leiden University in the Netherlands, Umeå University in Sweden, and has been academic consultant at King Saud University in Saudi Arabia. Dutton's other books include: *Meeting Jesus at University: Rites of Passage and Student Evangelicals* (2008), *The Genius Famine* (2015, jointly with Bruce Charlton), *How to Judge People By What They Look Like* (2018) and *At Our Wits' End: Why We're Becoming Less Intelligent and What It Means for the Future* (In Press, 2018; jointly with Michael Woodley of Menie).

Dutton was first to set out all the evidence for IQ decline across Europe, proposed the idea that non-religious people are low in instinct, and proved that traditional religiousness is a reflection of low levels of mutant genes. Dutton's research has been reported in newspapers worldwide. In his spare time, Dutton enjoys genealogy and has written widely on the subject. He is married to a Finn and has two young children.

Acknowledgements

I would like to acknowledge the assistance of the following colleagues who have generously forwarded me literature or provided useful critiques of aspects of this book: Dr Boris Bizumic, Dr Bruce Charlton, Dr Curtis Dunkel, Prof. A.J. Figueredo, Herra Aleksi Kari, Herr Emil Kirkegaard, Dr Kenya Kura, Prof. Guy Madison, Prof. Gerhard Meisenberg, Dr Frank Salter, Prof. Dimitri Van der Linden and Dr Michael Woodley of Menie.

EDWARD DUTTON
21st November 2018

CHAPTER ONE

'At Least They Hear the Things I Hear...'

1. Introduction

Ethnocentrism, argued the American economist William Sumner (1840–1910), is 'the view of things in which one's own group is the centre of everything and all others are scaled and rated with reference to it... Each group nourishes its *own* pride and vanity, boasts itself superior, exalts its own divinities, and looks with contempt on outsiders' (Sumner, 1906, p. 13). This kind of attitude is epitomized in words attributed to Socrates: 'He thanked Fortune for three things', it was said, one of them being, 'that I am a Greek and not a barbarian' (quoted in Coleman, 1997, p. 175). It is also very clear in the way that the British Empire produced maps with Britain at the centre, and longitude continues to be measured in degrees east or west of Greenwich in London (Benson, 2002, p. 37).

'Ethnocentrism', then, comes in two forms. On the one hand, 'positive ethnocentrism' involves taking pride in your ethnic group or nation and being prepared to make sacrifices for the good of it. Soldiers who regard their nation as being the best in the world and are prepared to risk their lives to defend it are 'positively ethnocentric'. In England, at the start of World War I, a huge propaganda campaign successfully persuaded thousands of young men to fight for their country, appealing to this kind of ethnocentrism. Recruitment posters included John Bull, the symbol of Britishness,[1] standing in front of uniformed soldiers and asking the reader, 'Who's absent? Is it you?' (see Messinger, 1992).

On the other hand, 'negative ethnocentrism' refers to being prejudiced against and hostile to members of other ethnic groups. The English soldier who is motivated by hatred of the Germans and is prepared to brutalize German civilians because they are German is high in negative ethnocentrism. During World War I, anti-German feeling in England reached such extremes that there were anti-German riots, assaults on suspected Germans, and the looting of stores whose owners had German-sounding surnames (Panayi, 1989). The British Royal Family, who are of German descent, were even forced to change their surname from Saxe-Coburg-Gotha to Windsor due to the anti-German hysteria generated by the War (Baldick & Bate 2006, p. 303).

'Ethnocentrism' combines these two dimensions. A person is 'ethnocentric' if they take pride in and make sacrifices for their country and are prejudiced against other countries, although, as we will see, there are people and groups who are high in one aspect of ethnocentrism but not in the other. Criticisms might be levelled against this division between positive and negative ethnocentrism. For example, it might be argued that people in many Western European countries — influenced by ideologies such as Multiculturalism — may profess a low level of national pride but will, nevertheless, hold to a view in which their own country is at the centre of the world and believe that everywhere should want to be like their own country, in the sense of being Multicultural.[2] 'Multiculturalism' generally refers to the promotion of a culturally diverse society combined with the view that all cultures are of equal value and their members should have

---

1   For a discussion of the history of John Bull see Hunt (2003).
2   I am grateful to Guy Madison for this observation.

equal status,[3] so it is, on the surface, inconsistent with ethnocentrism. However, it can be countered that, in this case, the sense of pride is in their country's ideology and if their country had a different ideology, such as a highly nationalistic one, then the same people would have far less pride in their country. Equally, people who adhere to such an ideology seem to be prejudiced against genuinely ethnocentric countries, such as Israel (Jayanetti, 17th April 2017), precisely because they reject Multiculturalism. National pride means being proud of your country simply because it *is* your country.

In this book, then, we aim to understand the causes of ethnocentrism and the reasons why there is variation in the degree to which different races and ethnic groups are ethnocentric. Put simply, we want to answer the question: 'Why are some races more ethnocentric than others?' and, indeed, 'Why are Europeans currently so low in ethnocentrism?' As we will see, there has been considerable discussion of the possible reasons for individual variation in levels of ethnocentrism. However, there exists no systematic attempt to understand why different ethnic groups may vary in the extent to which they are ethnocentric. Understanding the reasons for group differences in ethnocentrism is particularly salient during a period of mass migration (see Salter, 2007). Europe, in particular, has been experiencing this since the 1960s and it started to become particularly acute in the summer of 2015, when the mass movement of people from the Middle East into Europe, often via Turkey, was referred to as the 'Great Migration' (e.g. Nelson, 3rd September 2015). As many of the immigrants claimed to be 'refugees', supposedly fleeing violence in Syria at the hands of ISIS (Islamic State), the European Union instituted a policy whereby each nation should take 'refugee quotas' (*BBC News*, 22nd September 2015). The crisis evoked a fascinating array of responses from different countries.

---

3   See Dutton (2012) for more detailed discussions of the nature of this ideology.

The governments of the northern European countries, such as the Scandinavian nations and particularly Germany, were, initially at least, extremely welcoming, with Germany processing 1.1 million asylum seekers (Peev, 31st December 2015). Indeed, some national leaders used the crisis as a means of playing for moral status by virtue signalling.[4] The Finnish Prime Minister, Juha Sipilä, offered to take 'refugees' into his home (Withnall, 6th September 2015). However, attitudes soon hardened (Boztas, 5th February 2016), especially once the behaviour of some of the migrants came to light. This included the gang-raping of teenage girls (e.g. in Finland, YLE, 24th November 2015), the raping of children (e.g. in Austria, Dunn, 6th February 2016), the groping and widespread sexual assault of women (such as in large mobs on New Year's Eve 2015 in Cologne where approximately 1000 women were sexually assaulted; Richards, 11th February 2016), masturbating and defecating in public swimming pools (Wyke, 24th January 2016), and general threatening and criminal behaviour towards locals. The suicide bombings and a massacre in Paris on 13th November 2015 by ISIS terrorists hardened attitudes further. Some of the terrorists were French citizens of Moroccan descent who had gone to Syria to train as terrorists and had then re-entered Europe as 'refugees' that summer (Phipps & Rawlinson, 14th November 2015). 130 people were killed in the Paris attack. This was followed, on 22nd March 2016, by ISIS terrorists (Belgian nationals of Moroccan descent) suicide bombing Brussels Airport and a Brussels metro station, killing thirty-two people. Nevertheless, the initial reaction of Northwestern European governments can be summarised with the virtue-signalling Facebook meme 'Refugees Welcome'.

---

4   In a highly social species, emphasizing that you are generous is a way of playing for status because generosity is a likeable quality. This leads to a kind of competitive altruism. In addition, such behaviour can be seen to advertise one's qualities, including genetic qualities, rather like a peacock's tail. Your qualities are such that you have excess resources and you can survive despite giving away your resources. We will discuss the 'peacock's tail' in detail in the section on sexual selection.

The response of Eastern European governments and their people was very different. There were quickly huge protests in former Eastern Bloc EU countries against letting in any of the overwhelmingly Muslim and male migrants whatsoever (e.g. in Poland, Gander, 13th September 2015). Leading politicians from these countries, such as the Prime Minister of Slovakia, Robert Fico (BBC News, 19th August 2015) and the Prime Minister of Hungary, Viktor Orbán (Traynor, 3rd September 2015) spoke out strongly against letting any Muslims into their nations at all. Countries bordering Syria, such as Saudi Arabia and Qatar, refused to let in any supposed 'refugees' even though they are far more culturally and ethnically similar to the immigrants than are Europeans (Akbar, 4th September 2015). Israel also refused to admit any of them (Burrows, 6th September 2015). Furthermore, across Western Europe there were huge outpourings of public sympathy for the people killed in the Paris and Brussels attacks, with people changing their Facebook profile pictures to the flags of France or Belgium, for example, despite the fact that precisely these kinds of people had previously shared the 'Refugees Welcome' meme. However, interestingly, there was no such reaction among Europeans to ISIS bombings in Turkey, which happened around the same time (D'Angelo, 14th March 2016).

2. Previous Studies of Ethnocentrism

As such, why there should be racial and ethnic differences in ethnocentrism, and the potential consequences of this, is a very timely question. There have been a number of book-length studies of the topic. Psychologist Boris Bizumic (2017) explores the origins of ethnocentrism and the different theories behind it, though he does not explore group differences in its extent. LeVine and Campbell presented *Ethnocentrism: Theories of Conflict, Ethnic Attitudes, and Group Behaviour* (LeVine & Campbell, 1972). In this work they essentially argued that ethnocentrism was a result of conflict. In addition, an essay collection, *The Sociobiology of Ethnocentrism* (Reynolds et al., 1987) looked in depth at the relationship between ethnocentrism and indirectly passing on your genes; the concept of 'inclusive fitness', which we will examine later. Since these books were published there has been an abundance of research conducted relating to ethnocentrism and understanding its nature and causes. Indeed, research into ethnocentrism has been extended in many fruitful directions. This book will explore and extend that more recent research, especially by understanding race and ethnic differences in levels of ethnocentrism.

The concept of ethnocentrism has been highly relevant to more recent works such as Finnish political scientist Tatu Vanhanen's (1929–2015) *Ethnic Conflicts* (Vanhanen, 2012), Thayer's (2004) *Darwin and International Relations* and to narrower discussions of ethnocentrism in relation to specific contexts. These have included detailed studies examining the place of ethnocentrism in the education system (Schleicher & Komza, 1992), understanding American public opinion (Kinder & Kam, 2010), analysing the reaction of religious Dutch people to non-Christian immigrants (Cupucao, 2010), addressing the place of ethnocentrism in African Christianity (Tanye, 2010), and its place in anthropological fieldwork (Van der Geest & Reiss, 2005). It has also been explored in looking at the concept of 'culture shock', whereby people who encounter a new culture initially feel positive towards it but then become strongly ethnocentric, loathing the new culture and romanticizing their own (see Dutton, 2012), and even in understanding the development of English dictionaries (Benson, 2002).

3. Historical Observation of Differences in Ethnocentrism

Group and individual differences in ethnocentrism have always been an issue of significant concern, though I am not aware of any systematic historical analysis. During the so-called 'Age of Discovery' from the Renaissance until the nineteenth century, European explorers came into contact with many different ethnic groups with whom they had previously had no contact at all. Some of these groups were immediately friendly, others immediately hostile, while others still sat between these extremes and their attitudes noticeably altered according to the behaviour of the explorers. A fully comprehensive historical analysis of this area would be a fascinating study for any historian. But, to give a few examples, the natives of Hawaii were widely understood, when they were first contacted in the mid-eighteenth century, to be extremely 'friendly' (Wood, 1999, p. 30) until Captain James Cook (1728–1779) provoked their wrath by taking their king hostage. This geniality, however, was perhaps significantly because they thought that the white men were gods. But even putting aside the religious element, the Inuit have long been described by explorers as being very amiable to outsiders (e.g. Graburn, 2012). By contrast, the negrito tribes of the Andaman Islands, near India, have a reputation for being extraordinarily unfriendly and hostile to outsiders, to the extent that they are simply left alone by the Indian government. There is also intense inter-tribal warfare on these islands (Singh, 1994).

In terms of positive ethnocentrism, many descriptions of the Japanese by Early Modern European missionaries commented on the extent of their bravery in the service of their nation and the surprising degree of harmony in Japanese society; the degree to which they were prepared to co-operate with each other (e.g. Hawkes, 2016). By contrast, descriptions of the Yanomamö tribe of Venezuela portray a group characterized by extreme violence and lawlessness, unable to maintain a group membership of any significant size without splitting into rival clans. Known as the 'fierce people' even by neighbouring groups, the Yanomamö have also gained a reputation for being profoundly unpleasant to outsiders (Chagnon, 1968). These differences, in the extent of ethnocentrism, would appear to have resulted in observable differences in the fates of the different societies. The societies which are highly welcoming to outsiders, such as the Hawaiians and the Inuit, have both been substantially colonised by Europeans. The societies which are hostile in the extreme to outsiders, by contrast, are generally left alone. But they do not benefit, in either material or intellectual terms, from contact with outsiders so they do not develop into larger groups. Japan has developed a highly complex society with a very high standard of living, although, interestingly, its levels of genius — of innovating new inventions — appear to be much lower than in Europe and it has been suggested that its extreme cooperative nature may be a reason for this (Dutton & Charlton, 2015). Even so, the Japanese seem to have intense pride in themselves and their nation. By contrast, the Yanomamö remain in the Stone Age and are so internally divided into warring clans that it is unlikely that they could realistically mount a united front, let alone develop into a larger society. Group differences in ethnocentrism were even of interest to Charles Darwin (1809–1882) who commented in *The Descent of Man*: 'A tribe including many members who, from possessing a high degree of the spirit of patriotism, fidelity, obedience, courage, and sympathy, were always ready to aid one another, and to sacrifice themselves for the common good, would be victorious over most other tribes, and this would be natural selection' (Darwin, 1871).

In much the same way, some individuals can be said to be more ethnocentric than others. In the UK, perhaps the most striking examples of positive ethnocentrism can be seen in those who have received the Victoria Cross. The Victoria Cross is the highest medal for valour in the face of the enemy that can be bestowed upon a British soldier or soldier fighting for a country of whom the British monarch is the head of state. Since 1857, when it was established, the medal has only been awarded just over 1350 times and it has only been awarded fifteen times since World War II (Smith, 2008). Recipients include Private Edward Barber (1893–1915) who, on 12th March 1915 at the Battle of Neuve Chapelle in France:

ran speedily in front of the grenade company to which he belonged, and threw bombs on the enemy with such effect that a very great number of them at once surrendered. When the grenade party reached Private Barber they found him quite alone and unsupported, with the enemy surrendering all about him (*London Gazette,* 19th April 1915).

Private Barber lost his life due to this singular act of suicidal gallantry. By contrast, other people can be so low in positive ethnocentrism that they are prepared to spy for the enemy in return for payment or due to some shared ideology. In Britain, Guy Burgess (1911–1963), along with other members of the so-called 'Cambridge spy ring' (a reference to the university where they originally met), was a diplomat who passed information to the Soviet Union during the Cold War, making him a traitor to his country (see Lownie, 2016). By the same token, it is clear that some people are higher than others in negative ethnocentrism. Some people would be horrified by having someone of a different race as a neighbour, let alone a family member. In the UK, in the 1940s, a father threw his daughter out of his house because she insisted on marrying a man from Trinidad (Appleyard & Goldwin, 5th February 2016). Others will fall in love with and marry a person of a different race. It was not uncommon, for example, for British soldiers stationed in India during the Raj to marry local women. The products of these marriages were generally raised as Christian, and themselves married other mixed-race people, with the result that there remains a distinct Indian ethnic group known as 'Anglo-Indians' (see Muthiah et al., 2014). A famous example was Lt. Col. James Kirkpatrick (1764–1805), a soldier with the East India Company, who married Khair un-Nissa, an Indian noblewoman who was the grand-daughter of the Prime Minister of Hyderabad, in 1801. Indeed, he adopted Indian culture more generally. He wore Mughal-style costumes at home, smoked a hookah, and converted to Islam (Dalrymple, 2004), this being the religion of much of the Indian nobility at the time.

So, these differences in the level of ethnocentrism — at both the individual and group level — have long been observed, but what are their causes? What are the environmental and genetic factors which mean that some people are so much more ethnocentric than others? And are there different explanations for the same levels of ethnocentrism between different people and different groups? In this study, we will attempt a comprehensive examination of this area in order to answer these important questions.

4. Outline

In Chapter Two we will discuss the concepts of 'race' and 'ethnicity' and show that both can reasonably be accepted as valid scientific categories.

In Chapter Three, we will examine the nature of 'intelligence' and specifically evidence of population differences in intelligence. Examining the concept of 'intelligence' is necessary at this early point because it has been strongly criticised and impacts a number of dimensions of the discussion which follows. We show that the concept of intelligence is valid, IQ tests are reliable, and that we can reasonably accept that there are population differences in average intelligence.

In Chapter Four, we will define 'ethnocentrism' and look at 'ethnicity' in this light. We will argue in favour of what is known as the 'sociobiological' model of ethnocentrism and the nature of ethnicity, in contrast to the 'constructivist' model, which is more widely accepted in sociology and in anthropology. 'Sociobiology' is effectively what is now more widely termed 'evolutionary psychology'. Evolutionary psychology is the attempt to understand human behaviour from an evolutionary perspective. Proponents argue that human behaviour can be comprehended by examining evolved adaptations to the ancestral environment, and that behaviours that are common to all cultures are likely to reflect psychological adaptations. Certain psychological adaptations provided an evolutionary advantage, the adaptations spread, and, accordingly, only those descended from people with these adaptations are alive today. Of course, some psychological adaptations were less advantageous than others or advantageous only in certain environments or only in certain periods, so there is some population variance in psychological adaptations. Evolutionary psychologists argue that humans are best understood as an advanced ape, that the human brain is a physical organ subject to evolution like any other, that human nature is innate and that human behaviour is a product of this innate human nature reacting to a given environment. A large body of evidence has been presented in favour of this perspective (see Wilson, 1975). As we will see, evolutionary psychological explanations, when compared to purely environmental ones, explain the most, leave fewer questions unanswered and can be grounded in science and thus logic. The alternatives leave questions unanswered, explain less and involve significant assumptions.

In Chapter Five, we will present further evidence of the validity of sociobiological model of ethnocentrism. We will present all of the growing body of evidence in favour of Genetic Similarity Theory (e.g. Rushton, 2005); that is that people tend to associate with people who are genetically the most similar to them because so doing indirectly passes on more of their genes. We will argue that this theory helps to explain why people are prepared to fight for their ethnic group. The ethnic group is merely an extended genetic family and so, in certain contexts, it makes genetic sense to make sacrifices for the good of that family.

Having established our key models, we will turn to trying to understand why certain races are more ethnocentric than others. In Chapter Six, we will look at the evidence for there being an 'ethnocentric personality' and show that it is not persuasive. We will also examine a number of computer simulations which show that the more ethnocentric group will always ultimately triumph over the less ethnocentric group in the battle for group survival, all else being equal. Accordingly, this helps to explain why ethnocentrism would be selected for at the group level and it helps us to explain why certain groups are more ethnocentric than others. If what we will call group selection is more intense, then ethnocentrism will tend to be stronger. In order to test why there are group differences in the level of ethnocentrism, we will present data from the World Values Survey which can be seen as measures of positive and negative ethnocentrism at the country level. We will show that, at the group level, positive and negative ethnocentrism are unrelated and are thus underpinned by very different factors.

In Chapters Seven and Eight we focus on establishing key reasons why Northeast Asians, Arabs, Africans and Jews tend to be more ethnocentric than Europeans, despite these being relatively unrelated groups. In examining this, we show that a fast 'Life History Strategy' — evolution to an unstable environment — is associated with negative ethnocentrism, through looking at genetic polymorphisms. We will also see that high levels of cousin marriage are associated with both negative and positive ethnocentrism. High levels of religiousness are associated with ethnocentrism in general, while a slow 'Life History Strategy' is associated with aspects of positive ethnocentrism. We will see that both cousin marriage and religiousness can be seen as ways of promoting positive ethnocentrism without sacrificing aggressiveness to outsiders. We will argue that Europeans have developed a specific evolutionary strategy — where ethnocentrism has been sacrificed in favour of genius.

In Chapter Nine, we look at a number of other factors which may explain why the comparative ethnocentrism of different races or ethnic groups may vary across time. We show that stress — as manifested in environments which are poor or with high mortality — is associated with elevated ethnocentrism. The younger a country's population is, we find, the more ethnocentric it is; the lower the national IQ of the country is the more ethnocentric it is, and less intelligent people tend to be more ethnocentric, for reasons we will discuss.

In Chapter Ten, we speculate on possible causes of the decline in ethnocentrism in Western countries and argue that it may be a function of early industrialization and consequent dysgenics, the build-up of mutant genes in the population due to the extreme weakening of Natural Selection. In the pre-industrial world, we were under conditions of Natural Selection, in which only the fittest survived. This meant that only those who had very few mutant genes survived, those who were optimally adapted to the environment. As Natural Selection weakened, more and more people with mutant genes — who would not have survived under Natural Selection — survived and procreated, as did maladaptive ideas such as atheism and thus low ethnocentrism. We will show that having such ideas (mutations of the mind) is correlated with evidence of physical mutations, demonstrating that the ideas are likely underpinned by mutant genes whose carriers would not have previously survived to pass on their genes. The West had a strong head start in this process, further helping to explain its low levels of ethnocentrism. Finally, in Chapter Eleven, we summarise our findings and present what we regard as the most fundamental factors behind group differences in ethnocentrism.

CHAPTER TWO

What Is 'Race'?

1. Introduction

The term 'ethnicity' or 'ethny' is obviously at the centre of our analysis and, accordingly, we need to clarify precisely what we mean by it. There are different ways of defining the word 'ethnicity'. In common parlance, it is often conflated with the concept of 'race'. Thus, minority groups in Western societies who are conspicuously physically different from the majority are termed 'ethnic minorities'. Accordingly, in the UK, 'blacks' and 'Asians' are described as 'ethnic minorities'.

This conflation of the words 'ethnicity' and 'race' is problematic because we may as well reject one of the two words, if they mean exactly the same thing. Indeed, the pressure exerted by ideologies such as Multiculturalism and Political Correctness—including advocates' view that there is no such thing as 'race' or that it is merely a cultural construct—has led to the word 'ethnic' being used as a synonym for 'race' in academic research. This has been done either to avoid potential criticism or simply to avoid a lengthy digression in order to defend the concept of 'race' from its critics. In defining 'ethnicity' we must clearly distinguish it from 'race', though there is no scientific reason to dismiss the concept of 'race'. As such, we first need to define the word 'race', such that we can distinguish it from 'ethnicity'. We will also examine race differences in ethnocentrism in this study. In this chapter, we will, therefore, define the concept of 'race' and rebut the various criticisms of it.[5]

2. What Is Race?

'Race' is employed to refer to what in the animal world would be a subspecies: a breeding population separated from another of the same species long enough to be noticeably evolved to a different environment but not long enough to be unable to have fertile offspring with the other group. In other words, a race is a breeding population that differs genetically from other such populations as a result of geographical isolation, cultural separation, and endogamy, and which shows patterns of genotypic frequency for a number of intercorrelated characteristics compared with other breeding populations. The most obvious manifestations of these differences are observable differences in physical appearance and physical and mental characteristics which correlate together. These indicate that it is useful, following the scientific desire to be able to make correct predictions about the world, to divide humans into racial categories in much the same way that we might divide any other particular animal species into subspecies. As with any category, 'race' creates groups on the borders that do not fit neatly into one of two categories. Geographical contact zones may develop many thousands of years after races have separated and lead to racial hybrids. These hybrids, depending on the degree of admixture, have intermediate genes frequencies in relation to the two parent races and, if the hybrid subsequently becomes geographically and culturally separated from the parent races, a case may develop for terming it a separate race. These racial hybrids are known as clines.

The concept of 'race' is a scientific category because the essence of a scientific category is that it allows correct predictions to be made, and this is certainly the case with regard to 'race'. In evolutionary biology, it is a general principle that when two different populations of

---

5   An earlier version of this chapter was first published in Dutton and Lynn (2015).

the same species become geographically isolated from one another, such that they cease to interbreed, then they develop into different subspecies. Subspecies are adapted to different ecologies and thus differ, to varying degrees, in their physical appearance and behaviour. Subspecies are also known as varieties, strains, or simply as breeds. There are four interrelated processes through which different races or subspecies evolve:

1. **Founder Effect.** A particular population splits, with part of the population migrating to a new place. As they stop interbreeding, the two populations gradually become increasingly genetically differentiated, especially if the number of founders is small and the population remains isolated.

2. **Genetic Drift Effect.** Gene frequencies change over time as a matter of chance. As this effect is extended over a long period, it can lead to increasing differences between races.

3. **Mutation Effect.** Individual genes can take many different forms. The most well-known distinction is between the 'long form' and the 'short form' of certain genes, but there are many further possible distinctions. Genes come in pairs of alleles, with one allele inherited from each parent. Variants of genes are known, therefore, as alleles. When alleles are passed from parent to child, sometimes the process of copying the genetic information goes awry, leading to a mutation or in other words to a new allele. The Mutation Effect is when new alleles appear by chance in some populations and are highly advantageous for survival and reproduction in that population's particular environment. When this happens the allele in question spreads through the population. An advantageous mutant allele may appear in one racial population but not in another. This leads to genetic differences between the two populations.

4. **Adaptation Effect.** When one population moves to a new environment, alleles which were not especially advantageous in the old

environment may become advantageous in terms of survival and reproduction and will thus begin to be selected for. Accordingly, they will spread throughout the population.

In addition, subspecies can be artificially developed when a particular species is domesticated by another species. The most obvious examples can be seen in the various breeds of domestic dog, all of which have been deliberately engineered by humans to have certain physical and behavioural characteristics which render them useful in specific sets of circumstances or which simply make them friendly and aesthetically pleasing pets. The existence of separate races, usually termed subspecies, is uncontroversial when discussing non-human animals. Thus, if Darwin's Theory of Evolution is accepted, it should be likewise uncontroversial to assert that humans include distinct subspecies or races. As Baker (1974) has noted, there are a number of subspecies among our closest relatives, the chimpanzees. Each is slightly different because they have evolved in somewhat unique environments in line with the process previously outlined. The true chimpanzee is indigenous to West Africa, Guinea, and Nigeria; the bald chimpanzee lives in Cameroon and Gabon; the pygmy chimpanzee is found in the north and central areas of the Democratic Republic of Congo; while the Schweinfurth chimpanzee is found in the north-eastern regions of the same country. Each of these races differs in terms of physical appearance, distribution of blood groups, and even in terms of the kinds of cries they employ. Baker (1974) also examines similar differences between breeds of gorilla.

The human breeding of dogs is, of course, well known. Domestic dogs of different breeds can, in most cases, produce fertile offspring, thus conforming to the generally accepted definition of species (though it should be appreciated that the use of the word species does not always conform to this rule). Nevertheless, domestic dogs differ significantly in physical appearance, temperament (both of which are bred for specific purposes), and intelligence (used here to mean the ability to solve cognitively demanding problems at speed). For example, Coren (1994) observes that the most intelligent breeds of domestic dog include Border Collies (the most intelligent), Poodles, and Golden Retrievers. These dogs understand new commands after fewer than five repetitions and obey commands 95% of the time or higher. The least intelligent breeds require more than 80 repetitions to understand a new command and obey commands less than 30% of the time. These relatively unintelligent dogs include Basset Hounds, Pekingese, and Bulldogs.[6]

Evidently, race is useful among non-human animals because dividing these animals up into races permits correct predictions to be made about their physical and mental abilities, a finding which is of practical use when dealing with them or even in terms of keeping them alive. However, before looking at these differences among humans, we will examine the history of the concept of race as well as the criticisms which have been levelled against it.

3. Taxonomies of Races

Anthropologists began to systematically classify human races in middle of the eighteenth century, though an awareness of them can be found much further into history. Baker (1974, p. 12) presents an historical summary which indicates an awareness of racial differences in antiquity. When the Indo-Afghans began to penetrate into northern India in around 1500 BC, it was seemingly an awareness of hereditary racial differences which led to their establishment of what would later become the Hindu caste system, a system which was originally divided in terms of colour; the Hindi word for 'caste' ('Varna') literally meaning 'colour'. In the Old Testament, three separate ethnic groups are supposed to have sprung from the three sons of Noah (Genesis 10). As such, we seem to see evidence of the idea that different racial

---

[6] For a detailed examination of intelligence differences in dogs, see Arden and James (2016).

groups are distinct extended families. Many other examples of what we might cautiously call 'awareness of racial differences' might be provided, such as Pope Gregory I (540–604) seeing Anglo-Saxon slave boys at the marketplace in Rome and observing how distinct they looked from his own people, something recorded by the Venerable Bede in around 731 (Bede, 1890). However, it is unclear, in many cases, whether they understood these differences to be hereditary.

Moving forward in time, in 1684, French physician Francois Bernier (1625–1688) published his *Nouvelle division de la terre par les différentes espèces ou races d'hommes qui l'habitent* (*New Division of Earth by the Different Species or Races of Men that Inhabit It*; Bernier, 1684). He divided the world into four races, distinguished by a variety of inter-correlated factors including skin colour, facial type, cranial profile, and hair type and colour, which he understood to be hereditary qualities. He argued that there were four 'species':

1. The European, North African, South Asian, and Native American (which he saw as essentially one species);
2. The Asian;
3. The Sub-Saharan African;
4. The Lapp.

However, a more influential taxonomy of races was published by Swedish botanist Carl Linnaeus (1707–1778) in the year 1758 in the form of his book *Systema Naturae* (Linnaeus, 1758). He argued that there were four races: *Europaeus* (Europeans), *Afer* (Black Africans), *Asiaticus* (Asians), and *Americanus* (Native Americans). He described these races mainly in terms of physical differences, not limited to skin colour. In 1776, German physician Johann Friedrich Blumenbach (1752–1840) argued that there should be a fifth race. Accordingly, he divided between Caucasian (white), Mongolian (yellow), Ethiopian (black), American (red), and Malayan (brown). These categories were developed through the observation that different morphological features clustered together with skin pigmentation. Thus, he noted that the Europeans had white skin, straight hair, and narrow noses; the Sub-Saharan Africans had black skin, frizzy hair, and wide noses; the Mongolians (Northeast Asians) had black hair, yellowish skin, and flattened noses; the Native Americans had reddish skin and beaky noses; and the Malaysians had brown skin (Blumenbach, 1828). In addition, a variety of eighteenth-century philosophers including Immanuel Kant (1724–1804), David Hume (1711–1776), and Voltaire (1694–1778) presented relatively detailed descriptions of apparent inter-correlated physical and mental racial differences, arguing that these appeared to be passed from one generation to the next (Baker, Chapter 1). Towards the end of the eighteenth century, an increasing level of quantitative rigor was being added to racial classifications. The Dutch anatomist Petrus Camper (1722–1789) introduced the 'facial line', setting up a skull in the horizontal and then measuring the angle and distance from the most protruding part of the skull to the least. In this regard, he noted that the skull of the Sub-Saharan African was more sloping than that of the European, while the skull of the chimpanzee was more sloping still.

The issue of racial classification provoked particular interest over the course of the nineteenth century, with perhaps the best known racial taxonomist of this period being Count Arthur de Gobineau (1816–1882). His *Essay on the Inequality of the Races* (Gobineau, 1915) was first published in 1855. The issue of racial superiority or inferiority, upon which Gobineau focused, need not concern us here. But it is worth noting that Gobineau's taxonomy was composed of just three essential races with pigmentation used as the proxy for inter-correlated morphological and behavioural differences: White, Yellow, and Black. Within these broad categories, Gobineau examined various 'sub-races', including the Nordic strain of the 'White' race. Debate over the precise number of races continued throughout the nineteenth century, but there was general agreement that race was a meaningful taxonomy.

With scientific advances in the twentieth century, even more data were collected to show that a large number of important differences, which permitted important Life History predictions to be made, clustered along the kind of racial dividing lines suggested by the eighteenth-century scholars. In the early twentieth century, data were collected on differences in the frequencies of blood groups in various populations throughout the world. Hirszfeld and Hirszfeld (1919) proved that the frequencies of a number of blood groups significantly correlate with racial differences in pigmentation and morphology. For example, blood group A is present in 41% to 48% of Europeans but in only about 28% of Sub-Saharan Africans. Blood group B is present in between 10% and 20% of Europeans and in roughly 34% of Sub-Saharan Africans. Native Americans have almost no A or B blood groups and the overwhelming majority possess the O blood group.

Data on the distribution of the Rhesus (Rh) blood groups were employed by Boyd (1950) to propose a five race taxonomy. This was composed of:

1. *Europeans* with high frequencies of blood groups Rh cde and cde;

2. *Africans* with very high frequencies of Rh cde;

3. *East Asians* with high frequency of B and almost no cde;

4. *American Indians* with a very high frequency of O, absence of B, and few cde;

5. *Australids* (Aborigines) with high A, negligible B, and cde.

This analysis demonstrated that blood-group distributions were consistent with the morphological and pigmentation-based racial taxonomies of classical anthropology. A more detailed taxonomy of races was presented by Coon et al. (1950), who advocated seven major races based on available data, each of which was subdivided into two or more sub-races. These were:

1. *Caucasoids*: This category was composed of Nordics (Northwest Europe), Slavs (Northeast Europe), Alpines (Central Europe), Mediterraneans (Southern Europe, North Africa, and the Near East), and Hindis of India and Pakistan.

2. *East Asians*: This was composed of Tibetans, North Chinese, Northeast Asians (Koreans, Japanese, Mongolians), and the Inuit and similar Arctic peoples.

3. *Southeast Asians*: These were the South Chinese, Thais, Burmese, Malayans, and Indonesians.

4. *American Indians:* These were divided into north, central, south, and Fuegians.

5. *Africans*: These were divided into East Africans, Sudanese, West Africans, Bantu, Bushmen, and Pygmies.

6. *Pacific Islanders*: Melanesians, Micronesians, Polynesians, and Negritos.

7. *Australian Aborigines*: Murrayian peoples of southeastern Australia and the Carpentarian people of northern and central Australia.

Baker (1974) advanced a very similar taxonomy, composed of the five races suggested by Blumenbach, adding the Bushmen and Australids (Aborigines and Melanesians).

Moving into the 1980s and 1990s, increasing advances in the study of genetics further evidenced the meaningfulness of dividing humans into subspecies along the racial lines advanced by nineteenth century anthropologists. Nei and Roychoudhury (1993) and Cavalli-Sforza et al. (1994) developed a novel means of classifying humans into races on the basis of a variety of genetic polymorphisms. A polymorphism refers to a gene that can be composed of alleles which have different forms. Their technique involved taking polymorphic genes for blood groups, blood proteins, lymphocyte antigens, and immunoglobins, and calculating different allele frequencies in populations throughout the world. The results were then factor analysed to discern the degree to which the allele frequencies were associated into population clusters that were genetically similar to each other. Jensen (1998) demonstrated that factor analysing Nei and Roychoudhury's data from twenty-six populations reduced it to six population clusters. These six major groups of humans strongly corresponded to the six races proposed by classical anthropologists. These clusters were:

1. *Africans of Sub-Saharan Africa* (Pygmies, Nigerians, Bantu, Bushmen);

2. *Caucasoids* (Lapps, Finns, Germans, English, Italians, Iranians, North Indians);

3. *Northeast Asians* (Japanese, Chinese, Koreans, Tibetans, Mongolians);

4. *Southeast Asians* (Southern Chinese, Thais, Filipinos, Indonesians, Polynesians, Micronesians);

5. *Amerindians* (North and South Native American Indians and Inuit);

6. *Australian Aborigines* (Australian Aborigines and New Guineans).

It should be noted that this does not correspond precisely to the analysis of Coon et al. (1950), which was more strongly based around morphological features. It is, of course, to be expected that if the method employed to categorize (or the definition of a category) changes, then some subjects will end up within a different category, because it is in the very nature of categorizing that some subjects are in an ambiguous position, on the borders. But we can equally see that the results of categorizing employing a genetic method are substantially the same as when employing a morphological method. In addition, we would also expect changes because the method employed by Nei and Roychoudhury is more scientifically rigorous.

The same technique has been employed by Cavalli-Sforza, Menozzi, and Piazza (1994) to analyse a larger data set of 120 alleles for forty-two populations. These data were used to calculate the genetic differences between each population and every other population. From these, they calculated a genetic linkage tree that grouped the populations into what they termed 'clusters'. They found ten major clusters. These were:

1. Bushmen and Pygmies;
2. Sub-Saharan Africans;
3. South Asians and North Africans;
4. Europeans;
5. Northeast Asians;
6. Arctic Peoples;
7. Native American Indians;
8. Southeast Asians;
9. Pacific Islanders;
10. Australian Aborigines and the Aboriginal New Guineans.

So, what is seemingly the most rigorous analysis we have examined so far again closely corresponds to the racial taxonomies advanced by classical anthropologists. Cavalli-Sforza et al. use the word 'cluster' rather than 'race'. However, it appears that there is little discernible difference between a cluster and a race, and as race is a commonly understood term, we would suggest it is unnecessary and confusing to introduce a new one which means, in essence, exactly the same thing. This caution about the word race seems to be an example of reflecting the fashion of the time because Cavalli-Sforza expressed no such caution in 1976. Bodmer and Cavalli-Sforza (1976, p. 698) note that:

> races could be called subspecies if we adopted for man a criterion from systematic zoology. The criterion is that two or more groups become subspecies when 75 per cent or more of all individuals constituting the groups can be unequivocally classified as belonging to a particular group.

They continue by observing that when human races are defined broadly, it is possible to identify the race of many more than 75% of the population. Hence races certainly exist among humans.

However, the utility of race is not limited to physical environmental adaptations and blood types. There are race differences in a number of serious medical conditions which have a genetic basis, further evidencing the degree to which race is a predictive and useful category. Race-based differences exist in a number of genetically based conditions including in cystic fibrosis, PKU (phenylketonuria, this leads to retardation and seizures), hypertension, stroke, diabetes, prostate cancer, breast cancer, obesity, myopia, and schizophrenia. These differences have arisen through founder effect, genetic drift, mutation, and adaptation. There is an extensive body of literature on this subject (e.g. Martin & Soldo, 1997) and the differences can be simply illustrated by Bodmer and Cavalli-Sforza's (1976) examination of cystic fibrosis and PKU in Europeans, Sub-Saharan Africans, and East Asians. Cystic fibrosis is between 54% and 100% heritable (Willis-Owen and Moffatt, 2012, p. 14). PKU is 100% heritable, though its effects can be reduced by a specialized diet (Joseph, 2006, p. 35).

Table 1. Gene frequencies (prevalence rate in population, %) of cystic fibrosis and PKU in different races (Source: Lynn, 2006).

RACE	CYSTIC FIBROSIS	PKU
Africans	0.4	0.3
East Asians	0.3	0.5
Europeans	2.0	1.1

Austria	-	1.2
Australia	2.2	1.1
Canada	-	0.9
England	1.9	1.5
USA	1.9	0.9

The gene frequencies of cystic fibrosis in Europeans are four or five times higher than in Sub-Saharan Africans and East Asians, while gene frequencies of PKU are around twice as high in Europeans than in the other two races. However, the genes frequencies are quite similar in assorted European populations such as among Austrians, Australians, Canadians, the English, and European Americans.

Before moving on to criticisms of the concept of race, it is worth noting that there remains debate over the degree to which, and through what means, the different human races are related. The most widely known theory is the so-called 'Out of Africa Theory' whereby anatomically modern humans evolved in Africa and began to migrate between 125,000 and 60,000 years ago, displacing proto-humans and Neanderthals. An alternative theory, which is currently gaining traction, is the 'Multiregional Origins Theory'. This theory proposes that humans may have left Africa around 338,000 years ago. They interbred with Homo erectus and Neanderthals, the latter having limited genetic influence (1–10%) in all human populations with the exception of Sub-Saharan Africans.[7] The correct theory of human origins remains a matter of debate and, to the extent that we draw upon a theory in this study, we tentatively assume the veracity of the more widely accepted Out of Africa Theory.

---

7   See Cochran & Harpending, 2009, or Smith & Ahern, 2013, for a more detailed discussion.

4. Criticisms of the Concept of Race

From the eighteenth century to the middle of the twentieth century, almost all biologists and anthropologists accepted that the human species could be divided into biologically distinct races. Thus, in 1922, the Scottish anthropologist Sir Arthur Keith (1866–1955) wrote that:

> So clearly differentiated are the types of mankind that, were an anthropologist presented with a crowd of men drawn from the Australoid, the Negroid, East Asian or Caucasoid types, he could separate the one human element from the other without hesitation or mistake (Keith, 1922, p. xviii).

However, the scholarly mood, at least in the social sciences, began to change by 1945 when British-American anthropologist Ashley Montagu (1905–1999) published *Mankind's Most Dangerous Myth* (Montagu, 1945). Despite the fact that Montagu clearly stated in this book that different races do exist as we have defined them (p. 6), he attempted to suggest that the whole concept of race was fallacious, indeed subtitling his book *The Fallacy of Race*. Another anthropologist, the American Frank B. Livingstone (1928–2005), published a paper entitled *On the Non-Existence of the Human Races*, arguing that there were no races, only 'clines' (Livingstone, 1962). There is no such thing as a perfect example of a particular category. We conceive of a category when a number of features correlate together and distinguishing these into a category allows correct predictions to be made. A cline, by definition, sits on the borders between two conceptual extremes (i.e. on the borders between two races which we distinguish because so doing permits correct predictions to be made). Thus, there can be no clines if there are no races.

Perhaps the fiercest criticism of the concept of race in the latter half of the twentieth century has come from the very discipline that once did the most to promote the concept: anthropology. Since around 1900, anthropology in Western Europe and the USA has gradually moved from being a branch of biology concerned with the physical and social evolution of humans, to a highly ideologically driven discipline strongly influenced by such dogmas as cultural determinism (that differences are caused by culture), cultural relativism (all cultures are equal and cannot be compared), and postmodernism ('truth' is merely a reflection of the dominant culture, we have a duty to deconstruct that truth and so empower those who lack power). I would aver that these ideologies are highly problematic. As we will see, differences between humans are significantly genetic. Following the test of pragmatism, if all cultures are equal then seriously ill cultural anthropologists should go to witch doctors rather than hospitals, and should not be happy to fly to anthropology conferences, because this implies that Western science is objectively correct. And if truth is merely a construct, cultural anthropologists should test this by throwing themselves off a tall building. If truth is not objective, they should be fine. The precise history of, and reasons for, this shift have been discussed in depth elsewhere (see Dutton, 2012).

However, in 2004 the American Anthropological Association announced on its website that 'race is not a scientifically valid biological category'. In the multi-authored volume, *Race and Intelligence: Separating Science from Myth*, Graves (2002, p. 5) writes, 'The majority of geneticists, evolutionary biologists and anthropologists agree that there are no biological races in the human species'. Cohen (2002, p. 211) likewise asserts, 'Almost all anthropologists agree that races in the popular sense do not exist and never have existed'. This is simply incorrect. For example, a 2001 survey of Polish anthropologists found that 75% agreed that there were races (Kaszycka & Strzalko, 2003), and a 1985 survey of American anthropologists found that 59% agreed that there were races (Lieberman & Reynolds, 1996). Interestingly, the chapter summaries in the volume already mentioned include the line, 'There are no biological races. Human physical appearance varies gradually around the planet, with the most geographically distant peoples generally appearing the most different from one another'. Even if this were true, this does not undermine the utility of race. If a species varies in small ways due to slightly different environments, then those at the extremes will differ so much, and in consistent ways, that it becomes useful, in terms of making correct predictions, to distinguish between them. As we have seen, there exist population clusters which differ significantly due to varying degrees of evolutionary isolation. Nevertheless, there is clearly a vociferous movement in anthropology opposed to the use of the race category. We shall now examine criticisms of race which they and like-minded scholars advance.

The first criticism is that race has a history, problematic conceptual borders, and is a Western concept (e.g. Diamond, 1994). The same argument could be made about any concept in the English language. The central question is whether it is a predictive category.

Secondly, it has been noted that the word race can mean different things. Historically, it has been used as 'culture' or 'nation' is now used. This is irrelevant. We are clear that by race we mean breeding populations separated in prehistory and adapted to different environments. Accordingly, in categorizing an individual into a particular race, we must remember that as in all taxonomies there will be those who are borderline; but it is clear that by race we are referring to the birthplace of the majority of a person's ancestors within certain time constraints, based on the widely accepted theories of human origins (e.g. Wilson, 1978, pp. 48–49).

According to our current chronology (e.g. Stringer & Andrews, 1988), Man evolved in Africa. Humans came to Europe about 110,000 years ago and to North Asia about 70,000 years later. Africa ceased to be isolated about 2000 years ago. Assuming about twenty-five years to a generation, a black African is a person most of whose ancestors, forty to 4400 generations removed, were born in Sub-Saharan Africa. In that African Americans are, on average, about 10–25% European, an African American would be a person at least 75% of whose ancestors forty to 4400 generations removed were born in Sub-Saharan Africa. It has been demonstrated that numerous physical traits such as skin colour, lip eversion, hair texture, facial bone structure, and voice timbre (e.g. Putnam, 1975) are shared, to varying degrees, by Africans. This creates an African stereotype, but it is meaningful because all of the significant traits correlate, they are adaptations to the same environment and, as such, they permit significant predictions to be made. The fact that these correlations can be ascribed to most people whose ancestors were born in Africa means that the 'African' group can be compared to other groups, and that the average member of the group will react differently from members of other groups in set circumstances because they are adapted to a specific environment. At an obvious level, being dark skinned is useful for avoiding skin cancer. This is what we mean by race and why it is useful and meaningful, at least in terms of physical predictions. If anyone uses race to mean anything else, then our use of race and his are merely homonyms.

Equally, we could divide races, or even nations, in accordance with the percentage of genes the members share in comparison to outsiders. Populations that look physically different are evolved to different environments. As such, they are separate breeding populations, and thus have more genes in common with each other than with outsiders. In this sense, they are an extended family and a different race is a different extended family. Salter's (2007) analysis showed that if the world population were just English, then the kinship between any random pair of Englishmen would be zero. But if the world population consisted of both English people and Danes, then two random English people would have a kinship of 0.0021. This would make them sixth cousins when compared to a Dane. As genetic distances between populations become larger, the kinship coefficient between random co-ethnics within a population gets larger. But this again shows that the racial division is meaningful and has a clear statistical basis: members of a race have more genetically in common with co-ethnics than with members of any other race, as we have seen from research on polymorphism clusters. What it also means, and this should be emphasized, is that races are constantly evolving as different groups within the broader category breed according to different patterns.

The third supposed problem with race is that deploying it leads to bad consequences. It legitimizes 'racist groups' and so forth. That it does this is clearly of no relevance to whether or not it is a philosophically justifiable and predictive category. This argument commits the fallacy of 'appeal to consequences' and, depending on how the consequences are described, 'appeal to emotion'.

The fourth criticism is that there are more differences within races than there are between them. Likewise, you could argue that there are more differences within humanity than there are between humans and chimpanzees. There is, after all, only a 1.5% difference between humans and chimpanzees (Caccone & Powell, 1989). I do not think many people would argue that the distinction between humans and chimpanzees is meaningless. We are talking about comparative differences. Dividing between two racial categories, for example, permits accurate predictions to be made about each, even if the differences are very small (e.g. Hoffman, 1994). The genetic differences (in terms of heritable musical ability) between a standard musician and Mozart are probably rather small but these differences have clear and important consequences. Tiny genetic differences (humans only differ by 0.0012%) can have significant consequences. As we will see, it is possible to extend this understanding of within-group differences to between-group differences.

In addition, as Cochran and Harpending (2009, p. 15) have noted, there are more genetic differences within breeds of dog than between breeds of dog, but nobody would dismiss as insignificant the differences between a Great Dane and Chihuahua. In addition, they note that 'information about the distribution of genetic variation tells you essentially nothing about the size or significance of trait differences... If between-group genetic differences tend to push in a particular direction — tend to favour a certain trend — they can add up and have large effects'. Thus, we can conclude that the criticisms of the race concept can be successfully refuted.

6. Conclusion

In this chapter we have examined race taxonomies and the concept of race. We have argued that 'race' is nothing more than what would be termed 'subspecies' or 'breed' in the animal kingdom of which the human species is a member. We have demonstrated that, following our previous discussion of what constitutes a meaningful and scientific category, race is indeed a meaningful category, because it permits correct predictions to be made. We have seen that the traditional races of classical anthropology have a clear quantitative basis and that gene and disease frequencies cluster along racial lines. Finally, we have examined the criticisms of the concept of race and shown that they can be refuted.

CHAPTER THREE

What Is Intelligence?

1. Introduction

In this study of ethnocentrism, the issue of intelligence will be examined as a possible factor in explaining differences in group levels of ethnocentrism. Accordingly, in this chapter we will examine the issue of intelligence, as well as the evidence for racial differences in average intelligence.[8]

2. What Is Intelligence?

For the purposes of this book, it suffices to say that we define 'intelligence' as the ability to solve complex problems and to solve them quickly. The more quickly you can solve a given problem the more intelligent you are and the more intelligent you are the more complex the problem has to be before you are stumped.

Intelligence is a single entity that can be measured by IQ (intelligence quotient) tests. These tests are divided into three components testing linguistic, mathematical, and spatial intelligence. People vary in their performance on the components, but performance is positively correlated, proving that there is a single entity known as g (general intelligence) which underpins these intelligences. This model of intelligence is widely accepted by experts in the field such as Lynn (2006),

---

[8] Parts of this chapter were previously published in Dutton (2014).

Jensen (1998), and Mackintosh (1998). There are three fundamental forms of intelligence: mathematical reasoning, verbal reasoning, and spatial reasoning, with these three understood to be underpinned by g.

In statistics, a correlation refers to a relationship between two variables and the degree of its strength. So, if the correlation was 1, the two things always go together and if it's −1 then they never do. Usually, correlations are between 0 and 1. So, a 0.7 correlation is strong and means that the two variables often go together. Correlations tell us what percentage of the variance is explained by a particular variable. So, if the correlation between IQ and how well people perform in school leaving exams in 0.7 (which it is, see Jensen, 1998) then IQ explains 49% of the variation in how well people do in school leaving exams. The percentage of the variance is always the correlation squared.

The criticisms of the concept of intelligence, as defined above, are highly problematic. As we will draw upon the concept of intelligence and upon IQ tests, we will now look at these.

1. **But what do you mean by 'Intelligence'?** Critics argue that 'intelligence' is difficult to precisely define. Where do you draw the border between 'intelligent' and 'not intelligent'? This point could be made about any concept to varying degrees. It could be argued that 'tall' is difficult to define, but that does not mean we cannot talk about 'tall people'. The world is a mass of information which we make sense of through categories which allow seemingly correct predictions to be made. If we can't do that, then we wouldn't be able to do anything because we could never make any predictions. Insisting categories be perfectly defined fails the test of pragmatism.

2. **There are different kinds of intelligence, such as 'emotional intelligence'.** It has been shown that emotional intelligence correlates with g at 0.3 (Kaufman et al., 2011). Also, since in general (in

dictionaries, for example), intelligence is defined as we have defined it, it is confusing to use the concept differently. Additionally, if everyone has some kind of 'high intelligence' then the concept becomes meaningless in terms of making predictions.

3. **Intelligence means different things in different cultures.** We have stated what we mean by intelligence. If a different culture talks about something different, then they're not talking about intelligence.

4. **Intelligence is simply what IQ tests test.** As we will see below, IQ test results are statistically significantly and strongly correlated with other differences. These differences include health, law-abidingness, access to resources (Lynn & Vanhanen, 2012), and general knowledge (Spearman, 1904) so intelligence is germane in all cultures.

    Correlations, it should be noted, are tested for 'statistical significance'. This is a way of proving that the correlation is not a fluke, based on the sample size. For example, with a sample of twelve people you might find a strong negative correlation between education level and wearing blue clothes but this could just be down to chance. So, a p test, a test of significance, allows us to establish whether or not the relationship is a fluke. If we can be at least 95% confident that it is not a fluke ($p = < 0.05$) then we accept that the relationship is genuine. This, of course, involves drawing a random border. If something has a 94% probability of not being a fluke then we might say that 'near significance' has been attained. But the border of acceptability has to be drawn somewhere and it is accepted among scientists that this is at 95% certainty.

5. **We do not fully understand intelligence, so intelligence research is speculative.** It is true that we do not yet understand the precise brain architecture of intelligence, but this does not mean that we cannot talk about intelligence. We could talk about stars before we understood their architecture (Levin, 2005).

Criticisms have also been leveled against IQ tests. We respond to the most common of these below.

1. **A few dozen questions are insufficient to test mental ability.** It is quite true that, in a minority of cases, an IQ test score may be skewed by illness, stress, or even developing slightly later than one's peers, but there is a significant correlation between adolescent IQ score and later achievement in various fields which relate to mental ability. For example, IQ test scores predict educational success at 0.5 overall, 0.7 at school, 0.5 at undergraduate level, and 0.3 at postgraduate level (Jensen, 1979, p. 319). They also predict income, health, criminality (negatively), and many other factors (Lynn & Vanhanen, 2012).

2. **IQ tests are unable to measure intelligence.** To argue that intelligence is real yet IQ tests do not measure it is like claiming that weight is real, and some people are heavier than others, but bathroom scales do not accurately measure it. A pair of scales is reliable if its estimation of the heaviness of different people positively correlates with our own estimation when trying to lift the same people. Likewise, an IQ test is reliable if its estimation of the intelligence of different people positively correlates with differences in their intelligence as measured by more intuitive measures of intelligence, such as academic performance. The instrument, in both cases, may be imperfect, but it is the best instrument we have. In that IQ scores positively correlate with evidence of intelligence (such as educational attainment), they are the best (if imperfect) means we have of measuring intelligence, just as bathroom scales are the best (if imperfect) means we have of measuring weight. Different scales will give people slightly different weights just as different IQ tests will give different people slightly different IQs.

3. **Intelligence and IQ are not the same thing.** We have defined intelligence as ability in cognitive tasks. Academic exams involve

cognitive tasks, and successful performance in school exams is predicted by IQ at 0.7 (Jensen, 1979, p. 319).

4. **IQ tests are unreliable.** No test instrument is perfectly reliable. Modern IQ tests, in particular the Raven Progressive Matrices (first developed in 1938), have been argued to have a reliability of at least 0.9 (Jensen, 1998, pp. 49–50), so it is simply inaccurate to brand them unreliable.

5. **The tests are not predictive of life outcomes because some successful people, such as Einstein, are brilliant at mathematics but less good at linguistic tasks.** This criticism fails to appreciate that this kind of contrast is relatively rare. In general, those who perform above average on linguistic tasks also perform well on spatial and mathematical tasks, and this implies the presence of g (general intelligence). The correlation at age sixteen between verbal and mathematical intelligence on the NCDS (the UK-based National Child Development Study, N. 17,000) is 0.65 (Kanazawa, 2012, p. 42). The subjects generally perform better on one kind of task than on another, but the crucial point is that there is a strong positive correlation. Spearman's (1904) own research found a correlation of 0.64 between performance in English (mainly linguistic intelligence) and performance in Math. This demonstrates that many of the subjects were better at English than Math or vice versa. But it also evidences our ability to posit g and shows a strong positive correlation. With this in mind, IQ tests can be 'g-loaded' such that they more accurately test g, steadily eliminating aspects of the test which have been shown not to relate to g. This has led some IQ tests to have g-loadings of around 0.9, which means that the argument that they are unfair is very difficult to sustain.

6. **IQ Tests are culturally biased.** The tests are argued to be culturally biased and unfair on certain races and classes (e.g. Ryle, 1974, p. 54). This is simply inaccurate. With regard to race, East Asians score better on IQ tests than the Europeans who developed them,

and East Asian Americans score better than white Americans (Jensen, 1981, p. 205). In addition, reaction times correlate with IQ at about 0.4 (Hunt, 2011, p. 151), and racial differences in reaction times are in the same direction as racial differences in IQ scores (Jensen, 1998, Ch. 11). Also, relative brain size correlates with IQ at around 0.3, and racial differences in relative brain size are in the same direction as the differences in IQ scores (Jensen, 1998, p. 437). As such, IQ tests significantly correlate with objective measures so that it is very difficult to argue they are culturally biased.

In addition, the specific theory of bias known as 'stereotype threat' is not persuasive. The argument runs that blacks, for example, are stereotyped to do worse than whites on IQ tests, so they do worse solely because this expectation creates stress. However, in the case of blacks, this is a misreading of Steele and Aronson (1995) who actually found a 1 SD (standard deviation) difference between black and white IQ scores even when controlling for stereotype threat (see Ganley et al., 2013 for meta-analysis). Also, large-scale strongly controlled attempts to replicate stereotype threat, for example in relation to females and mathematics, have consistently failed (Ganley et al., 2013). As such, it seems clear that our definition of intelligence is the most useful one and that IQ tests are reliable.

3. Race Differences in Intelligence

The different races have adapted to their different environments through different modal personalities and average levels of intelligence. Beginning with intelligence, we will set out below the average IQs for different races. However, before doing this we must respond to the argument that though there are racial differences in IQ these are for environmental rather than genetic reasons.

Environment is a significant factor in understanding intelligence. Intelligence is less genetically predicted in a poor environment in which people are prone to serious childhood illnesses which might reduce IQ. British psychologist Richard Lynn (2006) has set out the following average racial IQs based on a detailed meta-analysis of average national IQs.

1. Ashkenazi Jews: 112.
2. Northeast Asians: 105.
3. Europeans: 100.
4. African Americans: 85.
5. South Asians/Middle Easterners: 80.
6. Sub-Saharan Africans: 70.

The average IQ of African Americans is especially interesting because it sits between that of Africans and Europeans. This implies that much of the difference between Europeans and Africans is genetic, since the environment of African Americans is much closer to the European one than it is to the African one. Thus, the African American IQ probably reflects an element of environment and some admixture with Europeans. African Americans are, as we have noted, up to about 25% European genetically. Interestingly, the IQ in Jamaica, where European admixture is much lower and living standards lower, is around 75 (Lynn & Meisenberg, 2015). These differences make evolutionary sense. A cold environment, such as that to which Northeast Asians are adapted, would have strongly selected in favor of intelligence because it would require the ability to plan, conceive of survival strategies (such as building shelters and making clothes) in extremely harsh conditions, and it would select in favor of very low time preference, of those able to think far into the future to plan for the colder times. This is known as the Cold Winters Theory. It is also possible that a trade-off had to be made, in terms of sexual selection, in selecting for parasite resistance or for intelligence. Intelligence would be more important in colder climates while parasite resistance (advertised through physical prowess) would be more important in tropical climates (Miller, 2000).

Lynn (2006) has found important differences in IQ within racial categories. Thus, for example, in Europe, though the average IQ is 100, there are clear regional differences. The average IQ of white British people is 100, but it is only 93 in the Republic of Ireland, possibly reflecting a long history of outward migration, with intelligence predicting migration (Lynn, 1988 or Lynn, 1980). The average IQs in Greece (92), Portugal (94), and in certain Balkan countries are around this level, reflecting the fact that they are clines between Europeans and South Asians in Turkey in the case of Greece and the Balkans or, in the case of Portugal, between Europeans and Sub-Saharan Africans (Lynn, 2006, p. 15). In Eastern Europe, some countries, such as Latvia, have IQs below 100. In the case of Latvia, for example, this is 97. If this is not down to sampling errors, then it is also likely to reflect emigration, especially during the turbulence of World War II. Northeast Asian IQs also vary, with the Mongolian IQ being only 100. Significant variation occurs within racial groups.[9]

4. Criticisms of Race and IQ Data

The criticisms of these data take three forms: (1) to question the national IQs per se; (2) to assert that IQ tests are biased against blacks; and (3) to assert that the tests are reasonable, but the reasons for the differences are not genetic.

1. THE NATIONAL IQs ARE ALL PROBLEMATIC

Critics have dismissed Lynn's (2006) IQ scores, variously, as being 'virtually meaningless' (Barnett & Williams, 2004) or 'technically inadequate...and meaningless' (Hunt & Sternberg, 2006, 133–136). The IQ data drawn upon have been described as 'highly deficient' (Volken, 2003, p. 411). Ervik (2003, p. 406) asserts, of Lynn and

---

9   For example, the IQ of most Sub-Saharan African countries is between 64 and 75 but in Sudan it is 77.5 (Lynn & Vanhanen, 2012). This is likely a reflection of significant Arab admixture among the Northern Sudanese.

Vanhanen (2002), that 'the authors fail to present convincing evidence and appear to jump to conclusions' while Nechyba (2004, p. 1178) has stated that there is 'relatively weak statistical evidence and dubious presumptions'.

Lynn and Vanhanen (2012, p. 7) rejoin that their national IQ scores are highly correlated with national scores in tests of mathematics and science as well as with many other social and economic variables which are predicted to varying degrees, at an individual level, by intelligence.[10] The validity of an IQ test is the degree to which it measures intelligence, and this can be shown by the extent to which its results correlate with other established measures of cognitive ability. Intelligence positively correlates with educational attainment, claim Lynn and Vanhanen (2012, Ch. 1), at between 0.5 and 0.8. Lynn and Vanhanen have shown that their national IQ scores correlate with national mathematics scores at 0.88, and with national science scores at 0.86. They correlate with PISA science scores (obtained by fifteen year olds) at 0.83, and subsequent studies using larger data sets have found a correlation of 0.9, with the results independently confirmed (Rindermann, 2007). In one study of 108 nations, Lynn found a correlation of 1 between national IQ scores and scores aggregated from PISA and other national tests (Lynn & Vanhanen, 2012, pp. 33–34). The national IQ scores also correlate in the right direction with other factors which correlate with intelligence such as health, wealth, and (negatively) crime. Accordingly, the critics are deliberately exaggerating the deficiencies. This is a straw man argument.

The next, and perhaps the most useful method, as it is the least overtly fallacious, is, as Allik (2008, p. 707) summarizes, 'to interpret the results as measurement error. A useful strategy is to discover a few small mistakes, declaring that all the results are equally suspicious'. MackIntosh (2007) is an example of such a critic. MackIntosh writes, albeit regarding Lynn's (2011) analysis of dysgenics, that, 'The errors

---

10   These are set out in Lynn and Vanhanen (2012).

may not be particularly important, and I do not know how typical they are. But they do not increase my confidence in Lynn's scholarship'. This criticism risks the fallacy of composition. That there is a particular error or relevant omission in one place does not mean that it will be the case throughout the work. Only a detailed analysis of the work can allow a person to argue that there are so many important errors in it that the argument is essentially undermined. Critics of these data have not done this and, as such, they engage in the fallacy of composition.

2. TESTS ARE BIASED AGAINST BLACK PEOPLE

We have already looked at this issue as part of our broader discussion of IQ tests and noted that this argument cannot be sustained.

3. TESTS ARE ACCURATE MEASURES BUT BLACK WHITE DIFFERENCES ARE NOT GENETIC

Firstly, blacks score worse on IQ tests than groups which can be understood to be more impoverished and more distant from white norms than them, such as Eskimos (Levin, 2005). This implies that their low IQ cannot be attributed to environmental or cultural reasons.

Secondly, the one SD difference between white and black intelligence in the USA is evident by the age of three. The earlier a difference becomes apparent, it is argued in genetics, the more likely it is to be genetic (Broman et al., 1987).[11] Levin (2005) calculates that it is extremely improbable on this basis, around a 10% probability, that such differences would not be at least partly genetic. Thirdly, race

---

11 Some researchers still cite the 1960s Milwaukee Project as evidence that race differences in IQ are not genetic. This project, which purported to show that environmental intervention could radically improve black IQ, was exposed as fraudulent, the results were never published in a refereed journal, the improvements were found to be temporary, requests for the raw data were refused, and the lead researcher was jailed for fraud (Jensen, 1998).

differences in IQ scores correlate in the expected direction with race differences in undoubtedly objective measures, such as reaction times.

Fourthly, compelling evidence comes in the form of interracial adoption studies, because these help to control for environment. Weinberg et al. (1992) show that the average IQ of black children adopted, usually by educated white families, is 96.8. This is significantly below the average white IQ of 100 and even further below the IQ of the adoptive parents, which is in the region of 110. The fact that it is higher than the average black IQ may reflect a much more stimulating environment from a very young age, but it is clearly closer to the average black IQ in the USA than that of the adopted parents. This would seem to indicate, argues Lynn (2006), that the racial difference in IQ is genetic.

Studies of Northeast Asian children adopted by white families demonstrate something similar. The IQs of Northeast Asian children adopted by whites are closer to the Northeast Asian average than to the white average. There have been six such studies. Winick et al. (1975) investigated Koreans aged between six and fourteen adopted by white families in the USA. Those who were severely undernourished as infants had an IQ of 102, those who were poorly nourished had an IQ of 106, while those who were well nourished had an IQ of 112, higher even than the average IQ of the adoptive parents. Another USA study (Clark & Hanisee, 1982) gave Koreans adopted by whites an IQ of 105, a study in Belgium (Frydman & Lynn, 1989) was 110, while a Dutch study (Stams et al., 2000) was 108. We have noted that intelligence is substantially heritable, so it makes sense that these children's IQs are higher than the average white IQ and, if well nourished prior to adoption, even higher than the average IQ of the white adoptive parents.

Fifthly, Italian anthropologist Davide Piffer (2016) has shown that the correlation between a country's average IQ and the percentage of the population who carry forms of particular genes which essentially predict high intelligence is 0.9, which is an exceptionally high correlation. It means that 81% of the variance in population differences in IQ is down to genetic differences. In effect, Piffer proves that race differences in intelligence are overwhelmingly a reflection of genetic differences. As such, the arguments against racial differences in intelligence being genetic can be refuted, and critics are merely left with moralistic arguments and other fallacies.

5. Conclusion

We have to conclude that the lexical definition of intelligence is justifiable and IQ tests can be legitimately administered to different cultures and races. Further, there are consistent racial differences in average intelligence and these are overwhelmingly genetic in origin.

CHAPTER FOUR

What Are 'Ethnocentrism' and 'Ethnicity'?

1. Introduction

We saw in Chapter Two that we must distinguish between the concepts of 'race' and 'ethnicity' or we may as well reject one of the two categories. In this chapter, we will clarify what we mean by the terms 'ethnicity' and 'ethnocentrism'. We will argue that the most useful definition of an 'ethny' is, in effect, what might be termed a sub-race; a group that is a substantially separate breeding population, such that its members are an extended kinship group who have more genetically in common with each other than with a random member of the neighbouring ethnic group. Thus, an ethny can be seen as on its way to becoming a separate 'race', just as a 'race' can be regarded as on its way to becoming a separate 'species'.

2. What Is Ethnocentrism?

The word 'ethnocentrism' combines the Greek words 'ethnos' (ethnic group, nation or people) with the word 'centre' — placing one's 'ethnic group' at the centre. According to historical research by Bizumic (2014), the word 'ethnocentrism' was coined by Ludwig Gumplowicz (1838–1909), a Polish sociologist, in 1879 (Gumplowicz, 1879) and employed in Gumplowicz's research, which was written in German and

Polish. American economist William Sumner (1840–1910) introduced the word into the English language and popularized the concept (Sumner, 1906). However, Sumner did not reference Gumplowicz's work, meaning that later ethnocentrism researchers have credited Sumner with coining the term (e.g. Adorno et al., 1950).

For Gumplowicz, ethnocentrism was similar to geocentriism or anthrocentrism, only the reference point was one's own ethnicity. He argued that it was the belief that one's own ethnic group was superior to and preferable to other ethnic groups. For Sumner (1906, p. 13) ethnocentrism involved 'the view of things in which one's own group is the centre of everything and all others are scaled and rated with reference to it'. Sumner included, under the umbrella of ethnocentrism, feelings of in-group devotion and cohesion, the rejection of out-groups, a sense of in-group superiority, and the exploitation of out-groups. He also assumed that in-group positivity would generally be positively correlated with out-group negativity. Subsequent researchers drew upon this concept of ethnocentrism, often defining it more narrowly. For example, Adorno et al. (1950) effectively used 'ethnocentrism' only to refer to out-group prejudice. However, more recent research has suggested that Sumner's assumption — that in-group love and out-group hate should positively correlate — is incorrect (Brewer, 1999). The fundamental dimensions to ethnocentrism can be found cross-culturally. These are:

1. A strong sense of group cohesion and group-devotion;

2. Preference for the ethnic in-group, a belief in one's own ethnic group's superiority, a desire to maintain ethnic purity, and approval of the exploitation of ethnic out-groups (Bizumic & Duckitt, 2012).

Accordingly, 'ethnocentrism' is more than simply out-group prejudice and in-group favouritism. It is conceptually distinct, though it crosses over with both of these. There is considerable debate regarding what causes ethnocentric behaviour. But before we look at this, it would be useful to understand the nature of the 'ethnic group'.

3. Lexical Definitions of Ethnicity

In defining 'ethnicity', it is useful to begin with 'dictionary' or 'lexical' definitions, as these reflect how the concept is commonly employed and understood. However, with regard to 'ethnicity' there is some implicit debate over the definition. According to the current *Oxford English Dictionary*, an 'ethnicity' is 'a social group that has a common cultural tradition', while for the *Collins English Dictionary* an ethnicity is a 'human group having racial, religious, linguistic and other traits in common'. For the *Merriam Webster Dictionary*, an 'ethnicity' is 'a race or large group of people who have the same customs, religion, origin etc.' There is a subtle disagreement between these three dictionaries regarding how the word 'ethnicity' is best defined and this disagreement reflects a broader division, over this subject, between scholars of ethnicity. The essential divide is between the older school of thought, known as the '*Primordialists*', and school of thought that has become popular since the 1960s; the '*Constructivists*' or '*Subjectivists*'.

For the *Primordialists*, ethnic groups are extremely ancient because they are ultimately based around common ancestry; in other words, bonds of blood. As such, they have a key point of commonality with 'race'. The ethnic group can thus be understood as a kind of extended family; a large-scale kinship group; something reflected in the way that members of ethnic groups do tend to have a folk sense of common ancestors and of being a kind of family. Indeed, this is consistent with genetic data, which has shown that ethnic groups really are distinct genetic clusters (see Salter, 2007). The *Collins Dictionary* definition is the most *Primordialist*, because it refers to 'race', which, as we have discussed, is generally a matter of genetics. Indeed, in common parlance, 'ethnic minority' is a term used to refer to a racial, rather than purely cultural, minority.[12] For the *Constructivists,* ethnic identities are merely a matter of 'culture'. They are relatively arbitrary and they are subject to change, meaning a person might change their ethnic identification during their lifetime. For this reason, ethnic groups are relatively unstable, because they are merely products of environmental factors. As such, *'Constructivists'* construct their theories around cultural or environmental determinism, the view that a phenomenon can be entirely explained by environmental or cultural factors. Culture and environment are assumed to explain the development of 'ethnic identity' and there is no space for a significantly genetic explanation.

We will look at both of these conceptions of ethnicity in some depth, and we will begin by examining the *Constructivist* school and the most important examples of it. Doing this is relatively complicated, because this school has itself divided into many sub-schools (perhaps we should call them 'classes', to extend the metaphor). But they are worth exploring, if only to understand just how much debate the concept of 'ethnicity' has engendered in social science. To make this easier to follow, I have italicised the names of the different schools and classes.

4. Constructivism

The Constructivist School can be divided into a variety of competing theoretical camps.

---

12 There can, of course, be a subjective element to 'race', such as in a situation where a mixed-race person or member of a cline is compelled, by legal procedure, to identify as one race or another. Most obviously, people who are Turkish or Greek are a cline, combining European and South Asian genes to varying extents (see Lynn, 2006). How should they identify themselves? Most Greeks will identify as 'white' and are widely accepted as being a European people. However, when Turks identify as 'white' this may be regarded as more contentious and many people would argue that they should be regarded as 'South Asian', or at least as non-European. But, in general, racial identification is clear and is a matter of genetics.

INSTRUMENTALISTS

Firstly, there are the so-called *'Instrumentalists',* epitomized by the Norwegian anthropologist Frederik Barth (1928–2016). In some respects, they have points of commonality with *Primordialists*. For Barth (1969), an ethnic group is a social organization based around a shared culture, with 'culture' employed to mean 'way of life'. It has symbolic social boundaries and the extent to which it maintains these boundaries is a function of environmental variables. The factors which distinguish one ethnic group from another are essentially arbitrary and the groups are mobilized by their leaders in times of crisis.

This model has a number of shortcomings from the viewpoint of other *Subjectivists*. Most obviously, it may explain identification in tribal groups, where members follow a fission-fusion model of frequently splitting and forming new groups, but may not work in nations, where a sense of ethnic identity is longer established. Olzak and Nagel (1989) have presented a variation on Barth's model called *'Competition Theory'* wherein a sense of ethnic identity is cultural and fluid but is periodically reawakened by competition between ethnic groups. Accordingly, ethnic identity is espoused in order to better access resources. However, this raises the question of why certain ethnic identities only begin to be espoused at certain points in history.

Then there are the *Rational Choice Theorists*, such as British sociologist Michael Banton (1983). They argue that people will behave rationally in order to maximize their benefits and they will adopt an ethnic identity, which is purely cultural and fluid, accordingly. This theory is highly problematic as there is strong evidence that people can act against their rational self-interest, following evolved tendencies which were useful in our evolutionary past. These include:

1. **Obedience to Authority:** Under laboratory conditions, it was demonstrated in American psychologist Stanley Milgram's (1933–1984; Milgram, 1974) experiment that the majority of people (more than 50%) would be prepared to knowingly administer a lethal electric

shock to an innocent person in another room simply in order to comply with the instructions of an authority, in the form of a white-coated scientist. Subjects were told that they were taking part in an experiment to see whether electric shocks increased learning ability. They watched as their 'student' (really an actor) was strapped into the electric device. Then, in another room, they had to ask the student questions over a speaker system, watched over by a scientist, with teachers increasing the electric shock level each time the student gave a wrong answer. Eventually, students were audibly screaming in pain and teachers questioning whether they should continue. Told that 'the experiment must go on', over half continued past the point where the machine said 'Danger: Severe Shock' and even after the students had fallen silent, presumably fainted or worse, simply because they were instructed to do so by an authority. This adaptation could explain why people can be induced, by an authority, to act against their interests.

2. **Consensus Effect:** We have evolved a strong capacity to conform to the group and this extends to the tendency to alter one's beliefs, even if one knows one is correct, in order to conform to the group. Indeed, the phenomenon of *cognitive dissonance* shows that people will alter their memories in order to ensure that their worldview is congruous with that of the group. This demonstrates that peer-pressure can be strong enough to cause us to behave in an irrational manner.

3. **Evolved Altruism:** We have evolved such a strong desire to be altruistic that it causes us to behave in a seemingly irrational manner. In Game Theory there is a game called 'Prisoner's Dilemma'. In experiments, two players will play on this game on networked computers and the two players will neither meet each other nor know anything about each other. Each player can decide to 'cooperate' with the other player or 'defect' on the other player. 'Cooperation' benefits the other player while 'defection' hurts the other player

but benefits the defector. In a 'two shot' game, it may be rational to 'cooperate' because if you don't then the other player can 'defect' on you in the future, so damaging you. However, in a 'one-shot' game it is always rational to defect, as you will always get a higher pay-off by doing so. Despite this, numerous experiments have shown that around 50% of people cooperate in a one shot game (Kanazawa, 2012, p. 32). This would mean that our evolved capacity to be altruistic is so strong that it can make us behave in an irrational way, in a way that actually damages our interests.

4. **Religion:** There is evidence that religiousness is an evolved capacity. Religiousness has been found to be 0.44 heritable based on twin studies while religious experience and fundamentalism are around 0.66 heritable (Koenig et al., 2005). A variety of evolved capacities would explain the development of religiousness including the tendency to find patterns in randomness and so-called 'Hyperactive Agency Detection', wherein we tend to assume an agent behind any inexplicable event (Boyer, 2001). In addition, it has been argued that religiousness developed as a means of reducing stress, especially that caused by an awareness of death or due to social exclusion, and both these tend to increase religiousness (see Lewis & Bates, 2013). It has been shown that the belief that one is being watched also makes one behave in a more pro-social manner, so those that had this belief would have been less likely to have been ostracised by the band for breaking its rules (Norenzayan & Shariff, 2008). As such, religiousness may cause us to behave in a highly pro-social way or in a highly rule-following way even if this is not rational.

MODERNISTS

But let us return to definitions of ethnicity. Secondly, there are the *'Modernists'*. They share with the *Instrumentalists* the assumptions of cultural and environmental determinism, but they insist that most contemporary ethnic identities — or nationalisms — are in fact 'modern' phenomena and that they are not a fixed part of a person's identity. Rather, they are strongly subject to change. This camp can be roughly divided into four different schools, which we will discuss one by one.

SOCIAL CONSTRUCTIVISTS

British sociologist Benedict Anderson's (1936-2015) influential book *Imagined Communities* (Anderson, 1983) can be regarded as the best example of '*Social Constructivism*'. In it, he maintains that the modern sense of 'national identity', something which has much in common with ethnic identity, is, indeed, very much 'modern'. There was, he maintains, no strong sense of Englishness prior to the sixteenth century. Most people hardly left their village, dialects were so pronounced that people might have difficulty communicating with others from the neighbouring county, and the cultural traditions in that county, at least beyond church rituals, might even seem rather foreign. People identified, argues Anderson, very strongly with their local area and there was little sense of feeling 'English' in England, for example.

With the rise of printing and literacy and the reading of the Bible during the Reformation, a particular dialect of English gradually spread throughout the country. In addition, as communication improved, local differences declined and English culture became increasingly homogeneous. Accordingly, there began to develop the sense of an 'imagined community' of the English: people began to perceive those whom they had not met as part of their in-group because they spoke the same language and held to the same common culture. This model would seem to raise the question of what held the English state together — in the face of foreign invasions and aggressive wars — if there was no sense of Englishness at all prior to the sixteenth century. At the very least, it might be suggested, there must have been some kind of sense of Englishness, especially among the elite, who would have been literate and would have had a relatively greater awareness of those who did not speak English at all. In addition, there is evidence of anti-foreigner — and especially anti-Jewish — riots in Medieval England, and even as far back as the Saxon period a clear sense in which the 'Norsemen' were not 'English'.[13]

ECONOMIC CONSTRUCTIVISTS

A variation of *Social Constructivism* is '*Economic Constructivism*'. This has been most forcefully advocated by British-Czech philosopher and anthropologist Ernest Gellner (1925–1995) in *Nations and Nationalism* (Gellner, 1983). This would seem to overcome some of the problems with Anderson's model, because it implicitly posits 'nationalism' as beginning with the elite and being imposed upon the masses by them. Gellner argues that a sense of national identity is a product of an increasingly educated and bureaucratic society. As society became more complex, the ruling class decided that it was necessary to foster a unified state. In order to do this, they had to break down strong local identities, based around folk culture, and impose their own 'high culture', which was based around a 'national identity'. In order to achieve this, they educated the masses, leading to the development of a single language. This not only meant that the masses developed more of a sense of being 'one nation' but they could also be more efficiently inculcated with this belief.

Of course, this raises the question of where the belief in a sense of, for example, Englishness held by the English elite came from. It would seem to at least imply that a sense of Englishness, at least among the elite, was relatively ancient; thus moving us towards *Primordialism*. If this is not the case, we must assume that the elite deceitfully manufactured national myths and a national past, which seems unlikely because there is at least some historical basis to many national myths.[14]

---

13 For a detailed examination of the extent of English identity in Medieval England see essays in Lavezzo (2004).

14 For a summary of the evidence of King Arthur's existence see Castleden (2003). With regard to Robin Hood, see Baldwin (2010).

Gellner's model assumes a dramatic chasm between the 'elite' and the 'masses' and fails to entertain the possibility that sometimes they have the same interests and that, sometimes, pressure can be placed on the elite by a mass movement. Most obviously, ethnic nationalism will often develop within larger multi-ethnic empires, rendering it a threat to the elite. It might be countered that this is spearheaded by a local elite group who are looking to gain power, however.

POLITICAL-IDEOLOGICAL CONSTRUCTIVISTS

A variation on economic constructivism is *'Political-Ideological Constructivism'*. Advocated most prominently by British sociologist Anthony Giddens (1971), this model suggests that Industrialization leads to the loss of a sense of time and space among the masses. They can regain this with nationalism and, as such, nationalism is propagated by the elite in order to control them. Not only does this model assume a highly distinct elite and mass, but it raises the question of how nationalism could possibly re-imbue the masses with a sense of 'time' and 'space' if it had no relationship whatsoever with their previous sense of folk identity. If it did have such a relationship, then this would be an argument for adopting a more *Primordialist* perspective.

MARXISTS

It may be argued that many of the *Constructivist* models which we have discussed are effectively variations of classical *Marxist Theory*. From a Marxist perspective, best articulated by historian Eric Hobsbawm (1917–2012), nationalism and related traditions were invented by the 'ruling class' in order to control and mobilize the proletariat (e.g. Hobsbawm, 1990). There are manifold problems with this extreme form of *Constructivism*. It is economically reductionist, assuming the people only act in their economic interests when there is evidence that people can act against these, at least to some extent, in order to attain other forms of status, something epitomized by Karl Marx (1818–1883) himself who, by advocating Marxism, became celebrated but damaged his economic prospects (see Dutton & Van der Linden, 2015). It assumes that all phenomena are the products of 'History' and thus effectively reifies History. History can surely be reduced to the interactions between people. These will be partly underpinned by significantly genetic factors, such as intelligence and personality (see Dutton, 2014). It also makes the unlikely assumption that 'nationalism' was simply invented as part of a giant conspiracy theory, rather than at least having a basis in prior ways of thinking. There are a number of other Marxist theories of nationalism. American sociologist Michael Hechter (1975) advocated the *'Internal Colonialism'* model, arguing that capitalism leads to the exploitation of ethnic minorities in a state and the resultant development of nationalism among them. Of course, even if this is true, it fails to explain nationalism among dominant ethnys, nor does it explain why nationalist conflict is more pronounced in some states, such as multiracial ones, than others, as we will see below. It raises the question of how capitalism brought a sense of ethnic nationalism into being if it did not already somehow exist.

PROBLEMS WITH CONSTRUCTIVISM

In general, a number of problems can be highlighted with all of the *Constructivist* theories. Most obviously, they are all underpinned by cultural or environmental determinism. Even focusing on Barth, if we ask why one ethnic group has adopted one cultural practice and its neighbour another, the answer must be because they have a different history. 'History', as already noted, is how culture behaves within a set period of time, so if we ask why the two groups have different histories then the answer must be because they have different cultures; and they, in turn, have different cultures because they have different histories. We end up with a circular argument, which can only be solved by reifying, for example, History and conceiving of different histories being thrown from the sky like thunderbolts and landing in different cultures.

In addition, there is a strong empirical case against cultural determinism. 'Culture', from an anthropological perspective, refers to a group's way of life. Differences in how individuals live their lives have been shown to be significantly predicted by genetic factors. For example, intelligence has been shown to be around 0.8 heritable. However, intelligence predicts education level at 0.5, income at 0.3, and school achievement at 0.7 (Jensen, 1981). Intelligence is a predictor of health and longevity and, at a national level, intelligence has been shown to negatively predict religiousness, criminality, fertility, and political liberalism, and positively predict national wealth, health, average educational attainment, sanitation, and even happiness (see Lynn & Vanhanen, 2012). Indeed, research has highlighted regional differences in the prevalence of different forms of specific genes and shown that these relate to regional differences in culture. As we will see later, it has been argued that A118G (OPRM1) is a genetic basis of the fear of social exclusion. G and A polymorphisms in this gene regulate μ-opioid receptors. A study showed that fMRI subjects with the G allele showed stronger unpleasant feelings when they were excluded in ball-toss games (Way et al., 2009). Way and Lieberman (2010) found a positive correlation between the frequencies of G alleles in a population and the collectivism of their culture. They also reported that the G allele frequencies among Asian populations are much higher than those in European populations. As such, there is a sound case for arguing that cultural differences are partly genetic in origin.

The *Constructivist Theories* are also highly question-begging. In the case of the *Modernist* theories, we must ask where this constructed 'nationalism' came from? Surely, it was not invented out of nothing as nothing is invented in a vacuum. Accordingly, ethnic nationalism must have some kind of a connection to an ancient past, which speaks in favour of some form of *Primordialism*. If, as Barth argues, the elements of ethnic identity are essentially arbitrary, then why are they relatively similar across cultures? If nationalism is imposed by the elite on the masses, then why does it sometimes take the form of a mass movement against the elite? Even if it is in fact led by those who want to become the new elite, they are not necessarily the elite in all but the most localized sense. Is it not possible, anyway, that the elite might have motivations in common with the masses, and be motivated by the good of their ethnic group rather than simply by money? And, most importantly, how can a cultural determinist model explain the extremes of self-sacrifice that people can be persuaded to engage in for the good of their ethnic group, including laying down their lives, anonymously, to invade a foreign country, despite this leading to no obvious economic benefit for their families? One possibility is that they have been 'brainwashed', but this raises the question of why even social animals will lay down their lives for relatively distantly related members of their group. If it is accepted that we are closely related to the chimpanzee (see Wilson, 1975), a theory is more parsimonious if it can explain both chimpanzee and human behaviour. It is most improbable that chimpanzees can brainwash each other in any complex sense as they lack the ability to speak. Furthermore, if nationhood is merely a construct imposed on the masses, then why is it that it tends to fail when a country is multi-ethnic? These countries will tend to Balkanize into separate ethnic communities, which often conceive of themselves as differing in terms of blood and ancestry (see Vanhanen, 2012). Accordingly, multi-ethnic societies tend to have an ethnic core, while other ethnic groups are more distant from the country's sense of identity. Indeed, in multi-ethnic states where the different groups are from conspicuously different races, this breakdown is along racial lines, as has been shown in detail by Tatu Vanhanen (2012). Vanhanen has demonstrated that extent of *Ethnic Conflict* (defined on a scale up to severe ethnic massacres) correlates with extent of *Ethnic Heterogeneity* (defined as differences in visible race, language or tribe, and religion), when controlling for other variables such as socioeconomic development level and level of democracy.

5. Primordialism

The opposite school seeking to explain ethnicity is known as *Primordialism*. The classic models of *Primordialism* or '*Perennialism*' were advocated in the nineteenth century during the rise in European nationalism. German Romantic nationalists, such as Johann von Herder (1744–1803), argued that the essence of a national community was ties of land, blood and language. These, argued Herder, meant that each nation was, in essence, different, and these differences were ancient, reflected in each ethnicity's folklore and traditions. As such, even though the nation-state may be of modern origin, it has emerged from a much more ancient sense of identity (e.g. Herder, 1784). Anthropologists, such as Englishman Edward Evans-Pritchard (1902–1973), also conceived of human societies in terms of layers of relatedness, beginning with the nuclear family, then the clan and finally the ethny (e.g. Evans-Pritchard, 1940). This would seem to explain a number of the problems which we have observed in relation to *Constructivism*. Again, there are a number of competing *Primordialist* schools, divided over the extent to which they regard genetic differences as significant to their model of ethnicity.

ETHNOSYMBOLISTS

British sociologist Anthony D. Smith (1939–2016; e.g. Smith, 2004) espoused what he called the *Ethnosymbolic* approach. For Smith, there is some kind of genuine 'ethnic' past underpinning modern conceptions of ethnic identity. Behind these identities are myths, folk memories, shared values, traditions and symbols. The most important of these myths is the myth of a 'Golden Age' or 'Glorious Past'. The 'Intellectuals' act as chroniclers of these myths, using the arts to reawaken the imagined community, and they reawaken a sense of ethnic identity when it is needed. A different group, the 'professionals' or 'intelligentsia' disseminate the ideas. Thus, the first stage of national or ethnic identity is some kind of shared, ancient history. The second stage is a group of intellectuals who act as a bridge between the past and the present, who spawn an image of the 'nation'. However, nationalism and ethnic identity can still exist without this second stage occurring at all.

The difference, however, between Smith and many other *Primordialists* is that he advocates something close to cultural determinism, the problems with which we have already highlighted. Smith defines the 'nation' as 'a named human population occupying an historic territory, and sharing myths, memories, a single public culture and common rights and duties for all members' (Smith, 2004, p. 65). The specifics of Smith's definition need not concern us, but it is clear that there is no engagement in Smith's definition of 'nation' — and by extension ethny — with bonds of blood. This kind of definition is, thus, incongruous with what is commonly meant by an 'ethnic' group in common parlance: a group that is held together by a sense of common ancestry.

KINSHIP GROUPS

A second *Primordialist* school regards ethnic groups as *kin networks*; as highly extended families. This raises the question of what is meant by 'family'. American political scientist Walter Connor (1994, p. 202) has emphasised that the 'nation' should be defined as 'the largest group that can command a person's loyalty because of felt kinship ties; it is, from this perspective, the fully extended family'. The use of the word 'felt' is extremely important here. From Connor's perspective, the important issue is that members of an ethnic group believe that they are kin; whether they *are* genuinely kin is a quite separate issue. That notwithstanding, there are a number of advantages to this definition. It is congruous with the shared cultural memory of common ancestry which is held by many ethnic groups, both in terms of many nation states as well as in pre-modern societies. It also assists in explaining the self-sacrificial behaviour that is associated with ethnic groups. If members genuinely believe that the group is their extended family then it follows that an element of the altruistic behaviour which they would display towards their family would also be displayed towards this highly extended family. This does not necessarily require a genetic explanation; though, as we will see, such an explanation is the most parsimonious because it explains why all social animals — not just humans — tend to behave in an altruistic way, especially towards members of their in-group. The crucial point is that members believe that they are kin and accept that they must act in an altruistic manner towards kin. This, however, raises the question of why we should be altruistic towards kin at all. Even if it is the case that enthys are extended kinship groups, and even if it is the case that such groups can be seen in the animal kingdom, why should we behave more altruistically towards kin?

6. The Sociobiological School

This brings us to the third form of *Primordialism*, the *Sociobiological Approach*. The most prominent advocates of this perspective are American biologist Edward O. Wilson, in his book *Sociobiology* (1975), and Belgian anthropologist Pierre van den Berghe (1978). Their approach is relatively straightforward. They apply Darwinian principles, which are readily applied to explain the behaviour of non-human animals, to human behaviour. If it is accepted, as Darwin argued and as subsequent genetic evidence has proven, that humans are evolved from a common ancestor with the chimpanzee and are essentially a form of highly evolved ape, then this approach should be entirely unproblematic. The fundamental question for *sociobiologists*, argued van den Berghe, was 'Why are animals social, that is, why do they cooperate?' After all, they are competing for scarce resources such that they can pass on their genes to the maximum extent, so there is no obvious reason why they should cooperate, yet some animals do cooperate, something which Wilson (1975) highlighted as being most extreme in the case of the social insects where sterile worker bees will readily lay down their lives by stinging intruders in defence of the hive.

Sociobiologists postulated the answer, long intuitively known, that animals are social to the extent that such cooperation is mutually beneficial in helping to pass on their genes. Clearly, it is accepted that an animal's fundamental instinct is to breed and thus pass on its genes to the next generation. British biologist Richard Dawkins (1976) goes further, arguing that the gene itself (or, specifically, the allele; the version of a particular gene) is essentially programmed to replicate itself and it achieves this by cooperating with other genes in the form of the organism, which is merely a vehicle for the replication of genes. Successful alleles are those which, in a particular environment, lead to the greatest reproductive success of their host, leading to that particular allele being more likely to spread through the population. In other words, successful alleles are those which lead to the host having the greatest 'fitness'. If these alleles lead to significant fitness advantages for their carriers, they will spread throughout the population, leading to a situation, for example, where having blue eyes, blonde hair, and pale skin is widespread in some parts of Europe. The alleles which underpin these adaptations permitted greater fitness, because the carriers, in an agricultural environment marked by winter darkness, could more easily absorb Vitamin D from the sun, rendering it more likely that they would live long enough to reproduce (Cochran & Harpending, 2009).

Sociobiology's main innovation was to posit the main genetic mechanism behind pro-social behaviour among animals, a mechanism which is termed 'inclusive fitness'. British evolutionary psychologist William Hamilton (1936–2000) argued that an animal can duplicate its genes in two ways. It can do so directly, through reproduction, or indirectly, through aiding the reproductive efforts of its relatives, with whom it will share specific proportions of genes, above a base rate of nil within the more general population of which it is a part (Hamilton, 1964). Animals can, therefore, be expected to behave cooperatively, and enhance each other's genetic fitness, to the extent that they are related to each other, and to the extent that doing so will be mutually beneficial in terms of genetic fitness. This idea has been termed '*kin selection*' (Maynard-Smith, 1964). '*Hamilton's Rule*' is that altruism will spread through a population if the cost to the altruistic individual is outweighed by his gain in terms of inclusive fitness, brought about by aiding his kin.

I will present detailed evidence for this later, but it is intuitively obvious that all animals, including humans, are *nepotistic*, at least to some extent. In general, they favour kin over non-kin and close kin over distant kin. They may consciously behave nepotistically, investing in their children whom they know to be their children, or, as we will see is often the case, unconsciously, such as by selecting a sexual partner that is genetically relatively similar to themselves. Van den Berghe (1978) adds, however, that the propensity to be altruistic will be proportionate not only to the coefficient of relatedness between the self and the other, but also to the benefit/cost ratio of the altruistic act with regard to one's own genetic fitness. Thus, a menopausal mother may be more likely to sacrifice her life for her only child than would a mother in her early twenties who was given a choice between her own death and the death of her first and as yet unborn child. The latter mother could go on to have many more children, but it would be in the interests of the former's genetic fitness to sacrifice herself for the sake of her offspring as she could not have any more. A simple formula can be used to calculate that if the cost/benefit ratio of the transaction is smaller than the coefficient of relatedness between the individual and the other, then altruism should be predicted.

Indeed, following van den Berghe, Australian political scientist Frank Salter (2007) has shown, in considerable mathematical detail, precisely how it is possible to predict whether kin-altruism is likely to occur at the level of the ethnic group or even at the level of the race. Salter notes that genetic interests can be quantified because gene frequencies within different ethnic groups have indeed been quantified.

For example, Salter draws upon an analysis of the mitochondrial DNA of 1,007 European males to show the degree of relatedness between different European ethnic groups. Consequently, Hamilton's theory, combined with data on population genetics, allows ethnic kinship to be estimated. Salter argues that kinship with other members of one's ethnic group is zero if the group is considered in isolation, though against that baseline one could obviously calculate kinship with one's family members, for example. However, Salter shows that the world's population is composed of many ethnies, some of which are far more closely related than others. Some ethnies are so distantly related that random co-ethnics become very closely related by comparison and even the difference between relatively genetically similar ethnies — such as the English and the Danish — is certainly sufficient that the genetic interests of an Englishman would be damaged by even a small degree of population replacement by Danes.

Clearly, noted Salter, in any given population of one ethnicity, an individual shares 50% of his genes with each of his parents, siblings, and children; 25% of his genes with each of his grandparents, aunts and uncles and grandchildren, 12.5% of his genes with each of his great-grandparents, cousins, and great-grandchildren and so on. He has zero genes in common with a random co-ethnic. However, this relationship changes if the baseline is changed. Numerically speaking, Salter calculated that if the world consisted simply of Englishmen and Danes then two random Englishmen would have a kinship coefficient of 0.0021 above the baseline. This would be akin to sharing a set of 6 x great-grandparents, in other words, being seventh cousins and so having common ancestors in the early eighteenth century. In that that one's genes can be replicated directly or indirectly, by kin altruism, the replacement of a random co-ethnic with a foreigner would damage one's genetic interests. However, this damage would be tiny, though not inconsequential, when comparing the English and the Danes. The replacement of a single, or small number, of co-ethnic English by a very small number of Danes, for example two, might actually be counter-balanced by the positive contribution of these Danes to one's genetic interests. For example, if one of the Danes became one's wife — allowing one to breed — and the other was a medical researcher who pioneered a cure for some rare condition affecting one's children, this small-scale Danish immigration would enhance one's genetic interests. But, in general, it would damage them, even if only modestly.

At the other extreme, if the world was divided between Australian Aborigines and Mbuti Pygmies, then two random Australian Aborigines would have a kinship coefficient of 0.43. This would render them almost as identical twins (where kinship is 0.5), meaning any replacement of even a single Aboriginal with a singly Pygmy would wreak enormous damage on the genetic interests of the Aboriginal. Following van den Berghe, we would expect that only a minimum risk would be taken by the English to repel a small number of a Danes, but it would be worth taking a very significant risk, as Australian Aborigines, to repel even a handful of Mbuti. On this basis, we would expect ethnic conflict to be more intense the larger the genetic difference between the two ethnic groups. As already noted, this is precisely what has been found by Vanhanen (2012), something we will explore in greater detail below.

The *sociobiologists* differ from extreme *Primordialists* in that they accept that the human development of 'culture' means that altruism is not as clearly predicted by relatedness as it is in non-human animals. The purely genetic hypothesis is complicated by a number of factors. The first significant factor is reciprocity, something we have already touched upon with the example of a Danish wife or Danish pioneering medical researcher. A rudimentary sense of reciprocity is present in some non-human animals but it is far more prevalent and complex in even the simplest human societies, due to longer time horizons and the ability to communicate complex information. Reciprocity is co-operation for mutual benefit or with the expectation of a return, and it can occur between kin as well as between non-kin. Thus, a human might be altruistic towards a human from a different ethnic group in the hope of receiving altruism in return at some future point. Due to our having longer time horizons than have our closest primate relatives, and our heightened ability to communicate, such an act could be better remembered and the response monitored.

The second factor is coercion: the use of force to ensure one-sided benefit and to allow the dominant partner to predate or act as a parasite upon the less powerful one. Van den Berghe argues that as societies become more complex and fluid, people have less and less contact with their close genetic kin and, consequently, reciprocity and coercion start to take on far greater importance, albeit within certain limits predicted by a desire to promote kin-altruism. We will look at the evidence for this model later in our discussion. But it seems fairly obvious that an individual could promote his own genetic fitness — and that of his close kin — by making an alliance with people even of a different ethnic group. He could then promote his genetic interests against competitors within his own ethnic group through a form of coercion. However, what this of course means is that though there may be a general trend towards kin-altruism in human societies this will obviously be less pronounced than is the case among simple human societies or among non-human animals. This can be observed in interethnic alliances in terms of friendship or mutually loving sexual relationships that cross ethnic boundaries (see Dalrymple, 2004). The point, however, which *sociobiologists* emphasize, is that kin-altruism will, nevertheless, be highly significant to human affairs. Moreover, it will become increasingly significant in explaining behaviour the more genetically distant two conflicting ethnic groups are. And though reciprocity and coercion are doubtless important, kinship will be the ultimate explanation, underpinning the more overt explanations. Thus, for example, a coercive relationship between two races will probably be more coercive and more unpleasant the more distantly related they are, while a mixed-raced sexual relationship may be more likely if the couple share certain highly heritable features, possibly even to the extent that their 'ethnic difference' is more than compensated for.[15]

Van den Berghe also looks at the question of why it is that most social groups — at least in relatively ethnically homogenous societies — tend not to be based around shared genetic characteristics, such as having blonde hair, but are more likely to be based around shared beliefs or hobbies. Van den Berghe argues that the answer is that there is significant inter-ethnic variation in particular traits, such as blonde hair, and this variation can be observed even within a nuclear family. Degree of kinship, therefore, cannot be easily inferred by one, or even a handful, of physical traits among relatively genetically closely related people. It is true, notes van den Berghe, that different European ethnic groups possess what he calls a 'somatic norm range', such that we may discuss people being 'Nordic-looking' or 'Mediterranean-looking', but these descriptions are often employed in the absence of more concrete information about the person's ethnic background, such as his accent or native language. Physical appearance is only a reliable measure of kinship when it is widely discrepant, such as when comparing Europeans and Sub-Saharan Africans or, possibly at some extremes, Northern and Southern Europeans. It is much less reliable when comparing, for example, the English and the Scottish. Accordingly, cultural markers actually become a more accurate means of assessing kinship coefficient than do genotypic traits, in this narrow context. This would, in turn, help to explain why most social groups tend to be cultural in nature and, also, why people can be so strongly motivated to defend the cultural group of which they are a part and attack its perceived enemy. An obvious example, in an English context, would be the accent with which a person speaks. This tells other English people the individual's regional and social background and can thus be

---

15   For example, Rushton (2005) notes the people in mixed-race relationships in Hawaii are more psychologically similar than are those in mono-racial relationships. He argues that this is a way of compensating for their relative physical dissimilarity.

employed to infer the level of kinship to self. Clearly, how one chooses to dress conveys subtle cues about one's social and, to a lesser extent, geographical background, which likely advertise small genetic differences from those of a different social or geographical background. Indeed, research by Italian geneticist Luigi Cavalli-Sforza (1997) has shown that divisions and sub-divisions of languages correspond remarkably well with populations (as defined by genetic distances) and boundaries of steep genetic gradients.

7. Criticisms of the Sociobiological School

A number of criticisms have been levelled against the *sociobiological school* but, unlike with the *Constructivists*, it seems to me that all of these can be satisfactorily answered.

Firstly, it may be argued that the model is 'reductionist', in that it reduces the mass of available information down to an ultimately biological theory. One can respond, following E. O. Wilson (1998), that science by its very nature is reductionist. The test of a successful scientific theory is three-fold. (1) It must be a unitary theory that explains a very large amount of data in the simplest possible way. As such, in this way, it must be 'reductionist'. (2) It must, in some way, unify separate fields of thought, such as social science and biology. This is known as 'consilience' (see Wilson, 1998). Advocates justify this arguing that, from a pragmatic perspective, we need to be able to make correct predictions about the world or we cannot survive. Science has shown that it achieves this aim, because it is underpinned by the empirical method and logic. As such, we can conceive of a hierarchy of disciplines, each reducible to the one that is closer to pure logic. Theories in psychology must be reducible to biology in order to be sound, biology to chemistry, chemistry to physics to pure Mathematics. The *sociobiological* model of nationalism does indeed reduce research in sociology and psychology down to the biological level. By contrast, the alternate, purely *subjectivist*, theories which we have examined do not pass the two tests of a scientific theory, for various reasons that we have already discussed.

The second criticism of the *sociobiological* model is that it is a form of 'biological determinism'. This criticism may legitimately be leveled against some forms of *Primordialism*. For example, American anthropologist Madison Grant (1865–1937) essentially argued that all differences between ethnic groups were a function of inheritance (Grant, 1916). However, this is a simply a straw man criticism if leveled against the work of scholars such as Wilson (1975) or van den Berghe (1978). Advocates of the sociobiological perspective clearly emphasize the significance of environmental variables in explaining differences in the behavior of different ethnies at different times. As we have seen, they note the significance, for example, of cooperation and coercion in human societies and especially more complex human societies and they discuss how the extent to which kin altruism will be displayed can be predicted by the risk balanced against the payoff, which will obviously vary according to environmental factors. In addition, van den Berghe has discussed the way in which purely cultural traits become an imperfect proxy for kinship in complex societies.

Moreover, anthropologists such as Cochran and Harpending (2009) have explored the way in which cultural changes — such as the introduction of agriculture — can alter natural selection in particular directions with regard to psychological adaptations and, by extension, with regard to cultural differences. As such, it is simply inaccurate to claim that *sociobiologists* are advancing a form of biological determinism. They are arguing that ethnic groups are ultimately defined by biological differences from other ethnic groups, but this is not the same as arguing that they are nothing more than this. Those who identify as, and are accepted as, members of a particular ethnic group will vary in the degree to which they are biologically related and, accordingly, there is clearly space for a substantially sociological dimension to ethnic identity. It is simply being argued that, in general, a random member of the ethny will have greater kinship with another random co-ethnic than he will with a random member of another ethny. Likewise, many of the overt differences between ethnic groups may be substantially underpinned by environmental variables. It is simply being argued that the most parsimonious explanation is that biological differences ultimately underpin the cultural differences.

The third criticism of this perspective has been leveled by many scholars but most prominently American psychologist Geoffrey Miller (2000) as part of a discussion of sexual selection called *The Mating Mind*. Miller rightly points out that we must be careful in attempting to explain all of human evolution in terms of Natural Selection; that is to say adaptions which assist an individual, or species, to better survive in a particular environment. *Sexual selection*, which was also originally proposed by Darwin, is also significant in explaining genetic variance. An obvious example of a 'sexual ornament' is a peacock's tail. This may have some use in terms of natural selection, in that the peacock can make himself look bigger to predators by displaying particularly large tail. However, Miller argues that it is also a 'fitness indicator'. A peacock with poor genetic fitness — and thus a high number of mutant genes — would have to invest proportionately more of its resources in simply staying alive than a peacock with fewer mutant genes. As such, it would not be able to grow or maintain as impressive a tail. The tail of a less fit peacock would be smaller, less bright, less ornate and asymmetrical. This is because we are evolved to be symmetrical, so symmetry shows that we have a lack of mutant genes which cause asymmetry and that we are fit enough to have grown a healthy phenotype in the face of disease or food shortage. With these considerations in mind, the tail would tell the peahen a great deal about the fitness of the peacock and we would expect the peahen to (1) select for peacocks than had such an ornament and (2) select for peacocks with the biggest and brightest tails. Miller argues that sexual dimorphism in humans and even psychological characteristics such as intelligence or a pro-social personality can thus partly be explained in terms of sexual selection.

This seems entirely reasonable, but from this he moves on to criticizing the sociobiological perspective and inclusive fitness. Miller seems to reduce human morality and pro-social behavior down to sexual selection for these traits. Males have little to lose from the sexual encounter, so the best strategy is to copulate with as many young and healthy women as possible, with beauty being a proxy for genetic health. Thus, men tend to be attracted to youth and beauty (Buss, 1989). Miller rightly notes that males, if they must invest in a female, will select for one who is honest and caring because she will make a better mother to his children and she will be less likely to cheat on him. Moreover, these qualities could imply a more complex brain and thus better genetic quality. Females will select for these traits even more so than males because they will want a male who will look after them while they are pregnant and who will care for the children they may already have by other men. Moreover, they will want a male who will not cheat on them, who will look after them and their children, and who can attain high status, with cooperativeness being, to varying degrees, associated with this. As such, Miller notes that 'kindness' is the single most important psychological characteristic, for both males and females, when selecting a partner. Miller summarizes the *sociobiological* argument (that it would have been adaptational to recognize kin and care for them more than non-kin) but he maintains that this cannot be used to explain kindness to 'non-kin' (Miller, 2000, p. 300).

This, I would suggest, is something of a misunderstanding of the *sociobiological* perspective which has occurred through the making of a binary division between 'kin' and 'non-kin' which does not exist in the real world. We may regard our 'second cousin' as kin and our third cousin as 'not kin' but this is simply a random border and there are probably those who see certain third cousins as 'kin'. From the *sociobiological* perspective, kinship is a spectrum, not an 'either/or'. It can be argued that we are evolved to be kinder to 'closer kin' than to 'distant kin' and that we are evolved, putting the social construct of kinship aside, to be kinder to the 'more genetically similar' than to the 'less genetically similar'. An organism that developed an unconscious way of discerning genetic similarity to self would be at a huge advantage because it could maximize the degree to which it passed on its genes; in other words it could maximize its inclusive fitness. It could do this by breeding with a person who occupied the optimum genetic distance from self to reap the maximum benefits from genetic diversification — avoiding harmful 'double doses' of mutant genes and passing on possible useful new genes to the offspring — and genetic similarity, passing on more of one's own genes. It could perform the same feat in terms of friendship: genetic differences permitting a useful *quid-pro-quo* relationship as against genetic similarity allowing one to help a genetically relatively similar person through life. So, the *sociobiological* argument is that, in general, how moral we are depends on whom we are dealing with, we will be more altruistic to those who are more genetically similar to us, and that this is explicable in terms of inclusive fitness. Below, we will survey the impressive amount of evidence for the veracity of this model, which is known as '*Genetic Similarity Theory*'.

The fourth criticism of the sociobiological perspective is a moral one. American biologist Richard Lewontin (1978), for example, effectively argued that the *sociobiological* model — wherein human behaviour is substantially explained by biology — implies that we cannot create a better world and those who are disadvantaged are in such position due to their own nature, rather than due to discrimination or poor circumstances. Moreover, the sociobiological perspective effectively argues that ethnic nepotism is a natural, evolved capacity, as it is an extension of general nepotism. *Sociobiology's* most ardent critics have argued that if we accept *Sociobiology* then we must accept the inevitability of 'racism'[16] and we must accept that eugenics is potentially

---

16 I have deliberately avoided using the term 'racism' in this discussion because it is not a neutral, analytical category. It is traditionally defined as the belief that some races are superior to others. However, the term 'racist' has been extended far beyond this to refer to anybody who is seen to deviate from

a good idea (as differences are mainly biological). Indeed, this kind of reaction manifested itself in Edward O. Wilson having a bucket of iced water poured over him by a Leftist group called 'Science for the People' in 1978. Such researchers commit the so-called 'moralistic fallacy' (Davies, 1978). Science is not moral and the morality of a position is completely irrelevant to whether or not it is logically and empirically justifiable. A more subtle moral criticism was presented by Richard Lewontin, who suggested that, for moral reasons, the burden of proof should be higher when making evolutionary speculations about humans. This renders humans somehow separate from animals when, from an evolutionary psychological perspective, humans are a form of ape. Moreover, it introduces the danger that biased scholars will tendentiously argue that there is never sufficient proof for hypotheses that they dislike.

The fifth criticism of *Sociobiology* is that it engages in speculation. Often disputes, once our definition of science is accepted, over whether or not something is science, relate to a specific debate within science. Finnish sociologist Ullica Segerstråle (2000, p. 255) argues that for those in the 'experimental tradition' of science, 'good science' is science which is, to a great extent, proven, beyond doubt (Segerstråle,

---

ideological orthodoxy with regard to the issue of race. Terming them 'racist' associates them with that which is accepted as somehow evil and immoral. As this association is damaging, the term 'racist' is an emotionally manipulative means of keeping people on the 'correct' ideological path and, clearly, an ad hominem criticism. The essence of the accusation is that the subject has strayed sufficiently far from orthodoxy that he is immoral; he is a heretic. There are many terms of this kind. As Walsham (1999, p. 108) summarizes in her analysis of Early Modern religious non-conformity in England, the accusation of 'atheist' was 'available for the expression and repression of disquiet about "aberrant" mental and behavioural tendencies — for the reinforcement and restatement of theoretical norms'. Both 'atheist' and 'papist' were 'categories of deviance to which individuals who were even marginally departed from the prescribed ideals might be assimilated and thereby reproved'.

p. 256).[17] Scientific *naturalists,* by contrast, are in an older tradition of science where you wish to understand nature and speculate, based on the available evidence, in an attempt to understand the natural world as a whole. Darwin's theory of evolution (Darwin, 1859) was in this tradition. Darwin was a naturalist and, based on his observations, he suggested his theory of evolution. It was not absolutely proven when he suggested it but there was certainly a body of evidence for it. It rendered the animal world congruous with the materialist underpinnings of science and made sense of various disparate empirical observations. Accordingly, there was a degree to which it was 'speculative' but it was also a contribution to science because it attempted to understand the nature of the world based on empirical evidence. Experimentalism is to be praised for its exactness but it is problematic because it demands such exacting standards of evidence before an assertion can be made. This leaves too little room for intelligent discussion, based on the evidence, and for the public, collegial dimension to science whereby ideas are freely discussed. Moreover, we may never be able to make any assertions if the level of proof required is so absolute that, for example, Richard Dawkins' attempts to understand, historically, why certain animals have evolved the features they have is 'bad science' as Richard Lewontin suggests it is (Segerstråle 2000, p. 257). In that scientific discovery is ongoing, it is always possible, as German psychologist Hans Eysenck (1916–1997; Eysenck, 1991, p. 41) observed, to claim that there is not sufficient evidence to reach a conclusion or that the evidence is open to dispute, as it always is. Scientists can merely reach conclusions based on what best fits the evidence.

---

17 For further discussion of this divide within science, see also Chalmers (1999). Kurzban (2010) has argued that, in fact, 'good science' is, in reality, science that does not challenge Political Correctness. He uses this term to refer to the ideology which seeks to avoid giving offense to cultural minorities and to promote the status of these minorities in Western nations. For further discussion see Ellis (2004).

Naturalism can be problematic if it becomes too speculative. 'Speculation' is generally defined as 'reasoning based on inconclusive evidence, conjecture or supposition'. As such, the exact border of 'speculation' is intuitive. This leads to an impasse which can be solved through philosophical pragmatism. So, in everyday situations, how much evidence, we might ask experimentalists, is enough for you to act differently in accordance with it? Would you, in everyday life, follow the method, used in this study, of making inferences from indirect or not wholly conclusive but nevertheless noteworthy evidence? Do you ever, for example, judge a person's intellectual ability based on their educational credentials? Does this lead to successful results? Based on such a method, whom would you call upon to solve a particular and specifically intellectual problem: the person with the PhD or the person with just a school leaving certificate who had dropped out of university? We suspect, all things being equal, it's the person with the doctorate rather than the university dropout, even if there are some highly intelligent university dropouts, such as Bill Gates or Mark Zuckerberg. This is because, on average, those with PhDs are more intelligent than university dropouts (see Herrnstein & Murray, 1994, p. 143). Likewise, naturalism permits successful predictions to be made, which have real life consequences, even if the perspective does not offer absolute proof.

So, the criticisms of this model can be responded to and it must be stressed that, of those presented, it explains the most with the fewest assumptions, rendering it the most scientific model. Firstly, it is congruous with Darwinian Theory and therefore consilient and based only on the assumptions of science: logic and empirical method. Secondly, it explains ethnic nepotism in all cases, in all time periods, and it even explains related behavior among animals. Thirdly, it neatly explains why ethnic groups tend to have a folk belief in common ancestry and kinship. They hold this belief because there is some truth in it.

8. What Causes Ethnocentrism?

The debate over the causes of ethnocentrism approximately parallels the debate over how 'ethnic group' should be defined. It divides between the *sociobiologists*—who advocate a significantly biological approach—and those who espouse an almost entirely environmental explanation. These explanations are effectively extensions of the model of 'ethnicity' which they employ.

THREAT AND CONFLICT EXPLANATIONS

It is argued that ethnocentrism is a defensive reaction by people or groups who feel under threat in some way. There are a number of explanations within this category.

REALISTIC CONFLICT THEORY

Sumner (1906) argued that ethnocentrism was instrumental in defending the in-group against the out-group and advancing in-group interests over those of the out-group. LeVine and Campbell (1972) averred that a group that finds itself in conflict is more likely to defend its own interests if it is ethnocentric. As such, ethnocentrism is a response to conflict. The problem with this as a standalone explanation is that people display some degree of ethnocentrism even if they are in no immediate conflict or they are under no immediate threat (e.g. Tajfel & Turner, 1979). We will see later that this is the case in ordinary, everyday life, such as when people select friends, sexual partners or even family members whom they wish to spend time with. In effect, they employ aspects of ethnocentrism—preferring those who are similar to them—but there is no obvious conflict situation when this occurs. In addition, this theory does not explain some of the more extreme examples of ethnocentric behavior. Why, for example, would people be prepared to sacrifice their lives for their ethnic group?

PSYCHODYNAMIC THEORY

Following Sigmund Freud (1856–1939), advocates argue that ethnocentrism is caused by 'intrapsychic' threats and conflicts. Freud argued that ethnocentrism occurs because living in a community causes tension and people cope with this by 'displacing' their feelings onto members of an out-group. The most well-known theory along these lines is German philosopher Theodore Adorno's (1903–1969) 'Authoritarian Personality'. He argued that strict parenting causes children to experience conflicting feelings, and to cope with these they employ the defense mechanisms of displacement and externalization. This can be seen in projecting negative feelings onto members of other ethnic groups. The difficulty with this theory is that it really only explains general prejudice, only partially explains ethnocentrism, and, moreover, fails to appreciate the highly heritable nature of personality, which we will discuss later.

TERROR MANAGEMENT

Prominent advocates include Solomon et al. (1991). According to this theory, people feel threatened by an awareness of death and their cultural value system buffers them against this existential anxiety. More generally, a large body of research has shown that prejudice and in-group ethnocentric behavior do appear to increase as a result of certain kinds of threat, especially threats to general group welfare, threats to group values, and finding an out-group irritating or frightening (e.g. Riek et al., 2006). Again, the problem with this model is that people have been shown to behave in an ethnocentric manner and hold to ethnocentric views when they are under no obvious threat at all. Moreover, animals are unable to experience existential anxiety but, as we will see later, they still display behavior which is effectively ethnocentric: they show a preference for those who are more genetically similar to themselves. So, having explored *'threat and conflict'* explanations, let us turn to the next kind.

SELF-AGGRANDIZEMENT THEORIES

Tajfel and Turner (1979) have been the most prominent advocates of these models. They argue that ethnocentrism makes people feel good by boosting in-group self-esteem and it is for this reason that ethnocentrism develops. They showed that under laboratory conditions strong groups can very easily be created and people can display group-centrism even when there is no interaction with the other group, almost no knowledge about it, and when discriminating against members of it would not be in the individual's self-interest. However, the difficulty here is that Tajfel's team were not dealing with groups divided along ethnic lines and it may that ethnic groups show even stronger forms of 'group-centric' behavior, raising the question of why there might be this qualitative difference. The theory also begs the question of why ethnocentrism — as distinct from other forms of group-behavior — should be so widespread and powerful. In addition, as we will see, even in groups that are mono-ethnic people will tend to consort along the lines of genetic similarity, in others words in a way that would be predicted by a *sociobiological* model.

THE MARXIST MODEL

A related model is the *Marxist Model*. This argues that by making the in-group feel good about itself ethnocentrism is useful in allowing one group to gain power over another group, whom they can then exploit. The problem with this model is that it begs the question of why ethnic identity, specifically, should be so appealing in this context? Why do dominant and submissive groups in the conflict divide along ethnic lines at all? Why is one ethnic group positive to its members but actively hostile to non-members? And, again, why should people engage in self-sacrifice in the interests of their ethnic group?

SOCIAL DOMINANCE THEORY

Another *Self-Aggrandizement Theory* is *Social Dominance Theory*. According to this perspective, a certain kind of personality — a 'dominant' personality that craves 'security' — tends towards ethnocentrism (Duckitt, 2001). Clearly, the difficulty here is that people of all personality types behave in a manner that is ethnocentric, and this can especially be seen in whom they socialize with, as we will see.

SOCIALIZATION AND NORMATIVE EXPLANATIONS

These are yet another form of explanation. Advocates of this model note that those with similar personalities still display differing levels of ethnocentrism. This is explained by the process of socialization. Children learn, it is argued, to be ethnocentric and they learn to divide people into racial categories. This raises the question of how ethnocentrism should have developed in the first place, such that it could even be taught. Moreover, there is evidence that babies will respond more positively to members of their own ethnic group than to members of another ethnic group (see Sagi et al., 1985), implying that ethnocentrism is innate rather than taught. Moreover, what we might call the 'building-blocks' of ethnocentrism — valuing those who are similar over those who are less similar — can be seen even in animal behaviour and it is not feasible that they have been taught to categorize in an ethnocentric way.

THE SOCIOBIOLOGICAL MODEL

We have already discussed why the *sociobiological model* is the most persuasive model of 'ethnicity' and it is also the most persuasive model of ethnocentrism. It is consilient as it grounds ethnocentrism in Darwinian Theory and it explains the most with the fewest assumptions, meaning that it does not leave questions unanswered, as the other theories do. To summarize, in-group preference and out-group negativity are useful because genes can be passed on not only from parents to offspring but also via kin. Accordingly, kin-preference will increase one's 'inclusive fitness'. This model explains the most as it is underpinned by evidence that animals prefer kin over non-kin and will sometimes engage in acts of self-sacrifice for relatively distant kin. So, this theory does not merely explain ethnocentrism in humans but also in animals — it explains more — and it is consilient, congruous with the Darwinian view that humans are an advanced form of ape. This model does not rule out the importance of conflict, stress, or personality differences in increasing ethnocentrism and these contributory factors will be accepted if they, likewise, can be shown to be consilient. The *sociobiological model* simply argues that ethnocentrism is most parsimoniously understood via a partly biological theory wherein the ethnic group is a kind of extended family.

9. Conclusion

In this chapter, we have examined the competing definitions of ethnocentrism and ethnicity and we have argued that the most persuasive and parsimonious definitions are those termed *'sociobiological'*. We have also engaged in a brief exploration of the proposed causes of ethnocentrism and similarly found that it is most reasonable to argue that the *sociobiological model* partly explains the development of ethnocentrism. In this chapter, we have noted a number of times that 'Genetic Similarity Theory' is compelling evidence for this model, because it shows that altruism is predicted by genetic similarity. We will now turn to more detailed evidence in favour of this theory.

CHAPTER FIVE

Evidence for Genetic Similarity Theory

1. Introduction

In this chapter, we will begin to survey more recent evidence for the *sociobiological model* of ethnocentrism and ethnicity. We will start by examining British-Canadian psychologist J. Philippe Rushton's (1943–2012) '*Genetic Similarity Theory*' (e.g. Rushton, 2005). We will demonstrate that there is a great deal of evidence in favour of this theory but that it does not fully explain all manifestations of ethnocentrism and, accordingly, it needs to be nuanced and carefully developed.

2. Genetic Similarity Theory

As we have discussed, the sociobiological model is predicated on the view that ethnic groups are extended families and that all animals will instinctively behave more pro-socially to those who share more of their genes. This inclination towards those who are genetically similar has been termed '*Genetic Similarity Theory*' and a great deal of evidence for it was presented by J. Philippe Rushton. We will begin with a detailed summary of this.

Rushton's theory is grounded in the sociobiological model of ethnic nepotism. As we have already seen, Hamilton (1964) posited the notion of 'inclusive fitness'. He argued that alleles which lead to altruism would usually not spread, because the altruistic individual would not survive. However, they would spread if they were directed specifically towards genetic kin and if the resulting boost to inclusive fitness exceeded the cost to individual fitness which would be borne by the altruist. This condition, for the evolution of altruism, is known as 'Hamilton's Rule'. As we have also seen, van den Berghe drew upon Hamilton's ideas and argued that insofar as the ethny is a putative kinship group, shared ethnic identity should lead to some of the same altruistic behaviour associated with families. He argued that people would look for kinship markers — such as language or dress — and these would release altruistic behaviour. At the same time, animal altruism, even to the point of self-sacrifice, was being massively confirmed (Wilson, 1975). Rushton's contribution was to argue that people could discern whether or not others were genetically similar to them, even in the complete absence of any kinship markers. Moreover, Rushton argued, this unconscious awareness of genetic similarity would be enough to release altruistic behaviour. This he called *'Genetic Similarity Theory'* and it requires a more detailed explication.

According to Rushton, kinship would have to be detectable and this could be through a number of methods including (1) proximity to self (2) familiarity through interaction (3) similarity to self — through imprinting of certain features (4) innate feature detectors allowing you to unconsciously discern similarity to self even in the absence of any mechanism to learn this. For the fourth mechanism to work, a gene would need to produce two effects: (a) a unique trait, such as a 'green beard' and (b) a preference for others who have that trait. This gene would be most effective if it made people the most interested in highly heritable traits. Some physical traits, it should be noted, are genetically influenced while others are more environmentally influenced.

Rushton argued that there is a large body of evidence that animals do indeed have *Innate Feature Detectors*, due to behaviour that cannot possibly be explained by conditioning, something he presented in Rushton (2005), an article aimed at scholars of nationalism and published in the journal *Nations and Nationalism*. In this article, Rushton noted that in a classic study of bees, Greenberg (1979) bred for fourteen degrees of closeness to a guard bee, which blocks the nest to intruders. Only the more genetically similar intruders were allowed to enter the hive. Rushton observed that in another classic study of frog tadpoles separated before hatching and raised in isolation, it was found that the tadpoles moved to the end of the tank where their siblings had been placed, even though they had never encountered them before, rather than to the end of the tank with non-siblings (Blaustein & O'Hara, 1981). Squirrels, explained Rushton, produce litters that contain both full siblings and half-siblings. Even though they have the same mother, share the same womb, and inhabit the same nest, full siblings fight less often than do half-siblings. Full siblings also come to each other's aid more often (Hauber & Sherman, 2001). Likewise, argued Rushton, the proposed feature would explain the ability of animals to mate assortatively, such that close kin are rejected. Even in species that disperse, the offspring typically show strong aversion to mating with close relatives. One study of wild baboons, discussed in Rushton (2005), showed that paternal kin recognition occurs as frequently as maternal kin recognition even though identifying paternal kin is much more difficult in a species where the mother mates with more than one male (Alberts, 1999).

From 1984, Rushton and his colleagues began to apply this Hamilton-inspired approach to human samples (Rushton et al., 1984; Rushton, 1989, Rushton, 2004, Rushton & Bons, 2005). As discussed, they dubbed the approach *'Genetic Similarity Theory'* and reasoned that if genes produced effects which allowed bearers to recognize each other, altruistic behaviour could evolve beyond merely near to actually very distant kin selection. People could maximise their inclusive fitness by marrying those who were genetically similar to themselves, making friends with those the most genetically similar to themselves, being friendlier to neighbours who were more genetically similar to themselves, and displaying ethnic and simply species nepotism.

Rushton and his colleagues presented a large body of evidence to support these hypotheses.

3. Social Assortment Studies

Rushton showed that people assort — choose their friends and their partners — in ways that would be predicted by *Genetic Similarity Theory*. In that these people are not kin, such a finding proves that *Genetic Similarity Theory* moves us beyond kin and helps in explaining ethnic nepotism. Both spouses and best friends are most similar on socio-demographic variables such as age, ethnic background and education level, where the correlation was 0.6. With regard to opinions and attitudes, the correlation was 0.5, a noteworthy finding which repudiates the idea that people are simply friends with those with whom they have a lot in common. On cognitive ability the correlation was 0.4 and the weakest but still statistically significant correlation was on personality type and on physical traits, at 0.2 (Rushton, 2005). It should be noted that intelligence — with a heritability of about 0.8 (Lynn, 2011a) — is more heritable than personality, which has a heritability of 0.5–0.6 (Nettle, 2007). Also, interestingly, research from Hawaii, where there are many inter-racial marriages, found that inter-racial couples seemed to compensate for physical *dissimilarity* with psychological *similarity*, as they were more similar in personality than were those marrying within their racial group (Ahern et al., 1981). There is an upper limit on like marrying like, as those who are too similar risk giving their offspring double doses of harmful genetic mutations. As such, the ideal partner is one who is genetically relatively similar but not a close relative. We will later discuss a study from Iceland (Helgason et al., 2008) which would appear to confirm this as it indicates that the most successful marriages are between third cousins.

Several studies have found that — within ethnic groups — people prefer those who are more similar to themselves and specifically more similar to themselves on more heritable traits. Rushton (2005) observes that for physical attributes, heritability is 80% for middle-finger length vs. 50% for upper-arm circumference; for intelligence, 80% for general intelligence vs. less than 50% for specific intelligence abilities; for personality items, 76% for 'enjoying meeting people' vs. 20% for 'enjoying being unattached'; and for social attitudes, 51% for agreement with the 'death penalty' vs. 25% per cent for agreement with 'Bible truth'. In a study of married couples, Russell et al. (1985) found that across 36 physical traits, spousal similarity was greater on attributes with higher heritability such as wrist circumference (71% heritable) than it was on attributes with lower heritability such as neck circumference (48% heritable). The same pattern was found with regard to attitudes and interests, while Rushton and Nicholson (1988) found that spouses were more similar on the more heritable aspects of intelligence than on the less heritable ones. When spouses assort on more heritable items, they report greater marital satisfaction (Russell & Wells, 1991).

In a study of best friends, Rushton (1989b) found that across a wide range of physical and psychological measures, best friends were more similar than random co-ethnics and more similar on the more heritable traits. These results were extended to liking strangers by Tesser (1993) who manipulated people's beliefs about how similar they were to others on attitudes pre-selected as being either high or low in heritability. Tesser found that people liked others more when their similarity had been chosen (by him) on the more heritable items.

4. Twin and Adoption Studies

Several twin and adoption studies show that the preference for genetic similarity is heritable, meaning that people are genetically programmed to prefer similar partners, but that there is individual variance in the extent to which they do so (reviewed in Rushton, 2005). Rowe and Osgood (1984) analysed data on delinquency from several hundred adolescent monozygotic (MZ) twin pairs, who share 100% of their genes, and dizygotic (DZ) twin pairs, who share 50% of their genes. They found that adolescents who were genetically inclined to delinquency were also genetically inclined to seek out other delinquents to be their friends. Daniels and Plomin (1985) examined friendships in several hundred pairs of siblings from both adoptive and non-adoptive homes. They found the friends of the biological siblings were genetically similar to each other. However, the friends of the adoptive siblings were only as similar as would be predicted by chance.

Rushton and Bons (2005) analysed a 130-item questionnaire on personality and social attitudes gathered from several hundred pairs of identical twins, fraternal twins, their spouses and their best friends. They found that: (a) spouses and best friends are roughly as similar as siblings, (b) identical twins choose more similar spouses and best friends to their co-twin than do non-identical twins. They also found that the preference for genetic similarity is around 30% heritable. This is important because it implies significant individual and probably also population differences in the degree of preference for genetic similarity and thus in the degree of ethnocentrism. It also leaves considerable space for environmental variables — such as conflict — to impact individual and population levels of ethnocentrism. Once again, matching for similarity was greater on the more heritable items showing that social assortment is based on the underlying genotype. In his review, Rushton (1989a) notes that adoptions are more likely to be successful if the parents see themselves as similar to the child and child abuse is disproportionately likely to be at the hands of a stepparent than a biological parent. These findings are in line with *Genetic Similarity Theory*.

5. Blood Tests, Bereavement, Scent and Faces

Rushton (1988) tested genetic similarity in relation to blood antigens. He analysed seven polymorphic marker systems at ten blood loci across six chromosomes (ABO, Rhesus [Rh], MNSs, Kell, Duffy [Fy], Kidd [Jk] and HLA) in a study of 1,000 cases of disputed paternity, limited to people of North European appearance (judged by photographs). Couples who produced a child together were 52% similar but those that had not were only 43% similar. Rushton (1989b) used these blood tests with pairs of male best friends of similar background and found that the friends were significantly more similar to each other than they were to randomly matched pairs from the same database. He noted that in Britain, blood type A is found to occur more frequently in SES 1, the highest socioeconomic group (57% of the time), than in SES 5, the lowest socioeconomic group (41% of the time). However, to eliminate this 'stratification' possibility, Rushton (1989a) calculated within-pair differences in age, education, and occupation. He did not find them to be significantly correlated with friends' blood similarity scores which they should have been if the stratification hypothesis was correct.

Within-family bereavement studies show that *Genetic Similarity Theory* operates even within the same small family. A study of 263 child bereavements found that (1) spouses agreed 74% of the time on which side of the family a child resembled the most, and (2) the grief intensity reported by mothers, fathers and grandparents was greater for children who resembled their side of the family than it was for children who resembled the other side of the family (Littlefield & Rushton, 1986). A study of bereavement in twins found that MZ twins, when compared to DZ twins (a) work harder in the interests of their co-twin; (b) show greater physical proximity to their co-twin; (c) are more affectionate towards their co-twin; and (d) show more intense grief when their co-twin dies (Segal, 2000).

It has been shown that women prefer the bodily scents of men who are more genetically similar to them than they do the scents of men who are less genetically similar to them. They also prefer this 'similar' scent to a scent which is almost exactly the same as their own (Jacob et al., 2002). Each woman's choice was based on the human leukocyte antigen (HLA) gene sequence—the basis for personal odour and smell preferences. This is inherited from the woman's father but not her mother. Penton-Voak et al. (1999) found that both men and women rated versions of their own face as the most attractive after they had been morphed into faces of the opposite-sex, even though they did not recognise the photos as images of themselves. DeBruine (2002) found that people whose faces were morphed onto the faces of strangers rated the ones who looked more like themselves as more trustworthy.

6. Genetic Similarity, Race and Race Proxies

A number of studies have shown that, in line with *Genetic Similarity Theory*, people will behave in a more pro-social way to members of their own ethnic group. One study examined street beggars in Moscow. Some were ethnic Russians, just like the vast majority of the pedestrians. Others were dressed in the distinctive costume associated with Moldova, where people speak Romanian. Also, some beggars were dressed as dark-skinned Roma.[18] The Russian pedestrians preferred to give money to their fellow Russians, then their fellow Eastern European Moldovans and finally to the Roma. This was despite the fact that the Roma went beyond mere begging to more persuasive tactics such as singing and dancing, importuning people, and sending out groups of children to beg (see Salter, 2007). Irwin (1987) tested Rushton's theory through an anthropological study of Inuit tribes in Northern Canada. He calculated coefficients of consanguinity within

---

18 For an interesting analysis of the Roma, see Cvorovic (2014).

and between these various tribes. He found that pro-social behaviour, such as wife exchange, and anti-social behaviour, such as the genocidal murder of women and children from another tribe during warfare, paralleled the degree of genetic distance in the expected direction.

Even very young children typically show a clear preference for others of their own ethnic group (Aboud, 1988). In fact, the process of making racial groupings has been shown to result from a natural tendency to classify people into 'kinds'. Children quickly begin to sort people into 'basic kinds' by sex, age, size and occupation. Experiments show that at an early age children clearly expect race to run in families (Hirschfield, 1996). Very early in life, a child knows which race it belongs to, and which ones it doesn't.

Finally, Rushton argued that many cleavages — such as social class, religion or political ideology — can ultimately be explained in terms of *Genetic Similarity Theory*. Indeed, he argued that people will tend to adopt the ideological or religious perspective which is the most likely to perpetuate their genes. In terms of proxies for genetic similarity, DNA sequencing of the ancient Hindu caste system has confirmed that higher castes are more genetically related to Europeans than are lower castes, these being genetically more related to other South Asians (Bamshad et al., 2001). Although outlawed in 1960, the caste system continues to be the main feature of Indian society, with powerful political repercussions. People can be predicted to adopt ideologies, argued Rushton, that work in their genetic self-interest. Examples of ideologies that have been shown, on analysis, to increase genetic fitness are religious beliefs that regulate dietary habits, sexual practices, marital customs, infant care and child rearing (see Lumsden & Wilson, 1981). Rushton (2005) noted that Amerindian tribes that cooked maize with alkali had higher population densities and more complex social organizations than tribes that did not, partly because alkali releases the most nutritious parts of the cereal, enabling more people to grow to reproductive maturity. The Amerindians did not know the biochemical reasons for the benefits of alkali cooking but their cultural beliefs had evolved for good reason, enabling them to replicate their genes more effectively than would otherwise have been the case.

The political pull of ethnic identity and genetic similarity also explains voting behaviour, Rushton (2005) argued. The re-election victory of George W. Bush in the 2004 US presidential election was largely attributed to white votes and to the higher value placed by these voters on 'values' than on the economy. A closer look at the demographics reveals that 'values' may be, at least in part, a proxy for ethnic identity and genetic similarity. The majority of white Americans voted based on which candidate — and candidate's family — they believed most appeared to look, speak and act like them (Brownstein & Rainey, 2004).

A number of criticisms of *Genetic Similarity Theory* have been highlighted and responded to by Salter and Harpending (2015). Firstly, it may be argued that inclusive fitness can only operate between genealogical kin because their genes are identical by common descent (e.g. Mealy, 1985). However, it can be countered that inclusive fitness will operate regardless of the how the similarity arises and this is evidenced by the kind of data which Rushton has presented.

Secondly, it might be argued that ethnic kinship is too slight to justify diverting effort from genealogical kin. However, this is simply untrue. The aggregate kinship within populations can be sufficient that it is adaptive to invest in ethnic kinship, as Salter (2007) has demonstrated. It is perfectly adaptive to contribute to collective goods, group defence and the punishment of free-riders.

Thirdly, Grafen (1990) pointed out that within an 'outbred population' (one that was relatively genetically diverse) assortment by phenotypic selection could not be a form of kin selection, as Rushton had argued. This was because sharing the kinds of characteristics which Rushton highlighted would involve sharing miniscule proportions of genes. These genes would only occur frequently on the genome among genealogical kin. Grafen argued that the percentage of shared genes would be insufficient, beyond genealogical kin, for the investment of friendship, for example, to pay off in terms of inclusive fitness. But, as Salter (2007) has found, if we compare different ethnic groups — calculating their degree of genetic separation — then co-ethnics, relatively speaking, share a significant percentage of their genes; more than sufficient to make ethnic nepotism adaptive. Indeed, Salter (2002) has found in an ethnically divided population, people will share 15% more genes with co-ethnics than with others, meaning that investment in those with shared phenotypic traits would pay off even more. Moreover, it might be countered that even in an outbred population, if a person shared a large number of phenotypic traits with someone else — as Rushton found was true of friends or sexual partners — then the investment could potentially pay off. But it is true that this is more likely within an inbred population, and Salter and Harpending (2015) note that most populations are inbred to some extent. In this context, kinship is highly variable even among complete strangers, and this would be even more likely in small, relatively isolated populations. For people in these populations, Rushton's model could apply even without the need to hypothesize collective goods and there would not need to be any ethnic conflict for the investment to pay off in terms of improved fitness. However, in more varied populations, altruism to strangers would not necessarily increase fitness.

Fourthly, it has been argued by some cultural anthropologists that tribal people are essentially peaceful and kind, except for disruptions caused by colonialism. Before the development of agriculture, people were relatively immobile foragers who moved only very short distances and only interacted with people like themselves. As such, there would have been no selection in favour of ethnic or racial discrimination. The fundamental problem with this criticism is that Rushton has presented evidence that people can detect even the slightest genetic differences, even within families. Moreover, there is no reason to believe that pre-agricultural humans were anything like some anthropologists portray them as being. Evidence from ethnographies with surviving foragers (e.g. Chagnon, 1968; Chagnon, 2013) indicates that their lives are characterized by extreme violence, including frequent battles with other tribes (and, so, other ethnic groups), territory invasions, and genocide. As such, a capacity to discriminate against members of a different tribe — and by extension ethnicity — would be highly adaptive.

Fifthly, it might be averred that Rushton's model does not fully explain variations in ethnocentrism. As we have seen, ethnocentrism is only modestly heritable, the region of 0.3. Accordingly, environmental factors must be significant in explaining variations in ethnocentrism and, in particular, why ethnic solidarity varies in cultures over time. Ethnic solidarity is generally of a moderate or low intensity but can reach fever pitch due to even the most minor attack on the group or even due to a slur against its identity. As such, threat to the interests of the ethny appears to be a highly significant dimension to ethnocentrism, meaning that it cannot be explained solely in terms of directly increasing inclusive fitness. A more subtle approach is required.

Further, it may be that a certain kind of personality is generally more ethnocentric and since personality alters throughout the lifespan, we would expect that the average age of a population would impact how ethnocentric it was. And this raises the broader question of why some populations are stereotyped as being particularly ethnocentric (e.g. MacDonald, 1996). Rushton's model would explain this in terms of greater genetic similarity in comparison to outsiders (in other words, inbreeding) and historically having been in conflict with another group, leading to greater selection for ethnocentrism. However, this raises the question of by what mechanism this ethnocentrism has developed. Also, Rushton (1995) has looked at population differences in modal personality and so-called 'Life History Strategy'. These may have some impact on the degree of a population's ethnocentrism. We will explore all of these issues later in this book.

Sixthly, research by Kurzban et al. (2001) has highlighted the degree to which ethnic nepotism is sensitive to cultural cues in a way which might be seen to challenge *Genetic Similarity Theory*. They found that the subjects of an experiment were less inclined to categorize fellow subjects in terms of race when the race of these subjects did not correlate with being or not being in their particular, experiment-manufactured group. However, this was not true of categorization by sex. This remained even when coalitions were composed of both males and females. This might be regarded as a challenge to the view that racial categorization is automatic and innate. But it can be countered that this does not seriously challenge the theory because *Genetic Similarity Theory* extends to intra-racial relations as well, based, often, around very weak ties. Also, it merely highlights the fact that — as already noted — humans can engage in mutual reciprocity and it is possible for this to be with somebody who is genetically very different, especially if such an alliance might be regarded as beneficial to one's own fitness in some way. In these circumstances, we might expect that people would regard an individual's genetic dissimilarity as less pertinent. An anecdotal example of this would be the way that, in the 1980s when I was a boy, those in England who might argue that 'the blacks should all sent back to where they came from' would sometimes add, 'Except Frank. He's one of us!' The heavyweight boxer Frank Bruno (b. 1961) had been born in London to Caribbean parents but had married an English woman, and had a 95% knock-out rate in the forty out of forty-five fights that he won. Despite his genetic dissimilarity from the native English, he fought successfully for England, and displayed the attractive qualities of toughness, physical strength, and general amiability. As such, we can see how otherwise ethnocentric people would see a benefit to their group's fitness in permitting him into their group, something that could potentially even outweigh (indeed, clearly outweighed) the negative side of this.

That said, the research by Kurzban et al. does highlight the degree to which ethnocentrism can be affected by environmental variables. The coalitions established by Kurzban et al. would, presumably, not have been under a great deal of stress. The suggestion is that were the coalition placed under stress then it would likely break down into infighting and members would start to categorize and even assort along racial lines—along the lines of genetic similarity.

7. Other Lines of Research

Various other studies have validated many of the predictions of *Genetic Similarity Theory*.

(A) ACADEMIC CITATIONS

The theory would predict that ethnic nepotism, or the influence of it, would be present in every area of life in which different ethnicities interacted. One obvious example of such an area is academia. Academia is international (especially in the hard sciences) and the medium of publication is English. *Genetic Similarity Theory* would predict that academics would be more likely to take seriously research conducted by members of their own ethnicity than by outsiders and would more likely want to assist the credibility of members of their own ethnicity by citing them. This could be tested by examining the propensity for academics to cite people of their own ethnicity (as judged by the academic's surname) in their research papers. Greenwald and Schuh's (1994) large scale study of academic social science journals classified citing and cited academics, according to their surnames, as Jewish or non-Jewish. The author's surname category was associated with a 40% increased likelihood of citing an academic with the same surname category. The authors noted that the overt leftist bias in social science adds credence to the view that this was probably an unconscious process.

However, it could be countered that it is laborious and moderately more time-consuming having to cite people with foreign names that you don't recognize and which you might therefore misspell. If you are using the Harvard method of citation, which I use here and which is standard practice outside of the humanities, you place the author's name in parentheses and then scroll down the document to your reference section to add the reference. If the name is English, and you are English, you don't have to then check again how the name was spelt and, accordingly, time is saved. It would be interesting to conduct a study like Greenwald and Schuh's that controlled, for example, for length of the surname or whether or not the author had heard of the surname. Even in writing the above paragraph, I had to check how 'Schuh' was spelt, as by the time I scrolled down to my reference section I wondered if it might be spelt 'Shuh'!

(B) TRUST

Following *Genetic Similarity Theory*, we would expect that people would be more likely to trust members of their own ethnic group. This would be because the feeling of trust would facilitate altruism which would boost the individual's inclusive fitness. In this regard, Salter (2002) has shown that trust, and the risky joint ventures underpinned by trust, are more common within ethnic groups than between ethnic groups. Indeed, Putnam (2007) has shown that in the USA in 'ethnically diverse neighbourhoods residents of all races tend to 'hunker down'. Trust (even of one's own race) is lower, altruism and community cooperation rarer, friends fewer'. Thus, not only do people trust members of different ethnicities less than those of their own ethnicity but the presence of those of a different ethnicity reduces societal trust, as the community is no longer ethnically homogenous, making people — overall — less trusting. It is interesting that immigration makes even the native population trust their own members less. One possible explanation is that any random fellow co-ethnic now has the opportunity to defect and one cannot trust whether or not he will do so. This phenomenon has also been found in Melbourne (Healy, 2007).

(C) THE WELFARE STATE

We have already noted research finding that people are more likely to give money to beggars of their own ethnicity. *Genetic Similarity*

Theory would predict that this would extend to any form of charity, including the compulsory system of wealth redistribution employed in welfare states. As such, we would expect that ethnic heterogeneity in a society would lead to people resenting their tax money going to non-co-ethnics and, thus, the whole society reducing the level of government expenditure. In this regard, Sanderson and Vanhanen (2004, p. 120) have found that ethno-linguistic diversity explains correlates at 0.3 with not supporting a system of welfare.

(D) ECONOMIC GROWTH

Genetic Similarity Theory would predict that ethnic heterogeneity would lead to a lack of social cohesion and consequently society would simply work less efficiently. It would have to deal with ethnic conflicts, organized crime along ethnic lines, more crime (due to lack trust between people) and so forth. Society would be less socially cohesive and we would expect that this would reduce the ability of the government to make rational economic decisions (Alesina et al., 1999). In this regard, it has been found that a nation's ethnic diversity is generally negatively associated with its extent of economic growth, except in the richest 10% of countries (Masters & MacMillan, 2004).

(E) ETHNIC CONFLICT

Genetic Similarity Theory would predict that the more ethnically diverse a nation was then the more ethnic conflict there would be, and the ferocity of ethnic conflict would be proportionate to the degree of genetic difference between the two conflicting ethnic groups, when controlling for socioeconomic factors. As discussed, Tatu Vanhanen has demonstrated that the extent of *Ethnic Conflict* (EC, defined on a scale up to severe ethnic massacres) correlates with the extent of *Ethnic Heterogeneity* (EH, defined as differences in visible race, language or tribe, and religion), when controlling for other variables such as socioeconomic development level and level of democracy.

Vanhanen found that *Ethnic Heterogeneity* correlated with Ethnic Conflict within nations at 0.66. He also found that socioeconomic variables were very weak in explaining ethnic conflict. Level of democracy was weakly negatively associated (−0.2) with level of ethnic conflict. Vanhanen also noted that even a tiny degree of ethnic diversity is sufficient to cause low level ethnic conflict, manifested, for example, in the development of democratic but ethnically based political parties. For example, he observes that in his native Finland there is a 5% Swedish-speaking minority and that this has its own political party and institutions. It has been appeased only by Swedish being made Finland's second official language as well as by various legal mechanisms that privilege the minority. Vanhanen highlights a number of outliers, where ethnic conflict is much lower than would be predicted by the levels of ethnic heterogeneity. He also notes possible reasons for their anomalous status, in particular institutional arrangements which appease ethnic minorities, strong autocracy, and a high percentage of ethnically mixed people. But, in general, it is clear that ethnic heterogeneity will lead to ethnic conflict, just as *Genetic Similarity Theory* would predict.

(F) GENOMICS AND KIN RECOGNITION

Salter and Harpending (2015) have employed the Human Genome Diversity Project database to test *Genetic Similarity Theory*. The database contains the genotypes of large numbers of individuals based on single nucleotide polymorphisms. The French sample confirms Salter's (2007) view that two random co-nationals — in this case, French people — are only minimally related. Helping one's nearest (stranger) kin would be worth only 2% of helping oneself, 4% of helping one's child and so on. As such, in a small community, there would be little value in placing fellow ethnics before oneself or one's family. The same is true of a Japanese sample. However, if these two samples were brought together then there is a clear benefit to inclusive fitness to helping a neighbour of the same ethnicity. In this context, a Frenchman would have a 0.06 kinship — equivalent to kinship with a great-grandchild — with any random Frenchman. Thus, offering a transient surplus to a fellow-Frenchman would increase a Frenchman's own fitness by 12% while offering it to a Japanese person would decrease it by 12%. So, the capacity to racially discriminate — in Malthusian conditions — would lead to a fitness benefit of 24%; a significant difference. 'Malthusian' refers to preindustrial conditions wherein the growth of population was exponential and outpaced the production of food. Accordingly, there was a constant struggle for survival with the population level being kept in check by disease, famine, starvation and war. Clearly, this was a situation ripe for Natural Selection.[19] In highly selective conditions, traits that favoured ethnic kin discrimination would be rapidly selected for and would spread throughout the population. The effect would be even stronger when the benefit was conferred on aggregated ethnic kinship via a collective good because this would not substantially damage anyone's individual fitness. We can thus see how this would lead to the extreme ethnic-altruism associated with ethnic conflict, such as suicidal attacks on members of other ethnic groups. But even if groups were not in conflict, there would obviously be a fitness benefit — if one had a surplus, for example — to favouring those who were more closely related even if not kin, and this would spread throughout the population.

(G) LIVING ARRANGEMENTS

Clark and Tuffin (2015) surveyed New Zealanders in their early twenties to early thirties who were involved in house-sharing with others of a similar demographic. They note that it is increasingly popular in Western countries for young, single people to 'house share' in this way. They found that people tended to prefer to house share with those of

---

19 The concept of Malthusian selection was originated by the Rev'd Thomas Malthus (1766–1834), an English vicar, in his book *An Essay on the Principle of Population* (Johnson, 1798), which was originally published under the pseudonym 'Joseph Johnson'.

the same ethnicity. This is in line with *Genetic Similarity Theory* as it shows that people are attracted to those who are more genetically similar to themselves and trust them to a greater extent.

(H) MOTHERS WHO USE EGG DONORS

It has been found that mothers who have babies using donor eggs create weaker bonds with their infants than do mothers whose infants are biologically their own. The mothers who have conceived via donor eggs make less eye contact with their infants and are less responsive to them than are the mothers whose infants are biologically theirs (Imrie et al., 2018).

8. Conclusion

We have seen that Rushton's *Genetic Similarity Theory* has a great deal of evidence in its favour, allows correct predictions to be made about human behaviour, and stands up robustly to the assorted criticisms which have been levelled against it. The problem with *Genetic Similarity Theory* is that it is not an all-encompassing theory of differences in ethnocentrism. Although it allows us to understand why ethnocentrism exists, it does not tell us why there are group or individual differences in the extent of it. We will now look at other explanatory mechanisms for variation in the level of ethnocentrism.

CHAPTER SIX

Ethnocentrism, Personality Traits and Computer Modelling

1. Introduction

We have almost completed our survey of the theoretical background. But there are two things we have to do before it is truly complete. We have to examine the concept of an 'ethnocentric personality' because, as we will see later, there are race differences in modal personality. So, if there is an 'ethnocentric personality' then this would neatly explain why race differences in ethnocentrism exist. We will then look at the concept of 'group selection' and we will show that ethnocentric groups are more likely to win the battle of group selection. As such, 'group selection' would appear to help us understand race differences in ethnocentrism.

2. Personality[20]

Personality is defined as 'the combination of characteristics or qualities that form an individual's distinctive character'. Thus, personality can be seen as a series of variable traits. McAdams and Pals (2006,

---

20 Parts of this discussion of 'personality' were originally published in Dutton and Charlton (2015).

p. 212) emphasize in their definition of personality the centrality of 'unique variation' in 'a developing pattern of dispositional traits'. In general, in current psychology, discussion of personality differences is focused through the prism of the so-called Big Five personality traits, all of which have been estimated to be somewhere in the region of at least 50% heritable (Nettle, 2007) and possibly up to around 0.66 heritable in some cases (Lynn, 2011a). The Big 5 have been developed since various personality 'aspects' — such as 'warmth' or 'depression' — have been found to correlate positively or negatively with each other, but to have no correlation, or only a very weak correlation, with other personality traits or with intelligence. As such, 'five' has been widely accepted as the number of separate personality variables and these variables are regarded as substantially independent of intelligence. The Big Five are:

1. **Extraversion:** Those who are outgoing, enthusiastic and active, seek novelty and excitement, and who experience positive emotions strongly. Those who score low on this express Introversion and are aloof, quiet, independent, cautious, and enjoy being alone.

2. **Neuroticism:** Those who are prone to stress, worry, and negative emotions and who require order. The opposite are Emotionally Stable and they are better at taking risks.

3. **Conscientiousness:** Organized, directed, hardworking, but controlling. The opposite are spontaneous, careless, and prone to addiction.

4. **Agreeableness:** Trusting, cooperative, altruistic, and slow to anger. This is contrasted with those who are uncooperative and hostile.

5. **Openness-Intellect:** Those who are creative, imaginative, and open to new ideas (this latter aspect being the 'intellect' component). This is contrasted with those who are practical, conventional, and less open to new ideas. This trait correlates positively with intelligence at 0.3 and the traits which compose it, such as 'unusual

thought patterns' or 'impulsive non-conformity', are often only weakly correlated.

In each case, the traits are conceived of as a spectrum and are named after one extreme on the spectrum. They are considered useful because variation in the Big Five allows successful Life History predictions to be made. For example, the 'Termites' were a cohort of 1500 Americans of above average intelligence first surveyed in 1921 and then finally in 1991. Drawing upon them, it was found that extraversion, independent of any other factor, was a predictor of early death, increasing the risk three-fold (Friedman et al., 1993). As already noted, the Big 5 are substantially independent of each other, though there is a correlation at the level of the aspects of which they are composed. Specifically, what we might call the socially positive aspects of each trait do correlate. These are the aspects which make you a socially effective person — friendly, diligent, cooperative, reliable — meaning, in essence, that you get on in life. As such, personality can be reduced down to a 'General Factor of Personality' and people can be positioned higher or lower on a spectrum measuring this General Factor of Personality (see Van der Linden et al., 2010).

As we have already discussed, in the wake of World War II the concept of the 'Authoritarian Personality' became popular as a means of explaining ethnocentrism (Adorno et al., 1950). According to Adorno, this kind of personality was tough-minded, strongly rule-following and profoundly insecure. For Adorno, this kind of personality would be strongly prone to prejudice against deviant groups or any group that was different, including those from different ethnicities. This 'authoritarian personality' has also been widely termed the 'ethnocentric personality' (e.g. Barrios, 1992, p. 227). But, as we have already discussed, there is a conceptual difference between ethnocentrism and simply racial prejudice. Just because a person despises foreigners it does not follow that he will lay down his life for his own ethnic group. Van Izjendoorn (1989), in the Netherlands, and Todosijevic and Enyedi (2002), in Hungary, found a positive correlation between 'authoritarian personality' and 'ethnocentrism' among student samples. But, as we will see below, this does mean that they are precisely the same concept.

A number of studies have found evidence that dimensions of personality impact aspects of ethnocentrism, though it would seem that 'ethnocentrism' cannot be explained simply in terms of the Big Five. Bizumic and Duckitt (2008) found a positive association between 'narcissism' (to some extent low Agreeableness) and intergroup ethnocentrism, that is to say prejudice towards out-groups. In a study of Canadian students, Altemeyer (2003) found a correlation between religious fundamentalism, religious prejudice, and Manitoba nationalism. However, this latter finding was part of a general prejudice against minorities, including homosexuals. In the USA, de Oliveira et al. (2009) measured students in terms of the Big Five and tested whether the Big Five predicted being prejudiced against foreign-born teachers and in favour of American-born teachers. They found that Agreeableness and Conscientiousness predicted a lower level of prejudice against foreign born teachers. They also found that students who liked one instructor group more tended to like the other one less. However, once again, though this study may provide evidence that prejudice is predicted by the Big Five traits — specifically, low Conscientiousness and low Agreeableness — it does not provide us with an 'ethnocentric personality'. It would seem to imply, however, that people who are low in Agreeableness extend this low Agreeableness to disliking people from groups of which they are not a part.

There is a growing body of research arguing that 'ethnocentrism' must be distinguished from simple 'prejudice'. For example, Swedish psychologist Robin Bergh (2013) directly tested the idea that there might be an 'ethnocentric personality'. He found that the only relevant traits on the Big 5 were Agreeableness and Openness and their contribution to variance in ethnocentrism was trivial. However, as Adorno's model would imply, low Agreeableness was associated with being 'prejudiced', but this was prejudiced against all minority groups — homosexuals as well as members of other ethnic minorities. Thus, low Agreeableness may contribute to the prejudice dimension of ethnocentrism to some extent but it is clearly conceptually distinct. As we have already noted, Bizumic and Duckitt (2012) have found that there are two dimensions to ethnocentrism and these are clearly distinct from mere in-group and out-group prejudice, something which Bergh's research substantiates.

As such, the body of evidence would indicate that the idea of an 'ethnocentric personality' cannot be accepted. This would imply that ethnocentrism is not the by-product of a particular or series of partly heritable personality traits, though aspects of it — such as prejudice against non-co-ethnics — are associated with certain personality traits. In this sense, it is comparable to religiousness. This is weakly (0.1) associated with certain personality traits, meaning that much of it is independent of these and 'personality' is nowhere close to being a full explanation. A meta-analysis of the relationship between religiousness and the Big Five (Saroglou, 2002) found that religiousness was weakly but significantly predicted by Conscientiousness and Agreeableness. In addition, Neuroticism was found to be positively associated with 'religious quest orientation', in other words periodic religiousness, such as at times of stress (Hills et al., 2004). This weak correlation would imply that an element of religiousness is a by-product of two personality characteristics, or of aspects of them, which we would anyway expect to be selected for by natural and sexual selection: Agreeableness and Conscientiousness. These characteristics would render a male a more attractive mate, not least because they tend to be associated with high socioeconomic status (see Nettle, 2007) and would likely convey to the female that the male would honest and so invest in her and her offspring. From the male perspective, these characteristics would imply that the female was rule-following and honest, meaning he could be more confident that his offspring would genuinely be his (Blume, 2009).

However, the weakness of the association strongly implies something else. Religiousness and ethnocentrism would seem to be 'instincts', which have been selected for because of their fitness benefits (see Dutton & Van der Linden, 2017). 'Instinct' is generally defined as 'an innate, typically fixed, pattern of behaviour in animals in response to certain stimuli' (*Oxford English Dictionary*). By implication, the behaviour is present — to a greater or lesser extent — in all normal members of the species in question. Instinctive behaviour is heightened at times of considerable distress. Thus, those who are extremely frightened will generally respond with predictable, instinctive behaviour patterns (Steimer, 2002), though there will be individual variation in how much stimuli is needed to induce these behaviours. 'Instinct' appears to be very similar to the concept of an evolved domain-specific adaptation. One of the fundamental ideas of evolutionary psychology is that the mind consists of a number of modules which have been selected because they aided survival in specific recurrent situations in the evolutionary past (Durrant & Ellis, 2003, p. 9). Likewise, the fact that there does not appear to be any large association between ethnocentrism and the Big Five would imply that it is not simply a by-product of a certain kind of personality. It is also a specific trait and it has become widespread because of the benefits it provides in terms of fitness. Individuals who were inclined towards those who were genetically similar to them — which can be regarded as related to ethnocentrism — would, in small and relatively inbred populations, as well as in those in conflict with others — see more of their genes passed on, helping to spread ethnocentrism and increase its intensity in the population. More importantly, however, groups which contained a lower percentage of ethnocentric people would have been more likely to have been wiped out by groups who were more ethnocentric in any given conflict situation. Accordingly, ethnocentrism would spread throughout populations, though we might expect that it would spread differentially and be selected for more or less intensely at certain points, which would explain why a desire for genetic similarity has been shown to have a heritability of only 0.3 (Rushton, 2005).

In this sense, once more, it can again be compared to religiousness. It might be argued that religiousness is not an instinct in itself but rather the by-product of a collection of instincts, such as to over-detect agency (leading to the assumption that anything unknown is caused by an agent, as in conspiracy theories), obey authority, and look for causation (see Boyer, 2001). However, as myself and Swedish psychologist Guy Madison (Dutton & Madison, 2017, p. 2), have summarised:

> It can be countered that there is strong evidence that religiosity is likely to be selected for in itself: it is a human universal, it is associated with increased fertility, it is substantially genetic *(around 0.4)*, it has clear physical manifestations (in terms of brain changes specifically associated with religious experiences, for example), and it can be argued to be adaptive, in promoting health, among many other positive dimensions (see Vaas, 2009).

Religiousness would be individually selected for because it would reduce stress and belief in an all-loving God would promote pro-social behaviour, meaning the religious would be less likely to be killed by the band (Norenzayan & Shariff, 2008). It would be sexually selected for because it would betoken trustworthiness, rule-following and co-operatives. In much the same way, we have seen that ethnocentrism is a human universal and is significantly genetic, in the sense that a propensity to genetic similarity is partly genetic. There is evidence ethnocentrism is associated with healthy behaviours, because negative ethnocentrism involves elevated levels of disgust and thus disease avoidance (Navarette et al., 2007). But, as we will see later, ethnocentrism tends to be associated with religiousness, meaning that it is often difficult to separate the two. Nevertheless, ethnocentrics would be more cooperative with other group members, meaning there would be individual and sexual selection for such behaviour. They would increase their inclusive fitness.

Clearly, the degree to which an instinct — such as ethnocentrism or religiousness — would be selected for would vary with the nature of the ecology. In so much as races and ethnic groups are adapted to different ecologies, we would expect there to be differences in the extent of ethnocentrism between different races and ethnic groups. So what would underpin these differences?

3. Tracking the Spread: Computer Modelling

And now we turn to the other kind of selection, which would select for ethnocentrism: group selection. It should be noted that there is considerable debate over the utility of 'group selection' as a construct. It has been defended by Dutton et al. (2017). They observe that Wilson and Sober (1994) have espoused the 'Multi-Level Selection Theory'. Wilson and Sober argue that selection can occur on multiple levels including on the individual, the kinship group, the group, and the entire species. Once cooperative groups develop within a species, selection will promote those groups which have the optimum level of qualities which allow them to outcompete other groups. This model, they argue, helps to explain the development of altruistic tendencies. 'Kin selection involves making sacrifices for your kin and group selection is a logical extension of this, as ethnic groups are extended kinship groups', they note. They further observe that even this nuanced version of 'Group selection' has been criticised in depth by Pinker (18th June 2012) because it 'deviates from the "random mutation" model inherent in evolution', 'we are clearly not going to be selected to damage our individual interests, as group selection implies' and 'Human altruism is self-interested and does not involve the kind of self-sacrifice engaged in by sterile bees'. They respond to each of these points. They note as group selection builds on individual selection the metaphor is bound to slightly differ. The group-selection model merely avers that a group will be more successful if an optimum percentage of its members are inclined to sacrifice themselves for their group. And they further note that 'it is clearly the case that a small percentage, in many groups, is indeed prepared to sacrifice itself for the group'. So, it seems to me that it is reasonable to accept multi-level selection and to regard ethnocentrism as group selected.

Were this to be the case then, all else being equal, the more ethnocentric group should always triumph in battles of group selection. This would mean that, all else being equal, races that were compelled, by the nature of their environment, to combat other groups (by being internally cooperative but externally hostile) would be more ethnocentric. And if it were indeed the case that the spread of genes for ethnocentrism was essentially inevitable then we would expect this prediction to be borne out with computer models. Computer simulation refers to a programme run on a computer which attempts to recreate a particular real-world system. The simulation uses an abstract model — known as a 'computer model' — in order to simulate the system in question. So, the 'computer model' is the algorithms and equations used to capture the behaviour of the system being modelled while the simulation is the actual running of the programme that contains these. Computer modelling has been employed to understand and predict a wide array of systems including weather forecasting, the design of noise barriers next to motorways, the behaviour of buildings under various types of stress, and the behaviour of cars during crashes. Clearly, computer modelling allows scales of events to be tested that would be beyond anything realistically possible using traditional mathematical modelling. The spread of ethnocentrism is one area to which computer modelling has been applied.

4. Prisoner's Dilemma

In the earliest work on this subject (e.g. Hales, 2000) agents played a one shot game of Prisoner's Dilemma. Prisoner's Dilemma is a game where you are in prison and have to make a choice with regard to how to behave towards another prisoner. The person with the most points ultimately wins. If you cooperate he gets points and you lose them, and if you 'defect' (don't cooperate) then you get points and he loses them. But the other prisoner knows what you've done and can punish you in the next round by 'defecting' himself. Clearly, there is reason to cooperate because you may benefit from the other prisoner's cooperation with you in future interactions. However, in a 'one shot' game you will never interact with that person again, so it is always rational to defect. In the simulation, the agents were divided into groups with different colour tags, but they only interacted with those of the same tag.

Axelrod and Hammond (2003) devised an ethnocentrism computer model that was more sophisticated. In the model, as before, each interaction involves a single Prisoner's Dilemma move: cooperate with the other agent or defect. An agent has three traits: a colour tag, the ability to cooperate or defect when meeting someone of their own colour, and the ability to cooperate or defect when meeting an agent of a different colour. This means they had four genetically transmitted strategies: humanitarian (cooperate with everyone), selfish (cooperate with nobody), treasonous (cooperate only with those of another colour tag) and ethnocentric (cooperate only with those of your own colour tag). Each agent has a 12% chance of reproducing. This is known as 'Potential to Reproduce' (PTR). Cooperating decreases an agent's PTR by 1% while being the subject of cooperation increases that agent's PTR by 3%. It can be seen immediately that if two agents both happen to cooperate this will be better for both of them in terms of reproduction and consequently better for their colour group. As such, defection always benefits the individual unless cooperation is mutual, which then benefits the entire group. Agents are placed on a grid where they can move in any direction until they run into others. They reproduce asexually with a mutation rate of 0.5% per generation and they have a 10% chance of dying at any given time. Axelrod and Hammond found that in the final 100 periods of ten 2000 period runs,

76% of the agents had the ethnocentric strategy, compared to 25% who would have had it by chance. In terms of behaviour, 88% of the choices made by agents were consistent with in-group favouritism. This high rate of in-group favouritism resulted from 90% of same colour interactions being cooperative, and 84% of the different colour interactions being non-cooperative. Thus, simulated conditions show how, over many generations, ethnocentric behaviour is likely to spread through a population and come to dominate it.

Their experiment also led to other findings which are approximately as sociobiological theories of ethnocentrism would predict. Ethnocentrism went down the higher the cost, because cooperating with 'same colour' cheaters would impose a penalty and the risk of altruism not paying off would, therefore, gradually become too high. Consistent with this, it is only a tiny minority of humans — like Private Barber whom we met earlier — who are prepared to make enormous sacrifices for their ethnic group. Also, the higher the number of colours on the grid, the higher was the level of ethnocentrism. This would be because as the variety of colours on the grid increases, colour becomes an increasingly accurate indicator of relatedness, making discrimination increasingly effective in perpetuating your own colour. However, when 'randomness' — via increased immigration (of any colour) and increased mutation — was increased, then ethnocentrism decreased because tags became less accurate indicators of relatedness, making discrimination less effective. But, when the extent of any of these variables was either halved or doubled, around two thirds of agents still adopted an ethnocentric strategy. This would imply that reducing ethnocentrism — using colour as a proxy — could only be achieved by rendering ethnic cooperation extremely costly to one's interests, creating a diverse population that all had the same colour tag, or by maintaining a highly ethnically homogenous population. As we will see later, these are some of the factors that reduce ethnocentrism in real life. Ethnocentrism became just as dominant even if the simulation began with a full lattice and no immigration was allowed.

Altering the programme so that an agent could distinguish all four colours rather than just between his own colour and colours that were 'other' also had very little impact on the results. The possibility that agents would misinterpret another agent's colour as much as 10% of the time, likewise, did not significantly impact the results. This is consistent with the argument that though there is diversity within races, as long as — on average — there are noticeable differences, races are meaningful categories and racial features are meaningful markers of ancestry.

The model allows a fascinating insight into how the ethnocentric strategy develops. In the early periods of a run, scattered immigrants create small regions of similar agents. Colonies of those willing to cooperate with those of their own colour arise relatively quickly but, over time, they face the phenomenon of free-riding egoists, who arise via mutation. Free-riding egoists cannot be suppressed by ethnocentrics of the same colour and consequently they gradually erode cooperative regions. At the same time, regions with different attributes will tend to expand until they are in contact with each other, with ethnocentric regions growing the most quickly. Once this stage is reached, ethnocentric groups will expand at the expense of less ethnocentric groups and, as such, the free-rider problem becomes, in essence, policed by this process. Egoists of one colour will fail to reproduce in the long term, because they will not receive cooperation from the other colour at their borders or from the egoists behind them. Accordingly, over time, the percentage of ethnocentrics inevitably rises even if there are periods where they decline in the history of a specific colour group.

One further result, described as 'remarkable' by the authors, was that the ability to distinguish between the in-group and the out-group actually promoted cooperation. As long as agents could clearly distinguish their own colour from that of others then even doubling the cost of cooperation sustained a cooperation rate of 56%. However, when agents — in the doubled-cost case — could not clearly distinguish their colour from that of others then cooperation fell to just 14%. As such, as the cost of cooperating increases, the ability to distinguish between in-group and out-group becomes increasingly essential in order to maintain that very cooperation. Indeed, the ability to distinguish between groups has been shown to be the basis for social capital (Putnam, 2000) within a group. This finding would be congruous with the importance of clear ethnic markers among relatively closely related ethnicities, such as scarring or distinctive dress. Even if we accept the veracity of *Genetic Similarity Theory*, there would be significant genetic variation within an ethnicity and, as such, cultural markers would sometimes be very important to discerning whether a person was part of your ethnicity and thus whether cooperation would aid the interests of the group, a desire selected for by ethnocentrism. But the authors' overall finding would seem to make intuitive sense when there are at least two colours and the possibility to cooperate or defect on that basis. Eventually, as the lattice fills up, the colour group with the most ethnocentrics will attack the colour tag with fewer ethnocentrics. The selfish agents will not be backed up by their own side while the humanitarian agents will be betrayed by other side, leading to a selection pressure for ethnocentrism.

5. Developments of the Model

A number of researchers have developed this model. Schultz et al. (2009), running a similar simulation though including more than one 'shot', found that ethnocentric clumps of agents directly suppress 'humanitarian' (those who always cooperate) agents from different groups. At the same time, they found that ethnocentrics were more effective than humanitarians at suppressing groups of free-riders from the same group. These findings were extended by Kaznatcheev (2010) who employed the Hammond and Axelrod colour-tag model. He argued that being ethnocentric was more cognitively demanding than being either selfish or humanitarian because it involved a complex, discriminatory decision. As such, he imposed a cognitive cost upon ethnocentrism as part of the model and found that ethnocentrism was, in this context, not very robust. Imposing only a small cognitive cost on ethnocentrism allowed humanitarians to dominate ethnocentrics. As such, he demonstrated that the cost of discriminating between in-groups and out-groups needs to be extremely low in comparison to the potential pay off for so doing or people will be less inclined to do it.

This raises some intriguing possibilities in terms of the nature of ethnic markers. It implies that ethnocentrism will be heightened if ethnic difference is conspicuous. This would potentially mean, for example, that if a group — such as fundamentalist Muslims — emphasized their ethnic difference through clothing, then they would arouse stronger feelings of ethnocentrism than precisely the same people dressed in normal clothes. But they would also evoke higher levels of positive ethnocentrism and its accordant benefits. Kaznatcheev's simulation also found that levels of in-group cooperation — within colour groups — quickly collapsed once humanitarians became dominant and cooperative action decreased. The implication of this is that humanitarianism cannot sustain high levels of in-group cooperation. Ethnocentrism does sustain this kind of cooperation and, as such, when the cost of cooperation is extremely high then ethnocentrism will be a necessary prerequisite of cooperation. This would imply that humanitarian societies will have trouble winning all-out wars.

In a related experiment using the Axelrod model, Schultz et al. (2006) found that areas of the lattice, later in the experiments, with substantial colour diversity often included lots of humanitarians. They theorized that this was probably because humanitarians cooperate with everybody and so boost the reproductive fitness of all adjacent agents. Accordingly, adopting a humanitarian strategy will causally foster a multi-ethnic region in a context of at least two competing ethnic groups. Moreover, agents — of any colour — who have selfish or ethnocentric strategies are likely to exploit the humanitarians thus diminishing the reproductive potential of populations which are dominated by humanitarians. A further noteworthy finding was that in the early stages of an experiment — before two colours began to come into contact — humanitarianism would dominate as much as ethnocentrism but selfishness and traitorousness never did. This is because by failing to cooperate with others at all, they reproduce less over time than if there were random mutual cooperation. So, the overall order, in terms of strategy success, is ethnocentrism, then humanitarianism, then selfishness, and finally treacherousness. Cheaters, it seems, ultimately never prosper.

The most recent deployment of ethnocentrism computer modelling is Hartshorn et al. (2013). They attempted to understand in greater depth what it is that always ultimately gives ethnocentrism the edge over humanitarianism. As with other simulations, they found that, in a 2000 generation simulation, early generations are marked by intense competition between ethnocentrics and humanitarians. In some worlds, ethnocentrism wins outright, in some humanitarianism attains a fleeting dominance, while in others the two strategies are neck-and-neck. This changes at around generation 300, when ethnocentrism begins to pull ahead. Hartshorn et al. argue, as have others that there are two possible explanations.

6. Why Do Ethnocentrics Always Win?

1. Ethnocentrism beats humanitarianism because ethnocentrics are better at suppressing selfish free-riders. If an ethnocentric group meets a group dominated by selfish individuals, they'll refuse to cooperate. Over time, thanks to the ethnocentrics' mutual cooperation and the selfish group's refusal to cooperate even with each other, ethnocentrics will reproduce faster than the selfish and thus expand at the selfish group's expense. Meanwhile the humanitarians will waste their precious reproductive potential helping out free riders who give them nothing in return. This is known as

the 'mediation hypothesis', and it is the mechanism favoured by Hammond and Axelrod (2006).

2. Another possibility is that ethnocentrism simply beats humanitarianism outright. If we imagine an ethnocentric group next to a humanitarian group, individuals on the group boundary benefit from the cooperation of their own group-mates behind them. But the ethnocentrics at the front doubly benefit from the cooperation of humanitarians of a different colour tag. This is known as the 'indirect hypothesis'.

Hartshorn et al. wanted to understand why a tipping point, followed by a dramatic rise in ethnocentrism, is reached specifically around generation 300. They found that 300 generations was the time when the world started to become increasingly crowded. In the early stages, the world is sparsely populated, intergroup contact is rare, so there is little opportunity for ethnocentrism to beat humanitarianism, either through the mediated or direct mechanism. In order to establish what then tipped the scales in favour of ethnocentrism, the authors restricted the simulation. They ran worlds with just humanitarian, selfish, and traitorous individuals; or just humanitarian and selfish, or even just selfish individuals. They established that, contrary to what Hammond and Axelrod had argued, it was not free-riders that doomed humanitarians, as in the absence of ethnocentrism the dominant strategy was humanitarianism. 2000 generations of non-cooperation simply led to a lower population than 2000 generations of humanitarianism. Thus, humanitarianism is nearly as good at free-rider suppression as ethnocentrism but ethnocentrism has the edge because ethnocentrics take advantage of foreign free-riders. Interestingly, they also found that the strategy order was the same except when ethnocentrism was removed. In that simulation, treacherous agents performed better than selfish agents. The authors explain this as follows:

> When traitorous agents of one cluster collide with ethnocentric agents of another, the ethnocentric agents earn outcome b, exploiting cooperating

traitors by defecting against them. Just as ethnocentrism is poisonous to humanitarians, it is also poisonous to traitors, who incur a cost of *c* in such interactions.

The authors found that chance is the factor behind early humanitarian dominance is some simulations. If a group of humanitarians of the same colour simply happen to end up together on the lattice by chance, isolated from others, then humanitarianism will spread through the population via a founder effect, a phenomenon we have already discussed. In general, however, ethnocentrism will always dominate humanitarianism.

7. Limitations to the Computer Modelling of Ethnocentrism

Clearly, there are a number of limitations to Axelrod and Hammond's model. Real-life inter-ethnic interaction is more complex because there are many markers of ethnicity rather than just one and reproduction occurs sexually rather than asexually and can happen across ethnic boundaries (although there is a degree to which the model controls for this by testing for the ability to distinguish colours). Also, all of the cooperation is 'one shot' whereas real life involves continuing interactions and thus, for example, a greater likelihood of cooperation between those of different 'colours' when they happen to be in close proximity. This is perhaps why, in real life, ethnocentrism is not as dominant as this model would predict even in conditions of natural selection, a point we will explore below. In real life, one's chance of dying is not random and set at 10%. It will depend on factors such as one's mutational load, one's lifestyle (and thus one's personality and intelligence), and one's environment. Moreover, the simulation assumes a high level of viscosity; that people do not move around much. This was probably quite true in the early evolution of humans but it is clearly less true now and, therefore, it would be interesting to see what impact this factor has on the different strategies. Indeed, in a critical examination of the Axelrod model, Jansson (2013) attempted to render the model more realistic by allowing people to discriminate not just in terms of ethnic markers, but in terms of kin; as in real life they would be likely to make this distinction. Janssen found that kin-discriminators soon came to dominate. Where ethnic markers coincided with kin-markers then the two strategies simply coalesced. So, this research would imply that a successful evolutionary strategy is to clearly display kin or ethnic markers, as can be seen in religious groups, for example (see Dutton, 2008).

These models are highly abstract and heavily simplify the human experience. However, they are useful because they are likely to have captured some fundamental principles of evolution that occur in all species and environments. These models would seem to imply that it is inevitable that some form of ethnocentrism is always likely to develop whether two ethnic groups are placed together or whether, due to mutation over time, one original group gradually splits into to two decreasingly similar groups. In addition, some of the models give us reason to believe that ethnocentrism requires strong rewards in order to be sustained. This allows us to cautiously make predictions regarding why ethnocentric behaviour might rise or fall in certain environmental circumstances. And if there was no longer a strong selection pressure for it then it would be especially likely to decline.

8. Bruce Charlton's Model

The computer modelling analysed above would appear to imply that ethnocentrism is a product of intergroup competition. However, English psychiatrist Bruce Charlton (15th December 2015) has argued that, though this is indeed the case, ethnocentric behaviour can also be selected for even if a group is isolated from other groups of the same species for a long period of time. In other words, a group can become 'group selected' even in the absence other groups. In many ways, the model Charlton proposes makes intuitive sense. If it is in the interests of the survival of the species to become pack animals, then certain kinds of pack will be more likely to survive the pressures of natural selection than others, even if there is no alternative pack of the same species against which to compete. Consequently, a certain kind of pack will be selected for meaning that, in a sense, the pack, in itself, will select for certain kinds of individual. As we have seen from the computer modelling, these will tend to be ethnocentric individuals who are prepared to make sacrifices for the good of the pack as a whole, and thus for other pack members. This being the case, it would be possible for high levels of positive and negative ethnocentrism to develop even if a pack was relatively isolated from other packs of the same species. This would happen if the group in question needed to be highly group selected; especially it was evolved to an extremely harsh environment in which the benefits of a cohesive group were very strong. We will see below that this would potentially make sense of the high levels of ethnocentrism found among Northeast Asians.

9. Conclusion

In this chapter, we first examined the Big 5 model of personality in an attempt to see whether or not ethnocentrism can be reduced to a certain kind of personality. We found that although there are dimensions of personality which are associated with elements of ethnocentrism it is not really possible to talk of an 'ethnocentric personality'. We have, however, noted evidence that ethnocentrism, like religion, may be regarded as an instinct. We then looked at the research attempting to discern the reasons for the spread ethnocentrism and we found that, drawing upon computer modelling, the more ethnocentric group will always outcompete the less ethnocentric group when other factors are held constant. Finally, we have looked at Charlton's theory that environmental conditions alone could select for ethnocentrism. We will now turn to ethnocentrism's specific genetic and environmental causes and how this explains differences between races and between ethnic groups.

CHAPTER SEVEN

The Genetics of Ethnocentrism

1. Introduction

We have seen so far that ethnocentrism is more likely to occur, and more likely to be selected for, when two or more different ethnic groups are in conflict under conditions of natural selection *or* when the ecology is particularly harsh. We have also noted that the disposition to be ethnocentric is partly heritable and that it is a trait in itself, which cannot be explained simply in terms of personality dispositions. Accordingly, we would expect to be able to find genetically based mechanisms which would cause certain races to be more ethnocentric and, in addition, we would expect certain ethnic groups to be more ethnocentric than others even when controlling for environmental variables which might influence the extent of ethnocentric behaviour. We will explore these possibilities in the following chapters by taking factors which cause differences in ethnocentrism at the individual level and testing whether they are behind such differences at the group level.

However, in order to properly test whether or not certain factors are causing group differences in ethnocentrism we must find data on this subject. Having done this, this chapter, and those that follow it, will look at a number of candidate causes to explain population differences in ethnocentrism. Dutton et al. (2016a) conducted a literature review to find the key individual level causes of differences in ethnocentrism and their research will be drawn upon and expanded upon here. In this chapter, we will look at: (1) Direct genetic differences (2) *Parasite Stress*, an alternative model (3) Differences in *Life History Strategy* underpinned by genetic differences.

2. Measures of Ethnocentrism

For measures of ethnocentrism, Dutton et al. (2016a) drew upon the World Values Survey 6 (2010–2014) which surveyed 57 countries. For Positive Ethnocentrism they looked at percentage who 'Would fight for your country' (Fight for Country) and, in reverse, the percentage who were 'Not at all proud of my nationality' (No Pride) This was superior to looking at the positive responses because they were divided into subjective qualifications such as 'very' and 'quite'. For negative ethnocentrism, they looked at the percentage who 'Would not want as a neighbour' 'someone of a different race' (No Other Race) or 'an immigrant' (No Foreigner). Obviously, it would be preferable to possess data on a far larger number of nations but, unfortunately, data from the World Values Survey was the best that they could find. As can be seen from Table 2, the measures of positive ethnocentrism strongly correlated in the expected direction, as did the measures of negative ethnocentrism, and they were statistically significant. However, the measures of the separate forms of ethnocentrism did not strongly correlate and were not statistically significant.

Table 2. Correlations between Positive and Negative Ethnocentrism (Dutton et al., 2016a).

	POSITIVE ETHNOCENTRISM	NEGATIVE ETHNOCENTRISM
No Foreigner	0.95	–0.193
	N = 56	56
	p = 0.001	p = 0.88

No Other Race	0.95	0.119
	N = 56	56
	p = 0.001	p = 0.41
Fight for Country	0.24	0.86
	N = 56	56
	p = 0.71	p = 0.001
No National Pride	0.13	−0.89
	N = 56	56
	p = 0.32	p = 0.001

Accordingly, they have what appears to be a sound measure of ethnocentrism with which they could attempt to test its causes. In the following, we will draw upon their research in order to test these causes.

3. Genes for Race Differences in Ethnocentrism

We will begin by looking at specific genes which might cause differences in ethnocentrism. And there is certainly good reason to suppose that there might be racial differences in ethnocentrism. Previous speculation on this has been evoked by supposed evidence of high ethnocentrism among Northeast Asians — and we test in the next chapter just how ethnocentric they are. There is, however, evidence from a variety of sources that Northeast Asian people are particularly ethnocentric, both positively and negatively. For example, Neuliep et al. (2001) conducted a survey with American and Japanese college students and found that on all measures the Japanese students were significantly more positively ethnocentric than were the American students and that, in both cases, the males were more ethnocentric than the females to roughly the same degree. Research with South Koreans and Chinese has garnered similar results. There is a large Chinese minority in Canada. A study of seventy-nine pupils in Toronto aged twelve to fourteen found that East Asian children were more positively ethnocentric than those of other races. There was a non-significant tendency for students to be more ethnocentric in their choice of best than in their choice of other friends. The East Asian participants rated their friendships with in-group members as being of higher quality than those with out-group members and this was a significant difference from other races. It was not true for the Anglo-European, West Indian or South Asian groups (Smith & Schneidner, 2000). Other studies with second generation immigrants have also pointed to a higher level of ethnocentrism among Northeast Asians. Stephan and Stephan (1989) found that Asian-Americans were significantly more negatively ethnocentric than Hispanic Americans and became significantly more anxious at the prospect of having to interact with white Americans than did Hispanic Americans. Li and Lui (1975) found that Taiwanese students in the USA were significantly higher scoring on all aspects of ethnocentrism than white American students. Accordingly, there would appear to be sound evidence that Northeast Asians are more ethnocentric than are Europeans, even when they are raised in multi-ethnic Western societies. The fact that this is noticeable even among Northeast Asian children in these societies would imply that it is likely to have a partially genetic nature, something substantiated by the more general evidence that ethnocentrism is partially genetic.

Candidate genes have been suggested for this, though we need to be relatively cautious of candidate gene literature as it is riddled with false positives and failure to replicate. De Dreu et al. (2010) hypothesized that ethnocentrism may be modulated by brain oxytocin, a peptide which has been shown to promote cooperation among in-group members. In double-blind, placebo-controlled designs, males self-administered oxytocin or placebo and privately performed computer-guided tasks to gauge different manifestations of ethnocentric in-group favouritism as well as out-group hostility. Results showed that oxytocin creates intergroup bias by motivating in-group favouritism and, to a lesser extent, out-group hostility. For example, in a computer war game subjects were more likely to self-sacrifice to save an in-group member and were more likely to permit the sacrifice of an out-group member if they had been injected with oxytocin. Oxytocin has previously been referred to as the 'cuddle chemical' as it makes people more affectionate. However, De Dreau et al.'s research demonstrates that it clearly has a darker side and that this relates to ethnocentrism.

Their research also means that there is at least one clear physical basis for differences in ethnocentrism: the degree of oxytocin that is transported and the strength of stimuli required to transport it. As such, we would expect Northeast Asians to disproportionately possess the short form of any gene relating to oxytocin, making them highly sensitive to it. In this regard, it has been reported that A118G (OPRM1) is a genetic basis of the fear of social exclusion. G and A polymorphisms in this gene regulate μ-opioid receptors. A study showed that subjects with the G allele showed stronger unpleasant feelings (based on fMRI) when they were excluded in ball-toss games (Way et al., 2009). Furthermore, Way and Lieberman (2010) found a positive correlation between the frequencies of G alleles in a population and the collectivism of the culture. They also reported that the G allele frequencies among East Asian populations are in fact much higher than those in European populations. Also, the G allele in rhesus macaques has been reported to strengthen mother-infant attachment and to be associated with higher oxytocin levels when lactating (Barr et al., 2008; Higham, et al., 2011). Thus, there is indirect evidence that Northeast Asians are more sensitive to oxytocin and that this, indeed, causes their cultures to be more collectivist and more ethnocentric than European cultures.

Pursuing this line of research, Cheon et al. (2014) reported that the serotonin transporter gene polymorphism (5-HTTLPR) has been associated with individual variations in sensitivity to context, particularly with regard to stressful and threatening situations. The authors examined how 5-HTTLPR and environmental factors signalling potential out-group threat interacted to shape in-group bias. Across two studies, they provided evidence for a gene-environment interaction on the acquisition of intergroup bias and prejudice. Greater exposure to signals of out-group threat, such as negative prior contact with out-groups and perceived danger from the social environment, were more predictive of intergroup bias among participants possessing at least one short allele (vs. two long alleles) of 5-HTTLPR. Moreover, this gene-environment interaction was observed for biases directed at diverse ethnic and arbitrarily defined out-groups across measures reflecting intergroup biases in evaluation and discriminatory behaviour. Accordingly, their research presents us with a candidate genetic mechanism for ethnocentrism. There would appear to be a biological mechanism, which means that evidence of out-group threat is more likely to lead to ethnocentrism of both kinds; that is, in-group bias and out-group prejudice. Further research on this topic found that 70–80% of an East Asian sample carried the short form of this gene, that is to say the form that makes you *more* ethnocentric. Only 40–45% of Europeans in the sample carried the short form of the gene. Indeed, it was found that across twenty-nine nations, the more collectivist a culture was the more likely it was to have the short form as the prevalent allele in the population (Chiao & Blizinsky, 2009).

Dutton et al. (2016a) tested the genetics of ethnocentrism using their own measures. They tested the association between 5HTTLPR and the measures of ethnocentrism. In this instance, they had a sample of twenty-five countries. They found that the correlations, which were generally weak, were nowhere close to significant. This would seem to highlight the problem with using 'collectivism' as a proxy for ethnocentrism. It involves some of the same dimensions as ethnocentrism, but is conceptually highly distinct. So, group differences in ethnocentrism do not appear to be strongly explicable in terms of this gene, though it may be germane to some extent.

4. Parasite Stress

But why exactly is there racial variation in these ethnocentrism-causing genes? There are two main evolutionary possibilities for explaining high levels of ethnocentrism at the group level. The first we will examine is the so-called *'Parasite Stress Model'*, though we will highlight a number of serious problems with it.

There is evidence that parasite stress is a factor in differential levels of ethnocentrism, especially negative ethnocentrism. Parasites are generally highly detrimental to health, meaning that in an ecology with a high parasite load, people will tend to differentially select as mates those who evidence a high level of health and disease resistance. However, we would also expect different forms of behaviour to be selected for when comparing environments of high and low parasite stress. In this regard, American evolutionary biologist Randy Thornhill and colleagues (2009) looked at parasite stress prevalence across countries based on twenty-two significant human diseases. They hypothesized and found that collectivism, autocracy, women's subordination relative to men's status, and women's sexual restrictiveness positively co-varied, and that they corresponded with a high prevalence of infectious disease. They further found that these values were linked to xenophobia and to ethnocentrism.

In effect, they argued that in a context of high parasite stress it would be sensible to avoid those whom you do not know — as they may carry new parasites to which you are not immune — and associate only with those whom you do know, as doing so has allowed you successfully to avoid parasites in the past. Clearly, even if the mechanism for the spread of disease — via pathogens — is not then known, nevertheless, genes which cause you to shun outsiders and focus strongly on insiders will become highly advantageous to survival in a context of high parasite stress. Accordingly, they will gradually spread throughout the population, rendering areas that are high (or have until recently been high) in parasite stress more ethnocentric than those which are lower in it, at least in general. Thornhill et al. found that, overall, less collectivist cultures tend to be at higher latitudes, meaning less parasite stress, and also that industrialism, and the consequent inoculation of the population against parasites, tended to reduce collectivist and thus ethnocentric behaviour. This being the case, we would expect that the length of time since a country industrialized would be negatively associated with ethnocentrism when other factors are controlled for and this is in fact what they find.

In another study, Fincher and Thornbill (2012) argued that strong family ties and heightened religiosity were both a reflection of parasite stress. They found that both within the USA and also between nations there was a positive association between parasite stress and heightened in-group assortative sociality and heightened religious commitment. The simplest explanation, they argued, is that in areas of very high parasite stress it pays to avoid strangers who may carry novel parasites into the community. These findings may even help to explain the relatively high levels of consanguineous marriage prevalent in Middle Eastern countries. Indeed, Thornhill and Fincher (2014, p. 334) note that ethnocentrism is comprised, partly, of 'nuclear and extended family nepotism' and 'cooperation with in-group non-family members with the same values and immunity'. This propensity for cousin marriage may even then be passed on as both a cultural and genetic legacy to future generations, though whether this is indeed the case remains speculative. As for the finding in relation to religiousness, in 137 countries religious belief and religious participation were positively correlated at 0.67 and these correlated with parasite stress at 0.4–0.64 (Fincher & Thornhill, 2012). As such, parasite stress is seemingly relevant to understanding religious differences worldwide but it is far from the only factor.

5. Problems with the Parasite Stress Model

However, there are a number of difficulties with the parasite stress model as a *total* explanation and, accordingly, it is not one I would be inclined at accept in this study.

Firstly, Thornhill and Fincher's theory may be criticized for over-emphasizing the importance of parasite stress to understanding human behaviour and especially to ethnocentrism. For example, we have already observed that in environments of relatively low parasite stress high levels of ethnocentrism can seemingly evolve for quite different reasons. Thornhill and Fincher specifically argue that low ethnocentrism involves prioritizing the nuclear family but otherwise caring relatively little about the broader, extended family; instead concentrating on more general alliances with non-relatives. They predict, and find, that areas that are high in parasite stress are, therefore, less likely to be democratic—as this involves trust of strangers—and are more likely to be autocratic (p. 334). In addition, the strong boundaries that will be produced by highly ethnocentric cultures will lead to high levels of civil war, as well as high levels of cultural and linguistic diversity within a given country (p. 335). As we have already discussed, genetic homogeneity is also a factor behind low democracy levels and ethnic conflict (Vanhanen, 2012). Further, low national intelligence has also been shown to be associated with low levels of democracy and high levels of political instability (e.g. Lynn & Vanhanen, 2012). This may be because less intelligent societies are less trusting, less cooperative (these both being associated with intelligence), less organized, have less self-control (necessary for democracy to function) and lack the necessary foresight to notice any decline into dictatorship before it is too late (Vanhanen, 2012). In drawing upon the parasite stress model, it is important not to reduce everything down to it. We need to appreciate that ethnocentrism can be explained by a variety of non-exclusive models of which parasite stress is only one. A superior model would be able to explain ethnocentrism variation in *all* cases.

Secondly, further difficulties with the parasite stress model also arise when attempts are made to extend it into national differences in modal personality. Fincher et al. (2010) distinguish between 'non-zoonotic' and 'zoonotic' parasites. Non-zoonotic parasites have the capacity for human-to-human transmission while zoonotic parasites do not. The research group found that it was specifically non-zoonotic parasite stress that was associated with collectivism and thus, by implication, ethnocentrism. However, they also averred that parasite stress was negatively associated with certain personality characteristics, especially extraversion. Likewise, Murray et al. (2013) have argued that high national levels of 'authoritarian personality' are associated with higher levels of parasite stress. The fundamental problem with these findings is that the quality of data comparing different countries on the Big 5 personality traits is very poor. It often involves small and incomparable samples and leads to extremely counter-intuitive findings, such as that the Japanese are lower in Conscientiousness than Sub-Saharan African countries (e.g. Schmitt et al., 2007). Moreover, serious questions must be raised over whether it is even possible to compare different nations on these measures (see Meisenberg, 2015). The personality surveys involve people subjectively evaluating the degree to which they are 'tidy', for example. But they will be making this evaluation according to different cultural norms of how tidy 'tidy' really is, meaning it is extremely problematic to compare different cultures in this way. Equally, as German psychologist Gerhard Meisenberg (2015) has also noted, national differences exist in how likely people are to opt for the most extreme of the numbered possible options in a survey. Also, many of the surveys rely on psychology students. Not only are these not representative of the population but they cannot be assumed to be approximately comparable across populations in terms of the way in which their personality differs from the norm.

Thirdly, related to this, we might question Thornhill's data on personality. Collectivism and Individualism have been found to be associated with Introversion (collectivism) and Extraversion (individualism). When comparisons are made within populations, those of Sub-Saharan African descent are consistently found to be the highest in Extraversion while Northeast Asians are found to be the lowest in it (see Levin, 2005). So, those evolved to the highest levels of parasite stress would appear to be, if anything, relatively individualistic, precisely the opposite of what Thornhill's model would predict. This being so, it would appear that parasite stress is likely only a weak predictor of differences in ethnocentric behaviour.

Indeed, it could be argued that Thornhill's assumption — that people in areas of high parasite stress would avoid strangers — is simply wrong. In an area of high parasite stress the population would need adaptations to survive the unpredictable parasites. This could be achieved by a high level of genetic diversity, allowing adaptations to the evolving parasites to continually develop, and this could in turn be achieved by a high level of friendliness to outsiders, *not* by ethnocentrism. Fourthly, it may be possible to explain these data more simply through *Life History Theory*, and we will now explore this and show that it is a more parsimonious explanation.

6. The Life History Theory Model of Ethnocentrism

Rushton (1995) examined the r–K continuum of evolutionary strategies and applied it to different human populations. At one end of the scale, the r-strategy (fast Life History Strategy) involves high reproductive rates, low levels of parental investment, and a fast life. This tends to develop in an ecology which is unstable but plentiful in resources. Due to the unpredictability of the environment, it would not be worthwhile for organisms to strongly adapt to that environment and, thus, a more successful strategy would be to have as many offspring as possible as quickly as possible. Such organisms rarely reach their maximum carrying capacity, because the environment is unpredictably dangerous and thus they are constantly being killed.

At the other end of the spectrum, a K-strategy (Slow Life History Strategy) involves lower reproductive rates, higher parental investment and a slower life. This tends to develop in environments which are stable. In such ecologies, r-strategists of the same species will not have sufficient predators and, accordingly, will breed until they have reached their environmental carrying capacity. When this occurs, they will have to start to compete with each other for scarce resources. They do this by diverting energy away from reproduction and towards competition within the species. The ones more likely to win this competition will be bigger, stronger, healthier, more intelligent, and more experienced. Accordingly, random mutations for these qualities will be selected for and, over generations, the entire species will become more adapted to the environment, increasingly breeding for *quality* rather than *quantity*. As such, a more stable ecology moves towards a K-strategy. In such an ecology, those who adopted an r-strategy may well find that none of their abundant offspring reach maturity at all.

As stated, Rushton argues that there are racial differences in Life History Strategy. Sub-Saharan Africans are argued to be the least K, Northeast Asians the most K, and 'Caucasians' (Europeans and South Asians) intermediate but closer to Northeast Asians. A summary of his findings can be seen in Table 3.

Table 3. Ranking of Races on Diverse Variables (Rushton, 2000b and other sources).

Variable	Measure	Mongoloids	Caucasoids	Negroids	Reference
Brain size					
Autopsy data (cm^3)	-	1,351	1,356	1,223	Rushton (2000b)
Endocrinal volume (cm^3)	-	1,415	1,362	1,268	Rushton (2000b)
External head measures (cm^3)	-	1,356	1,329	1,294	Rushton (2000b)
Cortical neurons (billions)	-	13.767	13.665	13.185	Rushton (2000b)
Cranial Capacity (cm^3)	-	1487	1458	1403	Rushton (2000b)
Intelligence					
IQ test scores (USA)	-	106	100	85	Rushton (2000b)
Decision times	Simple	361 mls	371 mls	398 mls	Rushton (2000b)
	Complex	423 mls	486 mls	489 mls	Rushton (2000b)
	Odd man out	787 mls	898 mls	924 mls	Rushton (2000b)
Cultural achievements	Number of times all 21 measures of civilization independently achieved	1	4	0	Rushton (2000b)
	Top 40 most important scientists, 800BC to 1950	0	100%	0	Murray (2006)

Variable	Measure	Mongoloids	Caucasoids	Negroids	Reference
	Scientists in Dictionary of Scientific Biography	2%	98%	0	Extrapolated from Murray (2006)

Maturation Rate

Variable	Measure	Mongoloids	Caucasoids	Negroids	Reference
Gestation time	Already born at 37 weeks	6.2%	6.9%	15.6%	Gage (2000)
Skeletal development	Bone age, measured by months in excess of chronological age among adolescent females	0	4 months	10 months	Ontell et al. (1996)
Motor development	Walking	13 months	12 months	11 months	Rushton (2000b)
Dental development	Age at permanent tooth eruption	8	6.1	5.8	Rushton (2000b)
Age at first experience	Sexually experienced aged 21	9%	40%	64%	Rushton (2000b)
Age of first pregnancy	-	29.5	27	24.2	Matthews & Hamilton (2016)
Life span (years, male, USA)	-	80.3	76.8	72.7	Washington State (2009)

Personality

Variable	Measure	Mongoloids	Caucasoids	Negroids	Reference
Psychopathic Personality	Assorted proxies	10.1%	14.6%	16.6%	Huang et al. (2006)

Social Organization

Variable	Measure	Mongoloids	Caucasoids	Negroids	Reference
Marital Stability	% married or cohabiting in middle age	66	63	35	Shi (1999)

Variable	Measure	Mongoloids	Caucasoids	Negroids	Reference
Law abidingness	Serious assaults per 100,000 by groups of nations	37.1	61.6	110.8	Rushton (2000b)
Mental health	Schizophrenia Odds ratio, UK	-	0	2.5	Coid et al. (2000).

Reproductive Effort

Variable	Measure	Mongoloids	Caucasoids	Negroids	Reference
2 egg twinning (per 1000 births)	-	4	8	16	Rushton (2000b)
Hormone levels	CAG Length (Low testosterone genetic marker)	23.1%	21.31%	20.23%	Dutton et al. (2016b)
Secondary sexual characteristics	Male Voice depth	108 Hz	110 Hz	117Hz	Rushton (2000b) & Traunmuller & Eriksson (1993).
Intercourse frequencies	Per week	1–4	2–4	3–10	Rushton (2000b)
Permissive attitudes	Promiscuity, 5 or more sexual partners in lifetime	8%	26%	38%	Schuster (1998)
Sexually transmitted diseases	Percent of population with AIDS	0.07%	0.4%	8%	Rushton (2000b)

It can be seen that in all of these measures, the races can be place on the r–K continuum in the same direction. In the unstable yet congenial environment of Sub-Saharan Africa it pays to live fast, die young and be evolved to be impulsive. Accordingly, Africans mature more quickly, are more sexually promiscuous, invest less in their offspring and even conspicuously advertise their sexual characteristics. Basic needs are met, so there is less selection for intelligence or cooperation. Northeast Asians are at the other extreme, strongly competing with each other and other groups in a very harsh, yet predictable, environment. Thus, energy is invested to a greater extent in personality and brain growth and less in secondary sexual characteristics, which might merely be signs of fertility. People mature slowly because there is so much to learn in order to survive.

American psychologist A. J. Figueredo and his colleagues (2012) argue that that parasite stress can be included within this model, meaning that r/K selection potentially permits a more parsimonious explanation for differences in behaviour than parasite stress alone. Put simply, a K-factor, including differences in General Factor of Personality, is proposed to explain the data presented by Thornhill's research group. Other critics have re-analysed Thornhill's data and found that it did not support his proposed hypothesis to the extent that his research group have argued (Currie & Mace, 2012). Moreover, we have already observed that ethnocentrism levels are relatively high in Northeast Asia. However, the peoples there are evolved to high latitudes with relatively low levels of a parasite stress. As such, this finding is incongruous with the theory and requires an *ad hoc* explanation. Accordingly, it can be argued that differences in Life History Strategy may significantly explain population differences in ethnocentric behaviour and we will now explore this in more depth.

The clearest presentation of the Life History model of ethnocentrism has been provided by Figueredo et al. (2011). Their own exploration of the model was partly motivated by a desire to test which theory of ethnocentrism was more plausible; the sociobiological theory or social identity theory (that people affiliate with certain groups because doing so enhances their self-esteem). Figueredo et al. maintain that the sociobiological model is really an extension of Genetic Similarity Theory, such that people will invest more in those who are genetically closer to them than they will in those who are genetically distant; and a member of your ethny is closer to you, on average, than a member of another ethny.

Figueredo et al. argue that in the context of a slow Life History, people are likely to form warm feelings and a strong degree of attachment to other people, including all in-groups of which they are a part. They will also form a more trusting and positive attitude to people in general, perceiving the world as a fundamentally good place and the authors note that individuals with cooperative personalities and secure attachments have relatively low levels of negative ethnocentrism. In contrast, fast Life History strategists will be the products of an unstable environment. As parental investment will be lower, they will have somewhat weaker bonds with their in-groups on this basis. They will also learn to see the world as a chaotic and nasty place and so learn to be extremely distrustful of members of out-groups in particular. So, slow Life History strategists will be more likely to engage in reciprocal altruistic relationships both with kin as well as with non-kin.

In addition, argue Figeruedo et al., slow Life History strategists will also be more able to control their emotions. Those who are evolved to stable yet selective environments will depend on many long-term and cooperative social bonds and, indeed, such bonds are fundamental to survival in such an environment. Accordingly, saying or doing the wrong thing at the wrong time will be a disaster for slow Life History strategists meaning that they must learn a high level of emotional intelligence, and perhaps simply have a high level of general intelligence, so that they don't make social mistakes. For the same reason they must also learn to control their impulses and not become easily enraged. By contrast, in an unstable environment, fast Life History strategists are likely to be killed if they carefully consider the right course of action in the face of an immediate threat. They must react decisively and immediately to crush the threat, something which might be aided by extremely high levels of aggression and thus low impulse control and low Agreeableness. As they will be more attuned to social norms, more cooperative and more controlled, slow Life

History strategists will also be more likely to internalize social norms and the current social norm in Western countries is to not be prejudiced against members of different ethnic groups (see Dutton, 2013).

Accordingly, Figueredo et al. predict that a slow Life History will be associated with a low level of negative ethnocentrism while a fast Life History will associated with high levels of it, something which they tested in Costa Rica and Tuscon, Arizona. They found a correlation of −0.26 between a slow Life History and negative ethnocentrism. They also found that men were more likely to be ethnocentric than women and less likely than women to follow a slow Life History. In addition, they found that greater in-group altruism is not necessarily associated with greater negative ethnocentrism. It is noteworthy that the correlation between Life History strategy and negative ethnocentrism was the same both in Arizona and Costa Rica. This being the case, it cannot be argued that the association is caused by conformity to the dominant political dispensation — for example, Multiculturalism in the USA — as the same correlation is found in Costa Rica. As such, the finding is likely to reflect an evolved capacity, just as Figueredo et al. argue. It is also worthy of comment that the correlation between Life History strategy and negative ethnocentrism is relatively weak, even if it is statistically significant. This would imply that though Life History strategy is important in predicting the degree to which people are likely to be ethnocentric, it is, again, far from the only factor that explains differences on this measure. However, it is a more parsimonious model than Parasite Stress.

8. Testing the Life History Theory Hypothesis

Dutton et al. (2016a) attempted to see if Figueredo et al's model also contributes to explaining ethnic and racial differences in ethnocentrism. They drew upon already published studies to accrue datasets on proxies for Life History strategy at a country level. These were:

1. **CAG repeats on the AR Gene (CAG).** Minkov and Bond (2015) tested national differences in Life History strategy using genetic polymorphisms. As part of their study they collected national-level data on the AR gene, which is a known androgen receptor gene and is polymorphic. Higher numbers of CAG repeats (i.e longer CAGs) have been linked to higher insensitivity to testosterone. They drew upon Minkov & Bond (2015) and Dutton et al. (2016b) who extended these data.

2. **Androgenic hair (No Androgenic Hair).** The level of male androgenic hair indicates higher androgen — that is testosterone — levels and Mid-Phalangeal hair is a proxy for androgenic hair. A large dataset was presented in Dutton et al. (2016b) and we employed this. It recorded the percent of the population with no androgenic hair. As Dutton et al. (2016b) explore, higher levels of testosterone make people more aggressive and are associated with a faster Life History strategy.

3. **DRD4 7-Repeat, National Frequency (DRD4).** This is a dopamine receptor genes which is associated with many aspects of a fast Life History, such as, on the 7-repeat, impulsiveness, financial risk-taking, gambling, and delinquency. Data was taken from Minkov and Bond (2015).

4. **5HTTLPR S-Allele National Frequency (5HTT).** This serotonin transporter gene is associated with sensitivity to context and especially stressful situations. Those possessing the s-form display higher levels of ingroup-bias and out-group hostility in such situations. Data was taken from Minkov and Bond (2015).

5. **Life History Strategy-GFI. (LHS) (N = 36).** This is a combination of the 3 LIFE HISTORY strategy measures presented by Minkov and Bond (2015).

DRD4 significantly positively correlated with negative ethnocentrism at −0.7. 5HTTLPR did not significantly correlate. In addition, CAG repeat did not significantly correlate with either of the variables and nor did Androgenic hair. However, LHS-GFI did significantly positively correlate with negative ethnocentrism, at 0.3. As noted, DRD4 also did. This implies a genetic basis for negative ethnocentrism in a fast Life History strategy. This being the case, these specific genes do not appear to explain the high levels of positive ethnocentrism that have been observed among Northeast Asians. That said, two markers of slow Life History—having low levels of androgenic hair and shorter CAG repeats on the AR gene—do almost reach significance in their association with positive ethnocentrism. Thus, although more research is required with a larger N to be truly confident in this, a liberal interpretation is that, at the population level, a slow Life History strategy, based on strongly genetic differences, can lead to higher levels of positive ethnocentrism.

9. Conclusion

In this chapter, we have looked at measures of Life History Strategy and demonstrated the degree to which they are predictive of positive and negative ethnocentrism at the group and individual level. In next chapter, we will test whether racial differences in ethnocentrism exist and explain these, primarily from the perspective of Life History Theory and Genetic Similarity Theory.

CHAPTER EIGHT

Race Differences, Cousin Marriage and Religion

1. Introduction

In last chapter, we established that ethnocentrism is partly predicted by Life History Strategy and that this is partly genetic. In this chapter, we will continue looking at the genetic explanations for differences in ethnocentrism that we commenced examining in the last chapter. We will establish that there *are* race differences in levels of ethnocentrism and we will then look at why these have developed by comparing the evolution of the different races. In particular, we will test the impact of cousin marriage and religion on group differences in ethnocentrism.

2. Race Differences in Ethnocentrism

With their ethnocentrism measures, Dutton et al. (2016a) classified each nation on the World Values Survey according to the largest ethnic group within their population, as African, European, East Asian, or South Asian (this included South Asians as well as those with significant South Asian admixture, such as Arab countries), excluding countries whose population is too variegated to allow one meaningful classification (e.g. Uzbekistan or Columbia). Absolute levels are relevant for this analysis, and they therefore used the population percentage that affirmed 'Fight for country' as the positive ethnocentrism measure, and also because national pride is known to vary widely and inconsistently across these small subgroups of countries due to tribalism and Life History. For Negative ethnicity they simply took the mean of the two 'Would not want as a neighbour' items: 'someone of a different race' and 'an immigrant'. Effect sizes were medium to large between South Asian and other populations, but only one pairwise difference in the sequence from African to South Asian was statistically significant ($p < .05$), partly owing to the small numbers of African and East Asian countries. However, all differences between Caucasian and South Asian countries were both large and significant, as can be seen in Table 4.

Table 4. Differences in Negative and Positive Ethnocentrism indicators as a function of race (adapted from Dutton et al., 2016a).

	N	NEGATIVE ETHNOCENTRISM	D	'WOULD FIGHT FOR MY COUNTRY'	D
African	6	15.1		57.5	
Caucasian	23	16.9	0.138	55.5	−0.160
East Asian	8	25.6	0.666*	58.0	0.154
South Asian	14	31.2	0.463	70.8	0.735
Caucasian	23	16.9	−1.141*	55.5	−1.143*

Note. South Asian includes Arab and North African countries, as justified by genetic assay data (see Lynn, 2006). Effect sizes refer to the pairwise comparisons between adjacent race groups, i.e. with that of the row above.
* = statistically significant ($p < .05$), referring to pairwise differences.

An alternative source of data, specifically on racial differences in ethnocentrism, is that which has been mined from the dating website OkCupid in the year 2016 by the Danish researcher Emil Kirkegaard. OkCupid is a US-based dating website in which people take various member-created quizzes, answer direct questions posed by other members, and rank each other's attractiveness, with a view to being able to get in contact with other members and go on dates with them. Kirkegaard provides us with a sample of roughly 68,000 people who have answered specific questions on their 'profile', with a view to persuading another user to go on a date with them (Kirkegaard, 5th May 2016). The findings here are very different not only — as we will see — from my own, presented in Dutton et al. (2016a) and in this broader study, but also from many other studies which hint in the same direction. The OkCupid data finds that women are more ethnocentric than men no matter what their race, (though the sex difference is very small, with a 0.12 correlation between being female and being ethnocentric), and that white people are more ethnocentric than black people.

However, there are a number of reasons why these data are more dubious than the World Values Survey, despite the very large sample. Most obviously, the people's views are being read by potential dates and so there would be a much stronger incentive to lie in order to make yourself look good. This could potentially explain why men come out as less ethnocentric than women. They are lower in Agreeableness and Conscientiousness than women (Nettle, 2007) and so are more inclined lie. And they may also understand that women sexually select, to a greater extent than do males, on personality traits (see Buss, 1989). It has been argued that racism (and in general being illiberal) is, in part, negatively correlated with intelligence because more intelligent people better understand the benefits of not being seen as 'racist' in a society in which Multiculturalism is the dominant ideology (Woodley of Menie & Dunkel, 2015). This would be congruous with the OkCupid finding that more intelligent members are lower in ethnocentrism, in the context of the other results. The more intelligent people, because they are being monitored, are more inclined to give the 'correct' answer — that which will best enhance their reputation.

It is very strange that 'white people' are reported to be the most ethnocentric. One possibility is that this site — in essence — appeals to people that want a one-night stand or similar superficial relationship. Being 'white' is found attractive by non-whites because 'whiteness' is dominant in the media and simply in the history of human achievement (Murray, 2006). This makes non-whites want to have sex with whites, as it means that whites have value. Indeed, it has been shown that females (who tend to select for status more than men) who are in multicultural marriages tend to have husbands from countries wealthier and more influential than their own. By contrast, males have wives from countries that are poorer and less influential than their own is. Thus, race and nationality are clearly dimensions of status in sexual relationships (Dutton & Madison, 2016). But this does not, of course, mean that black people would necessarily be more inclined to lay down their lives for white people, show preference for white interests over those of their own race, vote for whites over members of their own race or any other behaviour of that kind that might be regarded as low in ethnocentrism.

Further examinations of OkCupid have looked not just at people's stated preferences but at how they actually 'rate' other users, in terms of their attractiveness (Rudder, 14th Sept 2014). Under the OkCupid system, users were asked rate members of the opposite sex on attractiveness, so these are actual person-to-person interactions. White and East Asian men will penalize black women, while black men do not seem to care about race in terms of judging attractiveness to any significant degree. Women prefer men of their own race — they judge men of their own race to be the most attractive. But, when looking at other races, they also penalize East Asian and black men, whom they see as much less attractive than average. How can we interpret these findings? One possible interpretation relates to race differences in r/K strategy that we have already discussed. We can divide, approximately, between two dimensions to a potential mate: finding them highly sexually attractive based on appearance, and the psychological and social qualities which may make them a good mate. We would expect K-strategists to more interested in the latter dimension and, therefore, even if they were more sexually attracted to their own race it would not follow at all that they would be more ethnocentric more generally, because we would expect them to be somewhat less motivated purely by sexual attractiveness. For this reason, rating the sexual attractiveness of people in photographs cannot be regarded as a very good measure of race differences in ethnocentrism as we have defined it. It is certainly interesting that black men, according to these data, do not racially discriminate, whereas white and East Asian men do discriminate against black women. In the latter case, it is likely that black women are considered unattractive because they are high in testosterone, and therefore muscular and relatively unfeminine (see Rushton, 1995). In the former case, it may be that black men are attracted to white and Asian women due to their femininity and to black women due to genetic similarity and that they also have slightly different standards of beauty. For example, Freedman et al. (2004) found differences in the evaluation of the attractiveness of female figures when comparing white and African American male evaluators. Both racial groups were the most attracted to women with average weight and a Waist to Hip Ratio (WHR) of about 0.7. However, a higher proportion of African Americans favoured an extremely low WHR. In addition, both groups were the least attracted to overweight women, preferring underweight to overweight. However, African American men were less repelled by overweight women than white men were. In that being overweight is associated with low intelligence and low impulse control, it implies that black men care less about these issues as long as the female is highly fertile. It is possible that women, as they are more K-oriented, are slightly more prepared to trade physical attractiveness for genetic similarity (within certain boundaries) — hence their greater preference for men of their own race — but they are also more interested in status than are men, hence their greater attraction to whites, whom they do not penalise.

However, it should be stressed that the extent to which these data allow us to discern race differences in ethnocentrism is unclear. There is a difference between the kind of person with whom you will strongly bond and create a relationship and the kind of person whom you will simply find sexually attractive and, often, people will be prepared to make trade-offs between these two dimensions. Indeed, we would expect those who were *K*-strategy to make the trade-off against pure physical attraction. If it is so, the fact that black men do not care about race in rating attractiveness tells us nothing about how likely they are to bond with, befriend or lay down their life for a white person or black person differentially. Similarly, the fact that white men seem to find black women sexually unattractive doesn't tell us what their thoughts are about black people, or the likelihood that they would assist a black stranger over a white one. To give another example, a white man might find black women extremely sexually attractive but still regard black people as inferior to white people and be horrified by the idea of having a black family as neighbours or of marrying a black woman, where other considerations will come into play. As such, the OkCupid data, though fascinating, is not especially helpful in understanding ethnocentrism. So, we will draw upon the World Values Survey data in this study.

3. Why Are Northeast Asians More Ethnocentric than Europeans?

So, Northeast Asians really are more negatively ethnocentric than Europeans as well as non-significantly more positively ethnocentric. Why would this be the case? There are a number of interrelated possibilities.

Firstly, returning to Genetic Similarity Theory, the Northeast Asian gene pool is smaller than the European gene pool (e.g. Holtz, 1989). This small gene pool is caused by the ecology being extremely harsh, meaning you must be strongly adapted to it in order to survive. Accordingly, even if we controlled for environmental and cultural variables, we would still predict a relatively high level of ethnocentrism — both positive and negative — among Northeast Asians because there is less genetic diversity among them than there is among Europeans. This means that a random Japanese man, for example, is more closely related to another random Japanese man than two random English men would be to each other. For this reason, any act of ethnic altruism by the Japanese man would have a greater payoff in terms of inclusive fitness than would precisely the same act by an Englishman. As such, we would expect higher levels of positive ethnocentrism among Northeast Asians than among Europeans. By the same token, were a Japanese person to be confronted by a foreigner, this would potentially damage his genetic interests to a greater extent than would be the case if a European, from a larger gene pool, was confronted by a foreigner. Accordingly, it makes sense for the Northeast Asian to be more ethnocentric in both senses. This is congruous with research which we will look at below on cousin marriage, which would, of course, create a smaller gene pool by another means.

Secondly, we have observed a series of studies which imply that Northeast Asians are, in effect, less open to anything new or to change than are Europeans. Kura et al. (2015) have argued, based on these data, that Northeast Asians are simply less 'curious' than Europeans: they are more resistant to change, lower in Openness and more fearful of change. Eap et al. (2008) has found that second-generation Northeast Asians living in the USA are higher in Neuroticism (meaning a greater propensity to experience stress and fear) and lower in Openness than European Americans. Northeast Asians are also lower in Extraversion. A high score on this is associated with risk-taking and certain forms of intellectual creativity (Simonton, 2009). All three of these differences would lead to Europeans being more enthusiastic about new things than Northeast Asians. Openness predicts precisely this, Extraversion predicts taking risks and enjoying novel experiences, while low Neuroticism means you won't worry about the potential downside of these new experiences. These differences would make sense because in an extremely harsh ecology, such as Northeast

Asia, enthusiasm for the novel could be dangerous, high Openness would be accompanied by many impractical dreamers, and too little worry might mean insufficient planning for the future. Clearly, this could have an effect on how a group reacts to new immigrants and could lead to higher levels of negative ethnocentrism than exist among Europeans. Indirectly, however, low Openness has been found to be associated with being politically right-wing, prejudiced against the novel, and thus conservative in the face of change (Hodson et al., 2009). These 'conservatives' would, presumably, be less willing to trust strangers and less inclined to deviate from dominant thinking, leading to a more collectivist society and, as Kura et al. (2015) and Clark (2007) have shown, a society which tends to progress more slowly and is less likely to develop original ideas.

Thirdly, Northeast Asians can be understood to follow a slower Life History strategy than Europeans. This is most obviously evidenced in their higher scores on Agreeableness and Conscientiousness than Europeans (Rushton, 1995) and their lower levels of psychopathic personality (Lynn, 2011), a dimension of which is low Agreeableness and low Conscientiousness. But it can also clearly be seen in Table 3. It makes sense that they would follow this strategy because the extreme harshness of Northeast Asia would have necessitated greater degrees of cooperation and rule-following such that the group could survive. Such an environment would also select for a smaller gene pool for two reasons. At the individual level, the predictable nature of the environment will mean that it is possible to strongly adapt to it over generations and the harsh natural selection will ensure that only those who are strongly adapted will survive. At the group level, we would expect that the smaller gene-pool would leader to greater cooperation and general ethnocentric behaviour in situations of intergroup conflict.

As we have discussed, a slow Life History strategy would be expected to manifest itself in high positive ethnocentrism and low negative ethnocentrism. However, this is combined with a relatively high level of Neuroticism — selected for due to the dangerous nature of the environment, very low Openness, very high Conscientiousness (predicting a desire for rules and order), and a very small gene pool — meaning that foreigners will pose a particularly significant threat to the group's genetic interests. With this being the case, depending on subtle differences in the calibration of each factor, we can start to understand why the Northeast Asians would be more ethnocentric — both positively and negatively — than Europeans. It should be noted that intelligence is associated with K-strategy at the group level, though not at the individual level. As we will discuss in the next chapter, intelligence is associated with being more trusting — meaning, to some extent, more positively ethnocentric — and being less negatively ethnocentric. But, as already noted, it would be quite possible for this factor to be outweighed by other factors.

Finally, returning to Charlton's (15th December 2015) model, it can be argued that the harsh environment of Northeast Asia would itself select for high levels of both positive and negative ethnocentrism at the group level, for reasons already explored.

4. Arabs and South Asians

We can see from Table 4 that South Asians (primarily Arabs and other Muslim peoples in the sample) are more ethnocentric than Europeans. Why is this so?

If the Life History Theory Model of ethnocentrism is to be accepted then it must explain all population differences in levels of ethnocentric behaviour. It might be argued that Arab peoples are more ethnocentric than Europeans. We would expect this in terms of negative ethnocentrism, as they would perhaps be less K-evolved, due to the less harsh environment. Also they have an average of IQ that is around a standard deviation lower than that of Europe whereas that of Northeast Asia is only a third of a standard deviation higher. So, we would expect Arabs to be more negatively ethnocentric than Europeans due to relatively lower average intelligence.

Rushton (2005) has discussed, in some depth, the high levels of what he sees as positive ethnocentrism among Middle Easterners, and especially the Muslim population. The most obvious example is suicide bombing, where you lay down your life for your co-religionists, who are also disproportionately likely to be your co-ethnics. However, we need to be cautious here. The behaviour is mediated through religious belief, which may have independent effects on motivating self-sacrificial behaviour. Also, Vanhanen (2012) has observed that Arab societies are far from united. They are strongly canalized along the lines of separate — and conflicting — ethnic groups and clans and, indeed, the more unstable the ecology the greater the ethnic diversity appears to be. Thus, if Arabs are ethnocentric the nature of that ethnocentrism must be distinguished from that in many Western countries: it does not necessarily correspond with a nation state to the same extent. Assuming we accept that Arabs are highly positively ethnocentric, as evidenced in self-sacrificial behaviour, how can this be explained if Arabs are assumed to be lower in K than Europeans, due to a less harsh and less predictable ecology? We would argue that this can be partly explained by relatively high levels of cousin marriage. This would reduce the gene pool down to a series of competing tribes that would be internally strongly related. This would motivate high levels of both kinds of ethnocentrism.

There are a number of ways of understanding how a high level of consanguineous marriage might develop. One of the most widely accepted is that it is a means of enforcing social continuity. The husband-wife relationship will be more stable and involve less upheaval because they will already have very similar social relationships. Such marriages also make it easier for both sides of the family to help with the grandchildren, they keep property within a single family, and they mean that both sides of the union are already strongly bonded. In addition, when people live in small, isolated communities that already have a small gene pool, Rushton's research on *Genetic Similarity Theory* would predict that relatively closely related people would simply find each other attractive. He showed that couples who are more genetically similar tend to have happier marriages than those who are genetically distant. In line with this, a study in Iceland by Helgason et al. (2008), assessing population data between 1800 and 1965, found that fertility was highest among couples that were third or fourth cousins. Moving away from this 'sweet spot' in either direction seemed to lower fertility by consistent grades. The authors argued that owing to the relative socioeconomic homogeneity of Icelanders and the highly significant differences in the fertility of couples separated by fine degrees of kinship, their finding was likely to have a biological basis. For example, they found that contemporary Icelandic couples who are sixth cousins have higher fertility than do those who are seventh cousins. Thus, they argue that one possible explanation for the demographic transition associated with industrialization — where couples have fewer and fewer children — is that couples are decreasingly consanguineous in these societies.

However, it needs to be emphasised that among some ethnic and religious groups consanguineous marriage has proved highly resistant to social change. Research on Muslim marriage in India found that 22% of marriages were contracted between second cousins or closer and that there had been very little change in this percentage between the 1950s and the 1990s (Bittles & Huissain, 2000). In much the same way, 55% of British Pakistanis are the products of cousin marriages and this has remained a robust figure over 50 or so years (Bittles & Black, 2010). So, why do some groups — seemingly independent of environment — practice cousin marriage so much more than others? As already indicated, the answer would seem to explain high ethnocentrism among modern-day Arabs.

5. Cousin Marriage Among Arabs

We might argue that it does indeed make sense in terms of Life History Theory to practice cousin marriage at a certain point on the *r*–*K* continuum. If the ecology were unstable then we would predict that people would sexually select almost exclusively for signs of genetic fitness — such as symmetry, which is associated with physical attractiveness — as these would imply the ability to withstand the random and unpredictable calamities, such as disease outbreaks, which would befall a population. As such, in a highly *r*-oriented environment, we would predict that people would simply want to copulate with as many attractive people as possible in order to maximise the possibility of passing on their genes. We would also predict that they would be relatively unselective with regard to whom they copulated with. Though they would obviously choose the more attractive over the less attractive person, even copulating with an unattractive person — as part of a general *r*-strategy — would increase the probability of them passing on their genes.

Furthermore, deliberately copulating with somebody who was genetically very dissimilar to oneself would make sense in an unstable environment because such a person might possibly carry some genetic defence against a particular disease, which would seemingly not be the case among the local population. This strategy would lead to greater genetic diversity. Moreover, in a highly unstable environment the main selection is for general fitness, rather than genetic similarity, and those who are 'hybrids' will have 'hybrid vigour' due to a relatively low level of double doses of mutant genes. In other words, hybrids will be fitter. Consistent with this, it has been established that mixed-race people are, in general, more physical attractive, with beauty being associated with symmetry. This betokens a good immune system, as we have discussed, because such a person has maintained a symmetrical phenotype in the face of disease and thus a low percentage of double doses of mutant genes (Adams, 1st January 2006). Anyway, this being the case, we might expect that Sub-Saharan Africans, who have been shown to be strongly *r*-strategist, would be less inclined to engage in cousin marriage than those who were somewhat slower in their Life History, such as Arabs. Though they might engage in it to some extent, in a highly unstable ecology it would not be so strongly selected for. This being so, their instinct for cousin marriage or ethnocentrism would not be especially pronounced.

By contrast, in a more K-oriented environment, it would make sense to trade investment in partners who indicate just high fitness for partners who are genetically similar to oneself. This is because the adoption of a K-strategy, where you invest in your partner and child, could potentially reduce your 'fitness', because you would no longer be copulating with large numbers of people. You would be copulating with a small number of people but investing more in them so that they, and your children, could successfully negotiate the predictable dangers they would meet. Copulating with one person, who was genetically similar to you, would, thus, increase your fitness via inclusive fitness. There would be two ways of achieving this: consanguineous relationships and assortative mating. Let us look at them in turn.

COUSIN MARRIAGE

This can be supposed to be less K than assortative mating. Consanguineous marriage appears to be associated with those who live relatively difficult, unstable lives. Hampshire and Smith (2001) found that among the Fulani of Sudan levels of consanguineous marriage were significantly higher among brides whose families owned the fewest cattle. Likewise, British evolutionary psychologist Michael Woodley of Menie (Woodley, 2008) found a strong negative association between national IQ and levels of consanguineous marriage; also, countries with low average IQ tend to be poorer and so more difficult to live in (see Lynn & Vanhanen, 2012).

I would argue that one reason is that cousin marriage would help build a functioning society and would thus be group selected for. Fast Life History strategists are aggressive, uncooperative, distrusting, and mutually hostile. We would expect them, however, to be less hostile to those who were closely related to them, as it would be in the interests of their genetic fitness to be less hostile to these relatively close kin.

Any society of this kind, in which people began to interbreed with close relatives, would thus soon start to become less internally hostile, because all of its members would be relatively closely related. Even in an ecology, for example, in which the low levels of trust might mean that males could be less sure that their children were really theirs, high levels of cousin marriage would still mean that they were relatively closely related to these children and so it would be worth investing resources in the society as a whole. In other words, a relatively fast Life History society which developed a rule of cousin marriage would be likely to display relatively higher levels of positive ethnocentrism combined with high levels of negative ethnocentrism. A functioning society would need to be achieved in this way in an unstable ecology. It could not be achieved through a particular group adopting a very slow Life History strategy because the instability of the environment would mean that, in the long term, such a group would be unlikely to survive. So, the viable way to achieve a complex society would be a combination of the appropriate Life History strategy and high levels of cousin marriage. When this society then came into conflict with another band, there would be group selection for the band which was more ethnocentric, as predicted by higher levels of consanguineous marriage.

A second, more specific, reason for cousin marriage, as argued by Thornhill and Fincher (2012), is as a response to parasite stress. This creates a highly unstable environment which can potentially wipe people out at any moment. If parasite stress is extreme, then it makes sense to outbreed as the outsider may have some immunity which you don't have. However, once the level of stability is heightened slightly there will be an on-going arms race between humans and parasites. In this context, marrying your cousin will ensure that you breed with somebody who is as far ahead as they can be in this evolutionary arms race. So, we would expect a society that is middling in Life History to adopt cousin marriage, something which would elevate ethnocentrism.

ASSORTATIVE MATING

As the society becomes even more K, we would expect there to be a movement away from cousin marriage and towards assortative mating. This is likely due to the increased importance of tit-for-tat social relations. As the environment becomes harsher and more stable, the more K group — the group which can strongly cooperate — is more likely to survive. Through alliances with more distantly related kin, such a group will be able to develop into a very large group indeed. It will be able to trade, swap ideas, develop socio-economically and thus triumph over the kind of small, insular groups which would be produced by cousin marriage. Accordingly, members of such a group would be attracted to people — as friends and potential sexual partners — who were more distantly related, and this would aid their group survival. And they would be strongly repelled by what they would regard as incest.

This being the case, we can start to understand why high levels of cousin marriage can be found in the Middle East. American psychologist Kevin MacDonald (2002) argues that in this context, in pre-history, the environment would have been less stable but also less harsh than Europe. Clearly, this would lead to a relatively fast Life History strategy. However, it would be slow enough, compared to Sub-Saharan Africa for example, that the people would have the space to innovate combined with the evolved psychological factors necessary to do so. As such, it was here, in the Fertile Crescent, that the Agricultural Revolution began. This led, earlier than in Northeast Asia or Europe, to larger social groups, based around pastoralism rather than hunter gathering. In that the environment would be much less harsh than the Northeast Asian one, intergroup conflict would be, relative to Northeast Asia, a more significant selection pressure than environmental harshness, which would select for a slower Life History. As these Middle Eastern pastoralist groups came into conflict, we would expect the more ethnocentric groups to survive better and their being more positively ethnocentric would be underpinned by the practice of cousin marriage. Such a practice, accordingly, may have become gradually partly genetic: groups would be more likely to survive if more of their members were more inclined to copulate with their cousins. This would, in turn, lead to large numbers of conflicting tribes and clans.

6. Testing the Relationship between Cousin Marriage and Ethnocentrism

In order to test this, Dutton et al. (2016a) drew upon the percentage of the population in either a cousin or second cousin marriage for which they had data for thirty-four countries. Where there were a number of studies in a given country they took the median value. They found that cousin marriage was significantly positively associated with negative ethnocentrism. As discussed, this practice would only be necessary because of the very low levels of trust and a general fast Life History strategy. So, anyone who was not relatively close kin would be strongly distrusted and this would include people of different races and ethnic groups. In addition, the practice of cousin marriage would help to create a small gene pool, rendering such a group very strongly different from any other group. Following Salter (2007), the damage that immigration would thus inflict on the genetic interests of such people would be proportionally higher than if they had a larger gene pool and thus were genetically closer to any foreigner. We would not expect cousin marriage to predict fighting for your group, and it would also predict the inability to create large ethnic groups because this would be based on trusting people with decreasing degrees of kinship. Instead, it would create states that were Balkanized along tribal lines, tribes being overt kinship groups with a common ancestor. Dutton et al. found that cousin marriage was not significantly associated with positive ethnocentrism but it was very close to significance in the expected direction, at 0.3. It was significantly positively associated with willingness to fight for your country at 0.6. This is likely because societies which practice cousin marriage have only a weak sense of nationalism, because they are divided along tribal lines. As such, they lack 'pride in their country'. But they are strongly prepared to defend their community from a foreign invader — who would be even more genetically distinct from them than a neighbouring tribe — and this manifests itself in being prepared to potentially sacrifice their lives. So, cousin marriage predicts negative ethnocentrism and aspects of positive ethnocentrism in such a way that it would seem to neatly explain relatively high levels of ethnocentrism among Arabs. Further, it could be argued that cousin marriage is effectively a way of reducing the gene pool and so, following Genetic Similarity Theory, it implies that if a group had a small gene pool for different reasons than cousin marriage, such as intense Natural Selection, this should heighten their general ethnocentrism. This would be in line with high levels of ethnocentrism among Northeast Asians.

7. Religiousness and Ethnocentrism

So, we have examined the issue of cousin marriage and the way in which it explains how a less K group can be more positively ethnocentric than a more K one. Another possible explanation, which we have already touched upon briefly, is a high level of religiousness, and meta-analyses have found that religiousness is in the region of 0.44 heritable (see Dutton, 2014).

In terms of the r/K model, religion is something of an anomaly. In many ways, religiousness is associated with a slow Life History strategy. Religious people are (weakly) higher in Agreeableness and Conscientiousness than are non-religious people (Saroglou, 2002) and they maintain strong and ordered communities. Religiousness is generally seen as a marker of morality and of sexual control. In monogamous societies, religious people have stronger pair bonds (evidenced in lower levels of divorce), are less likely to have sex outside of marriage, are less likely to have illegitimate children, are less likely to engage with drugs of any kind, are less likely to have mental health problems (Blume, 2009). They also have a longer life expectancy than the non-religious (Koenig, 2012). In all of these ways, religiosity can be regarded as slow Life History strategy and Figueredo et al. (2006) have actually employed religiousness as a measure of K. However, there are a number of key ways in which religiousness appears to reflect a fast Life History strategy. Religiousness is negatively associated with IQ at about −0.2 (Dutton, 2014) and, at the group level, intelligence tends to be part of a K strategy. It is also associated with a desire to have lots of children and with actually having lots of children, meaning that the fertility of the religious — when controlling for sociological variables — is higher than the fertility of the non-religious (Rowthorn, 2011).

How can this anomaly be explained? It could be argued that r-strategists are simply programmed to have lots of sex with lots of different people. If children are the consequence of this, then so be it. However, they have no desire to invest anything in these children. Modern Western societies compel us to do this — by tracking fathers down and making them pay child maintenance or prosecuting neglectful mothers. This means that r-strategists don't really want to have children and if they have them then they have them by accident. By contrast, the religious actually want to have children. But the problem is still that the more religious they are then the more children they want to have and this is surely a sign of fast Life History strategy. If you have lots of children then, by necessity, you are minimising the level of investment in each child, when holding everything else constant. Moreover, having large numbers of children is normally associated with an unstable environment wherein organisms produce many offspring to ensure that at least some survive to adulthood. Further, the clearly documented relationship between religiousness and stress, which will discuss below, would imply that religiousness is at least partly a function of an unstable environment.

I would suggest the solution to the problem is quite similar to the solution that we have seen to the issue of cousin marriage among Arabs. Religiousness, like cousin marriage, allows you to be ethnocentric—and thus group selected—which means that you will simply outcompete groups who are otherwise the same but are not as religious. Most recently, American psychologist Curtis Dunkel and myself (Dutton & Dunkel, 2016) have shown that the more religious a group is then the more group-centric it is, based on MIDUS (America in Mid-Life survey) data. Thus, once a group in an unstable environment—that is still relatively aggressive and impulsive—adopts religiousness, and especially religiousness where there is a God concerned with morality and group purity, this will lead to a number of positive effects for the group. In terms of positive ethnocentrism:

1. They will believe that their lives—and their group—have eternal significance, meaning they are more likely to engage in self-sacrifice for the group.

2. They will believe that a morally judgemental God is watching them, which will help to motivate co-operative behaviour; in other words positive ethnocentrism. This may also be motivated by the belief that their associates are Godly.

However, religion will also make them more negatively ethnocentric, meaning more *r*-strategy, in certain specific respects. They will believe that those who do not share their religion are wholly other. They are either damned—in the case of moralistic religions such as Christianity or Islam—or they might be regarded as 'impure' and 'barbarous' by followers of polytheistic religions, where the focus is more on ritual and blood bonds than belief (de Benoist, 2004). The evolutionary benefits to this would be quite clear. At times of stress, such as during a war, there are roughly two possible reactions, one of which will be far more beneficial than the other. On the one hand, you can respond to stress by becoming depressed, anxious and withdrawn.

During this withdrawal, rather like during sleep, you can process what may have got you to this problematic situation and gradually become better. But this is not going to help a society in a situation of immediate peril. As such, there will likely be evolution for religiousness.

Furthermore, the religion will justify, with all the power implied by it being God's will, various modes of behaviour which allow the group to outcompete rival groups. As such, religions can be seen to encourage behaviour which is simply beneficial to group selection. These include:

1. **Fertility:** Encouraging adherents to have lots of children. This means that the group will both be relatively K-strategist *and* highly fertile, giving it a clear advantage over groups which are simply more cooperative in general or more aggressive in general.

2. **Matrimony:** Encouraging a system whereby children should be born within a committed marital union and thus encouraging men to invest in females and their offspring. Females, to a greater extent than males, will sexually select for the psychological qualities of their potential mates (Buss, 1989). This is because they must invest more in any sexual encounter — as they may become pregnant — and will thus want a male who will look after them and their child. Accordingly, they tend to be attracted to the status of the male. In that women will thus sexually select the males with such qualities as Conscientiousness and intelligence (as these predict social status), an emphasis on the divinely ordained need for marriage can be seen to encourage cooperative behaviour in the group as a whole.

3. **Violence to Children:** Being physically violent to their children in a controlled way. The use of controlled physical chastisement to children has been found to be much more common and severe among the religious than the non-religious when controlling for social factors. Indeed, it is sanctioned by many religious texts (Sela

et al., 2015). This kind of treatment can be understood to prepare a person to endure hardship, and make them rule-following and cooperative; in other words more *K*-strategist. Indeed, studies have shown that children who are raised by strict yet loving parents will tend to be more law-abiding and stable than the children of loving parents who are not strict (see Wilson & Herrnstein, 1985). We would expect that a religious upbringing would be associated with precisely this kind of method. Religiosity would encourage you to invest in others and be kind to others but also to strongly punish any transgression.

4. **Mutilation,** in particular genital mutilation. Undergoing this painful procedure can be understood to prepare you for pain and show that you are prepared to undergo pain to show your commitment to group, whether you are male or female. Accordingly, it can be regarded as a way of raising levels of trust. Genital mutilation is a mark that you are a trusted member of the in-group and so we would expect those who refused to be sexually selected against. In that it interferes with the ability to enjoy sex, especially for females, genital mutilation can also be regarded as a means of promoting *K*-strategy. Females who have undergone circumcision have shown (a) that they are cooperative and rule-following and (b) they are unlikely to enjoy having sex. Female Genital Mutilation is more common in societies with low levels of trust (Sela et al., 2015). This is presumably because it means that a male can better trust that his children are genuinely his. This will mean he is more likely to invest resources in them and more likely to trust his wife. Thus, it can be seen to boost *K*-strategy.

5. **Honour Killing** and practices related to sexual honour. In that the practices outlined above are likely to boost positive ethnocentrism, failure to follow these practices should be severely punished and this should be religiously mandated. As such, in Islam and other religions we see the practice of 'honour killing' whereby a

female who has broken the rules is ritually murdered by her family. Killing their close relative is also a means by which the family show that their commitment to the broader group outweighs even their commitment to each other. A high level of commitment to the broader group would obviously be associated with a K-strategy.

6. **Martyrdom:** Many world religions encourage martyrdom. Martyrs can be understood to inspire group members, provoke pity and awe in the group's enemies or simply be a function of intense military bravery, which will potentially benefit the group. Such behaviour is encouraged as the will of God, in certain circumstances, and something which will be rewarded by God.

7. **Celibacy:** The maintenance of a celibate caste would be useful as, having no family, they would work for the benefit of the group. Divinely encouraging celibacy would also mean that unattractive or low-status males, who could not find mates, would be less likely to gang together and cause disorder, such as through gang rape. Instead, they could be funnelled into this celibate caste.

8. **Intense violence** or enmity directed at non-believers. Sela et al. (2015) note that religion will 'make things worse' in terms of violence and this would be true in terms of negative ethnocentrism because killing or subjugating non-believers becomes the will of God.

So, religiousness will make the group highly ethnocentric. This being so, we would expect more religious groups to dominate groups in the same ecology that are less religious as well as groups that are slightly more K-oriented but, nevertheless, not religious. We would also expect that specific doctrines of any given religion would tend to change in order maximise group selection and survival at any given point. Accordingly, it should be emphasised that the kind of behaviour that is divinely ordained will vary depending on what is most adaptive for the survival of the group, and the group that adapts successfully will survive. Thus, some religious groups, such as the Amish, have adopted a policy of pacifism towards outsiders, as anything else would be very difficult considering their desire to live an essentially seventeenth century lifestyle, with some technological exceptions, in modern day America. In much the same way, some religious groups begin life as aggressively evangelistic and ultimately turn in on themselves, and withdraw from society, if this appears to be the most useful way to survive. In each instance, they will be able to theologically justify this decision thus making followers more likely to adhere to it. So, in some cases, the group might conform to the desires of a more dominant group in order to survive. But they will still be more likely to survive as a united group if they maintained a feeling of enmity, a kind of negative ethnocentrism, towards the dominant group.

But, with this model, we can see how it is possible for the religious to be broadly *K*-strategist but with certain specific *r*-strategy traits. In other words, religion makes the group highly ethnocentric and strikes the optimum balance between a fast and a slow Life History. This is why religiousness will often help a group to triumph over its competitors. We tested the relationship between religiousness and ethnocentrism by drawing upon Lynn et al.'s (2009) data on levels of atheism. Dutton et al. (2016a) had fifty-three countries where there was data for both atheism and our ethnocentrism measures. They found a weak but significant negative correlation between atheism and both positive ethnocentrism ($r = -0.4$) and negative ethnocentrism ($r = -0.2$), as we would have predicted. So, it appears that both religiousness—Arab countries are much more religious than their average IQs predict (Lynn & Vanhanen, 2012)—and cousin marriage explain high ethnocentrism among Arabs.

Of course, we would also expect to find differences in the form of religiousness practiced, and these may even be underpinned by differences on the *r*–*K* spectrum. It has been argued that one of the reasons for the development of a moral God is that people who feel they are being watched will behave in a more pro-social way, meaning they are less likely to be caste out of the prehistoric band (see Norenzayen & Shariff, 2008). In a highly unstable ecology, in which cooperation is not especially important, there will be less of a need for a moral God, who encourages cooperation and impulse control, because bonding with people is simply less important to survival. Accordingly, religiousness, in such an ecology, would simply be concerned with allaying stress (see Boyer, 2001) which you would achieve by following certain rules, thus keeping the gods happy. As the environment becomes more stable and harsh, cooperation becomes more important and so adaptations that will cause people to believe in an all-knowing, moralistic God will be more useful because they will make people more pro-social and so more likely to survive and pass on their genes. As the environment continues to change in this direction, we would expect the religion to become increasingly open to conversion from people who are not members of the clan or tribe, permitting large, cooperative social organizations to develop and be group selected for. In such a context, religion, not kinship, would be an increasingly important marker that a person could be trusted. Other markers, such as mutilation, would, therefore, be less necessary. So, the group whose concept of kinship extended further would be larger, and it would have a larger gene pool. Its sense of ethnocentrism would relate to a much larger group. This would have certain advantages, under conditions of Natural Selection, which we will explore shortly.

8. Genes for Ethnocentrism and Jews

Much has been written on the ethnocentrism of Jewish people (e.g. MacDonald, 2002). The Jews can be roughly divided into three groups:

1. *Sephardic Jews*, who settled in Iberia.
2. *Ashkenazi Jews*, who settled in northern and eastern Europe.
3. *Mizrahi Jews*, who settled in the Near East and Middle East.

The largest group and the one which is the most influential, both in the state of Israel and worldwide, are the Ashkenazi Jews. Indeed, it has been found that this ethnic group has the highest IQ of any ethnic group with an average of 112. This is half a standard deviation higher than Northeast Asians and a standard deviation higher than Europeans (Lynn, 2011).

The ethnocentrism of the Jews — and, in particular, the Ashkenazi Jews — has been explored in depth by Kevin MacDonald. In a series of books and articles (e.g. MacDonald, 2002; MacDonald, 1998), MacDonald has argued that Judaism should best be understood as a pronounced example of a group evolutionary strategy. He argues that European anti-Semitism can be regarded as a similar group evolutionary strategy (MacDonald, 2004). In classical Judaism, MacDonald claims, Jews strongly identify as separate from Gentiles even if there is minimal physical difference. They actively maintain cultural separation from the broader society, they actively maintain genetic separation, they are highly inbred, they strongly control individual behaviour, and they harshly punish free-riders, among other strategies. These policies ensure a high level of in-group altruism and out-group hostility, argues MacDonald, thus promoting the genetic interests of Jews.

MacDonald argues that Ashkenazi Jews, in particular, have long been persecuted with intermittent pogroms, in the areas of Eastern Europe in which they originally found themselves. This persecution by gentiles, often involving extreme anti-Semitic violence, can be understood as a form of group selection. In such circumstances of harsh selection, genes for ethnocentrism are particularly likely to be selected for, something which we have already explored in relation to computer modelling of this process. After a period of harsh selection, we would expect the remnant group to be highly ethnocentric and this, argues MacDonald, is the case with Jews. MacDonald provides a number of lines of evidence in favour of the view that Jews are highly ethnocentric, but much of this is of a qualitative, subjective kind, involving interpreting significant Jewish texts and providing historical examples of supposedly representative Jewish behaviour.

It has been argued that Jews have maintained a small gene pool, something which has led to their maintaining an unusual constellation of genetic disorders, especially among the Ashkenazi Jews. These disorders are so significant that medical organizations have been established specifically to offer Ashkenazi Jews screening for them (Ostrer, 2001). The most prominent conditions are:

1. **Tay-Sachs Disease:** This appears in children and causes progressive deterioration of physical and mental abilities, culminating in the child's death. In the USA, 1/27 Ashkenazi Jews carries this condition compared to 1/250 of the general population (National Human Genome Research Institute, 2011).

2. **Gaucher's Disease:** The defective gene for this is carried by 1/10 Ashkenazi Jews in the USA, but only by 1/200 Americans more generally. Four genetic mutations account for 95% of Gaucher disease in the Jewish population in the USA but for only 50% of cases in the general population (National Gaucher Federation, 2015). Those who develop this condition suffer seizures and brain damage, and it reduces life expectancy moderately.

3. **Riley-Day Syndrome:** Also known as Familial Dysautonomia, this causes vomiting, speech problems, an inability to cry and false sensory perception. It is found among 1/30 Ashkenazi Jews but 1/3700 of the general American population. Indeed, it is essentially exclusive to Ashkenazi Jews. In addition, there are a number of other genetic or partly genetic conditions which disproportionately affect Ashkenazi Jews including Bloom's Disease and highly genetic forms of cancer (Center for Jewish Genetics, 2015).

It cannot be argued that these findings have some sociological basis, such as more Jews being scientists and thus studying Jewish issues, meaning that Jews are not significantly more inbred than European gentiles. Many of the conditions which they have developed are found disproportionately among other inbred, isolated populations. For example, very high levels of Tay-Sachs Disease have been reported among the Amish and the Louisiana Cajun, both of them highly endogamous populations (Sutton, 2002). Moreover, genetic disorders are less problematic among Sephardi and Mizrahi Jews, the reason being that the gene pools of these groups are significantly larger (Lynn, 2011). More importantly, there is direct evidence that Jews are particularly closely related. Atzmon et al. (2010) conducted a genome-wide analysis of various Jewish groups, including the Ashkenazi, and compared them with Non-Jewish groups. They found the Jews in their study had such high levels of genetic commonality compared to the Gentiles that the Jews were roughly the equivalent of 4th cousins. This finding was despite clear evidence of European genetic impact on the Jewish gene pool.

It appears that Founder Effect and Genetic Drift combined with centuries of endogamy—with many Jews marrying out but very few Gentiles permitted to 'marry in'—partly explains why the current Jewish population has such a high prevalence of these rare disorders. It has been found that the world's 10 million Ashkenazi Jews are all descended from about 350 Ashkenazi Jews who found themselves in Eastern Europe in about the year 1400. This led not just to Founder Effect but a genetic bottle neck—due to endogamy—and thus Genetic Drift (Carmi et al., 2014). Accordingly, there were relatively high levels of inbreeding among Jews, either through choice or due to the pressure to marry another Jew in the context of small local population which would be more likely to survive if it was ethnocentric. There is direct evidence that consanguineous marriage is relatively high, or has been relatively high, in Jewish populations. G. H. Darwin, writing in 1875, found that 20% of Jews living in England were in cousin marriages. This was compared to 4.5% among the landed gentry, 3.7% in rural areas and 2.2% in London (Adler & Jacobs, 1906). An Israeli study of Jewish women between 1990 and 1992 (Cohen et al.,

2004) found that 2.3% of new mothers were second cousins or closer (consanguineous) to their husband. In 0.8% of cases they were first cousins. Among Mizrahi Jews the rate of consanguineous marriage was as high as 7.1%. A survey between 1972 and 1975 found that 25.4% of married Jews living in Iran were in consanguineous marriages. This was compared to 0.3% among Chinese Singaporeans in 1980 and 0.4% among people living in Japan in 1981 (Bittles & Black, 2015).

In understanding Jewish marriage patterns, it might be argued that, historically, Jews are effectively of Middle Eastern origin. As such, we would expect that a propensity towards consanguineous marriage would anyway be relatively high among them, making them both positively and negatively ethnocentric when confronted with non-Jews. Their persecution at the hands of non-Jews would further strongly select in favour of ethnocentrism because many non-ethnocentrics would defect and ethnocentrism is the most successful group strategy in these circumstances. This process would render the Jews, relative to other ethnic groups, even more ethnocentric. With a small pool of potential marriage partners to choose from, relatively high levels of consanguineous marriage would be the result of these circumstances and this could be expected to further boost ethnocentric behaviour among the Jewish minority under harsh conditions of pre-Industrial Natural Selection. In these circumstances, the defective dimensions of inbreeding would likely be selected out while the positive ones would be retained. Small founding populations of already relatively ethnocentric Ashkenazi would have moved into Europe in around the year 1400. As the Jewish population was both genetically homogeneous and possibly evolved to ethnocentrism, it became especially ethnocentric when confronted with a hostile host population who also intermittently persecuted it. Due to cultural endogamy and this environment, its levels of cousin marriage become relatively high, further boosting its levels of ethnocentric behaviour as the population became increasingly internally genetically similar when compared to outsiders.

CHAPTER EIGHT. RACE DIFFERENCES, COUSIN MARRIAGE AND RELIGION

An alternative argument has been presented by Cochran et al. (2006). They maintain that the Jewish disease profile is a function of Natural Selection because when a person has a recessive form of the mutant gene — when they are a carrier — their intelligence is boosted. According to their model, a short-term natural-selection event — due to a sudden change such as the arrival of the Jews in Europe — increases heterozygote fitness but there is a cost in terms of homozygote fitness. An example is the way that having one copy of a gene provides resistance to malaria while having two causes sickle cell anaemia. In pre-modern times, those with two copies would die young and only the benefits would be reaped. Intelligence, they argue, would have been very strongly selected for among Ashkenazi Jews because they were forced into cognitively demanding professions, such as banking, and fertility was positively associated with economic success in the pre-industrial world (see Clark, 2007). This explains why Jewish linguistic and mathematical intelligence is very high but their spatial intelligence — not being so significant in this context — is actually lower than the European average. (Europeans would have been mainly farmers, using tools.) Moreover, the influence of these genetic disorders among the Ashkenazi is too severe to be a matter of chance, the authors argue. In addition, they dispute the argument that the Jews have a small gene pool, so their work would imply that high Jewish ethnocentrism has been group selected for due to their being a persecuted and isolated population.

Direct evidence of Jewish ethnocentrism (in comparison to that of Germans) can be seen in the behaviour of babies, such behaviour being very likely to be strongly genetic in origin. Developmental psychologists have found unusually intense fear reactions among Israeli infants in response to strangers, while the opposite pattern is found for infants from North Germany. The Israeli infants were much more likely to become 'inconsolably upset' in reaction to strangers, whereas the North German infants had relatively minor reactions to strangers. The Israeli babies therefore tended to have an unusual degree of stranger anxiety, while the North German babies were the opposite—findings that fit with the hypothesis that Jews are more (negatively) ethnocentric than Europeans (Sagi et al., 1985).

However, there is an important way in which the causes of Jewish ethnocentrism diverge from those of Arab ethnocentrism. Data from the MIDUS study of middle-aged Americans shows that among white Europeans there is a significant positive correlation between how religious they are and how group-oriented they are, an association that also exists in the Jewish sample. However, the Jews were the most ethnocentric (or group-oriented) religious group despite being the least religious and they maintained this status when factors such as religiousness and intelligence were controlled for (see Dunkel & Dutton, 2016). A plausible explanation is that their high levels of ethnocentrism are a function of their small gene pool or, if this is incorrect, their isolation and persecution has selected for ethnocentrism. It may be that the experience of the Holocaust boosted Jewish ethnocentrism, but Jewish ethnocentrism was criticized long before this happened (see Lynn, 2011b).

9. Low Ethnocentrism: Europeans and Africans

The above discussion implies that Europeans—focusing solely on a genetic explanation—are likely to occupy a kind of 'Goldilocks Zone' of very low ethnocentrism. They are less ethnocentric than the Northeast Asians because they are less K-selected, they have a larger gene-pool, and their environment has been less harsh, leading to lower levels of group selection. However, they are also less ethnocentric than groups which are relatively more r-selected than them, such as Arabs. This is because at a certain point along the r–K continuum it would appear that a propensity towards cousin marriage is group selected for. This factor sets off high levels of positive ethnocentrism alongside the high levels of negative ethnocentrism which we can already expect to exist and the more ethnocentric groups then win the battle of group or natural selection. In much the same way, the less *K*-environment of Arabs means that they are more religious than Europeans. As we have discussed, religiousness can be understood to parallel and even exaggerate ethnocentrism and Europeans are clearly less religious than those from Arab countries (see Dutton, 2014).

Further, Life History theory would predict that Sub-Saharan Africans would also be relatively high in negative ethnocentrism compared to Europeans. Certainly, Judd et al. (1995) review four studies which all find that African American youths are more negatively ethnocentric than white youths, consistent with a Life History model. From Dutton et al.'s research (2016), Sub-Saharan Africans do not differ significantly in ethnocentrism from Europeans, so this needs to be investigated further with a larger sample. Part of the reason for this may be low levels national identity in tribally Balkanized African countries. However, Africans are clearly less ethnocentric than South Asians. As we have discussed, one possible reason for this is their relatively fast Life History. This would mean that they would engage in cousin marriage to a lesser extent and benefit more from exogamous relationships, leading to greater genetic diversity between individuals and between tribal organizations.

The consequent low level of societal development might also lead to a lower level of selection for a religious ideology based around an all-knowing, moral God of the kind that you find in Islam. This kind of god, it has been argued, be more useful in societies that developed more complex social structures in which non-relatives had to cooperate (see Norenzayan & Shariff, 2008). They were more likely to cooperate if they felt that a moral god was watching them, demanding they cooperate with co-religionists. Such a god might strongly promote marrying within the faith and rejecting deviants, providing a strong means of judging genetic similarity, as we have discussed. It would also promote positive ethnocentrism and negative ethnocentrism as being the will of God, providing an environmental way of promoting such behaviour as well as shunning or killing, and so damaging the breeding chances, of dissenters. Studies have indeed found that levels of religiousness are higher in South Asian and Arab countries than in African ones when average IQ is taken into account. South Asian and Arab countries are simply far more religious than their average national IQ would predict (see Lynn & Vanhanen, 2012, p. 305). So, these two factors may explain higher ethnocentrism among South Asians when compared to Africans. The South Asian environment is such that cousin marriage and a certain type of religion, involving a moral God, will be more strongly selected for, leading, in turn, to a group that is more ethnocentric without any of the main disadvantages associated with either type of ethnocentrism.

10. Selection for Low Ethnocentrism in Europeans?

It could be argued that the low ethnocentrism of Europeans could, like a propensity for cousin marriage, be a group-selected trait. In other words, a European sub-population developed these traits and then came to dominate all of the other European populations, causing the traits to spread. Low ethnocentrism would permit a greater ability to trade and pool resources and so, ultimately, the creation of an extremely large coalition with a very large gene pool. This group would be more likely than a smaller group to produce geniuses. There is much research on the nature of genius but it is widely agreed that there is a specific 'genius' type. The genius is characterized by extremely high — outlier — intelligence and moderately high psychoticism; that is to say moderately low Agreeableness and moderately low Conscientiousness (Dutton & Charlton, 2015; Feist, 2007 & 1998; Simonton, 2009 & 1988). This is because original, ground-breaking ideas will always cause offence and involve thinking outside the box. Low Conscientiousness predicts breaking the rules while low Agreeableness predicts not caring if your ideas cause offence. Very high intelligence predicts the ability to solve extremely difficulty problems. This is an extremely rare combination because, at the group level, intelligence tends to be correlated with *K* strategy and thus high Agreeableness and Conscientiousness (Rushton, 1995). For this reason, genius will occur due to unlikely, but possible, combinations of genes and geniuses will usually be born to parents who are not themselves geniuses, though they may have relatively high intelligence. For this reason, a relatively large gene pool will be necessary in order to produce a significant number of geniuses, but they will also be more likely to occur in societies that have evolved relatively high intelligence (see Dutton et al., 2016a).

According to Lynn and Vanhanen's (2012) extensive research, there are consistent racial differences in average intelligence as would be approximately predicted by Cold Winters Theory. Harsh yet stable ecologies — such as Northeast Asia and Europe — have selected in favour of relatively high average intelligence. National IQ is placed at 100 among European countries, 105 in Northeast Asia, and below 100 among all other large racial groups. This kind of harsh ecology would necessitate planning, the ability to design and create effective shelters and clothes, future orientation, cooperation, impulse control, and the ability to solve complex problems quickly. These are all functions of high intelligence.

However, the genius is not merely extremely intelligent. Precisely because he is anti-social, he is unafraid to challenge conventional thinking and is able to think in an unconventional way. In addition, as he is highly unconventional, he is not distracted from his quest to solve a particular problem by worldly distractions such as sex or, within reason, socioeconomic status. As such, the genius contributes at the 'group level' and a group that produces the optimum relatively low number of geniuses will be more successful than a group that is otherwise the same but produces fewer geniuses (Woodley & Figueredo, 2014). We can, it might be suggested, infer a relationship between low genius and ethnocentrism. There are two kinds of groups that will lack genius. Firstly, there is the group which is extremely *K* evolved, such as the Northeast Asians. This will have a very small gene pool and, hence, a lower level of genius than a group that is only slightly less *K* evolved and has slightly lower average intelligence but has a larger gene pool. And it has been shown elsewhere than Northeast Asians have lower levels of genius than Europeans based on per capita Nobel Prizes (e.g. Kura et al., 2015; Dutton et al, 2014); it has also been argued that this is precisely because they have a small gene pool, IQ bunched around the mean (itself likely a reflection of a small gene pool), and very low levels of psychoticism (Dutton & Charlton, 2015). Indeed, it has been shown that when national IQ is controlled for it is the more *r*-strategy countries who win the most Nobel Prizes (Van der Linden et al., 2018). But highly *r*-strategy countries win very few Nobel Prizes because they have low average intelligence and are simply too uncooperative.

The 'genius' group evolutionary model will involve a trade-off between 'genius' and 'ethnocentrism'. Groups with high levels of genius but low levels of ethnocentrism will triumph over groups with high levels of ethnocentrism but low levels of genius so long as certain conditions are met. Specifically, the effectiveness of the genius-driven innovation combined with the genius group's (low but activated) level of ethnocentrism must be sufficient to triumph over the higher level of ethnocentrism present in the more ethnocentric group. As long as this is the case, the genius group will be able to win in situations of group conflict. However, this is less likely to be the case when the ethnocentrism of the genius group drops too low in comparison to that of the ethnocentric group.

This model, which we might call the *Genius-Ethnocentrism Trade-Off Model*, would seem help to explain the available data implying low ethnocentrism among Europeans. This new model would imply that Northeast Asians are more ethnocentric than Europeans because, although they share a recent hunter-gatherer past, the conditions of extreme harshness to which Northeast Asians are evolved have also led to a very small gene pool and extremely low levels of psychoticism. This would be because, in general, an environment of extreme harshness would lead to a small gene pool because those who were not ideally adapted would not pass on their genes at all. In addition, there would be strong selection against any form of psychoticism and, anyway, the negative side of genius — uncooperative dreamers — would be even more intolerable in such an ecology than it would be in Europe. Northeast Asians are highly K evolved and highly intelligent — indeed, more so than Europeans — but their strategy is, by necessity, more ethnocentric than that of Europeans because of their limited capacity to produce genius. In addition, following Charlton, the extreme K-strategy of the Northeast Asians would also render them more ethnocentric as well.

If we move further south, we see the second kind of group that will be unlikely to adopt a genius strategy. The strategy of Middle Easterners must also be more ethnocentric than that of Europeans. Their average intelligence is considerably lower, as is their general level of K, due to a relatively more unpredictable, though relatively more easy, ecology. This would lead to high levels of conflict. In this context, any sub-group that began to practice a system of kinship marriage would be at an advantage because it would increase the degree of ethnocentrism in that subgroup, as its members would all be strongly related. Indeed, this would allow that sub-group to begin to build a more complex society. This would eventually lead to large numbers of separate tribes which would be internally strongly genetically related, meaning lots of small gene pools. In addition, we would expect such a group to become strongly religious, which would also help it to build a complex society. However, this would simply make it more ethnocentric, reducing the gene pool by forbidding marrying out, and likely to suppress those with deviant thoughts. For this reason, and due to their lower average intelligence, they would produce low levels of genius compared to the Europeans. But they would also produce very high levels of ethnocentrism in relation to their specific tribe or subgroup and, sometimes, this would be enough to triumph over a group that adopts a genius strategy. Europeans would be in the middle of these two extremes and so able to adopt a genius strategy.

11. The Fleeting Nature of Race Differences in Ethnocentrism

It should, of course, be emphasised that these racial evolutionary strategies are not written in stone and have changed over time. Clearly, in the Medieval period, Europeans were far more ethnocentric than is now the case, something that is most obviously embodied in the Crusades. Indeed, kinship, and thus consanguineous marriage, was more significant in this period as well (MacDonald, 2004). Civilization was higher in the Medieval Middle East than was the case in Europe at the time and it may even be the case that, at the time, the average IQ of Europe was lower than it was in the Middle East, while levels of positive and negative ethnocentrism were higher. Meisenberg (2007) has presented evidence that the collapse of the Roman Empire was partly caused by the development of contraception, and its use among the more intelligent, leading to declining IQ. Certainly, in the Medieval era, though cousin marriage was commonplace in Islam, girls were often married to the daughters of powerful neighbours or even outside the tribe in order to secure protection (Guthrie, 2013). Men might take a cousin as a first wife by non-relatives as further wives (Rosenthal, 2014). Some high-status males would maintain harems that had many non-Muslim members (Preston & Preston, 2010). Though we might expect the harsher ecology of northern Europe to produce a more K-strategy people than the Middle East, the collapse of civilization, in the form of the collapse of the Roman Empire, reflected civilization leading to declining IQ. Moreover, the wars this unleashed would have augmented this decline in K-strategy because it would have been those of the higher classes, who tend to be more K-strategist (Rushton, 1995), who would have primarily been sent off to war (Tobin, 2004, p. 82).

Equally, few people in the Classical period remarked on the high intelligence of the Jews in comparison to Romans (see Lynn, 2011b). This was something which developed later. Indeed, it might be argued that, in the beginning, Islamic civilization could not possibly have practiced cousin marriage to any significant degree, as it was an expansionist civilization. It likely practiced something much more similar to the 'genius' model later adopted by Europeans, as evidenced in the high civilization inventiveness of Islamic civilization during the Medieval period. For whatever reason, Islamic civilization went backwards, reverting to a strategy of religiousness and cousin marriage. Meisenberg (2007) suggests that the up-take of contraception by the higher classes and consequent declining intelligence may have been the central issue. European civilization overtook it, moving away from cousin marriage and especially from religiousness. Medieval Europe was a kinship society, involving numerous social obligations. Even in the Early Modern period, the establishment of even distant kinship with somebody was of great significance (e.g. Anon, 1901, Ch. 9). But, over time, this became less and less important in Europe, as developing a larger and larger group of contacts, based around trade and innovation, became more and more successful. Europe adopted the simple household system where teenagers would be sent off to live with relative strangers (see MacDonald, 2004), so extending contact way beyond the kinship group. Kinship was not needed, to the extent that it once was, to create a functioning society. A relatively K-strategy, including high intelligence, permitted this and managed to outcompete remaining kinship societies.

The possible reasons for this change may include the massive boost to Europe's intelligence provided by the Black Death which killed about 80% of English serfs (see Dutton, 2014). This would have, presumably, elevated K-strategy and trust levels. Other reasons would have pushed this even further, including Christianity's religious extremism and its complete prohibition on contraception. It has been suggested that at a certain level of development civilizations develop contraception and that this is better employed by the more intelligent who, anyway, see less of a need to have children because they are less instinctive, less religious and suffer lower child mortality. Accordingly the positive association between intelligence and fertility in pre-industrial societies (see Clark, 2007) goes into reverse, society becomes less intelligent, and it goes backwards (Meisenberg, 2007). The West managed to reach the Industrial Revolution before this happened because it was so intolerant of religious deviation, selected very strongly for religiousness (see Dutton & Madison, 2017), and had a strong taboo on contraception (see Meisenberg, 2007). Accordingly, in understanding race differences in ethnocentrism, it must be understood that races are in constant evolution, altering relative to other races, and are doing so at different rates. This study attempts to understand what the differences are and why they exist at the time of writing. The seemingly fleeting nature of the differences between European and Arab and South Asian peoples may be because they are relatively closely related, all ultimately 'Caucasian' (Rushton, 1995).

12. Conclusion

It is fairly clear that a fast Life History is associated with negative ethnocentrism while a slow Life History is associated with positive ethnocentrism. High levels of cousin marriage are likely to occur in a fast Life History context and boost negative and possibly positive ethnocentrism. Religiousness will, in general, boost ethnocentrism as will genetic similarity, as Rushton has observed. Likewise, as Charlton has argued, it is possible that a strong level of Natural Selection will boost positive ethnocentrism. This allows us to understand why Northeast Asians, Arabs, and Jews may display higher ethnocentrism than Europeans. It may also be that a 'low ethnocentrism' strategy has been specifically useful for Europeans, though more research would be needed to conclusively demonstrate this.

CHAPTER NINE

Stress, Demographics and Diversity

1. Introduction

In the previous chapter, we examined very fundamental reasons why there are race differences in ethnocentrism. In this chapter, we will examine more superficial reasons, which may also better explain differences between relatively similar ethnic groups. In this chapter we will examine (1) stress, especially as caused by poverty and mortality salience; (2) intelligence and education; (3) the median age of the society; (4) the society's gender balance; (5) the level of ethnic heterogeneity and ethnic conflict in the society.

2. Risk, Stress and Ethnocentrism

Danger appears to be a crucial environmental variable which promotes ethnocentric behaviour. This would make sense from an evolutionary perspective. Danger leads to the release of adrenaline and high levels of adrenaline are associated with highly instinctive — survival-focused — behaviour. Accordingly, under intense levels of stress, we would expect evolved psychological adaptations to become more prominent. Accordingly, it is not surprising that a body of evidence has found that highly stressful situations appear to increase ethnocentric behaviour. These are potentially 'survival' situations and in such situations we would unconsciously be acting in our genetic interests. We have already observed that extreme self-sacrifice for the good of the ethnic group can, in some circumstances, be in our genetic interests.

For example, Pratto and Glasford (2008) examined how the stressor of competition might influence the extent to which subjects value other human lives, by asking them their views on certain hypothetical policies. They showed that Americans value American and Iraqi lives equally when outcomes for those nations do not compete but when there was competition Americans valued American lives more than those of Iraqis. They extended this experiment, showing that even when large numbers of lives were at stake Americans valued a smaller number American combatant lives over a much larger number of Iraqi civilian lives. This would seem to imply that at times of competition ethnocentrism is heightened and heightened to such an extent that the very lives of members of other ethnic groups come to be worth relatively little. It is also congruous with the evidence that ethnocentrism is strongly an adaptation to intergroup competition. Interestingly, Greitenmeyer (2014) has found that playing violent video games not only increases feelings of aggression but particularly increases aggression in relation to members of perceived out-groups; in other words it increases negative ethnocentrism. This finding would be in line with view that stress — which is likely to be induced by playing a violent video game — is a key factor in negative ethnocentrism.

Agroskin and Jonas (2013) studied how 'mortality salience' (fear of death) impacted ethnocentric behaviour. They found that mortality salience made people behave in a more ethnocentric way, in the sense that they felt more inclined to defend whatever 'in-group' they were part of. The researchers argued that loss of control mediated this effect, so, in essence, the feeling that one is not in control of one's life — for example, due to mortality salience — leads people to behave in a way which is highly defensive of their in-group. This finding would be congruous with the idea that stress — which would be caused by uncertainty among other factors — is associated with ethnocentric behaviour.

We have already looked at the way in which oxytocin is associated with ethnocentric behaviour. Olff et al.'s (2013) literature review found that oxytocin increases ethnocentrism in a particularly pronounced way among subjects who are already prone to experiencing high levels of stress, due to suffering from anxiety, borderline personality disorder, or having undergone childhood maltreatment of some kind. Cheon et al. (2014) found, as we have already noted, that people are more ethnocentric when they carry a particular gene form which has been found to make people more sensitive to stress and danger.

We have already looked at Thornhill's 'parasite stress' model of ethnocentrism and we have found it to be problematic in a number of respects. However, it is potentially congruous with the finding that ethnocentrism is increased by stress. Thornhill has found, in essence, that the more industrialized countries — those that have been industrialized for longer — are, in general, less ethnocentric than less developed ones. He has put this down to parasite stress, but the problem with this argument is that it fails to explain ethnocentrism differences all over the world. Parasite stress might explain why Ghana would be more ethnocentric than England but it wouldn't really explain why Poland or East Germany would be more ethnocentric than England. Thus, a broader explanation, which would encompass parasite stress and which would readily explain all these differences, would simply be general stress. Industrialization reduces stress by combatting the causes of many of our fears. It allows widespread inoculation against and cure of illness, so reducing child mortality to tiny levels while allowing most people to live well into old age, and it ensures an extremely high standard of living such that even the poorest have high living standards by the standards of a century ago. It puts an end to famine, and tends to lead to high levels of political stability and low levels of war precisely because of the resource abundance which it produces. As such, we would expect the more industrialized areas to experience lower levels of all forms of stress than the less industrialized areas and, if stress causes ethnocentric behaviour, then ethnocentric behaviour would generally be lower in societies that were more industrialized, at least when controlling for other factors.

However, as stated, we cannot entirely reduce this to parasite stress. Differences between some countries may also be explained by slight differences in living standard, geographical position (for example, if the country is next to a dominant and aggressive neighbour), and even the genetic proneness of the population to experience stress. For this reason, differences in general stress levels are a more parsimonious explanation for differences in ethnocentric behaviour than are differences in parasite stress levels alone. In addition, as discussed, Figueredo et al. (2011) have shown that an unstable environment and consequent fast Life History strategy does lead to higher levels of negative ethnocentrism and we have also observed mechanisms which might cause the very same environment to result in high levels of positive ethnocentrism. Accordingly, a society that was under stress and which became less stable — due, for example, to fear of invasion or due to an economic slump — would move towards a faster Life History strategy and would therefore be likely to become more negatively ethnocentric.

Dutton et al. (2016a) tested this by looking at levels of ethnic conflict (N = 48; Vanhanen, 2012), per capita income in 2008 (N = 56; Lynn & Vanhanen, 2012), Life expectancy 2008 (Lynn & Vanhanen, 2012), Infant Mortality 2008 (Lynn & Vanhanen, 2012), crime rate in 2008 (Lynn & Vanhanen, 2012) and GDP in 2008 (CIA World Factbook). All of these variables could be regarded as stressors. Ethnic conflict was not significantly associated with ethnocentrism. In terms of significant correlations, per capita income was negatively associated with negative ethnocentrism ($r = -0.35$), infant mortality rate was positively associated with positive ethnocentrism ($r = 0.4$), and GDP was negatively associated with it (-0.3). Accordingly, on the surface at least, the more stressful a country is to live in then the more ethnocentric it is, though there may be other relevant factors underlying these differences.

So, in addition to differences in religiousness and cousin marriage elevating ethnocentrism among Arabs, the greater stress induced by living in an Arab society would also do so. And with reference to our discussion of the response to the Great Migration in Chapter One, the relative poverty of Eastern Europe would predict stress and thus ethnocentrism.

3. Age Profile and Gender

Indirectly related to the above discussion is the issue of the age-profile of the population. Rekker et al. (2015) assessed 1302 Dutch youths aged twelve to thirty-one years. They found that around late adolescence — approximately the age of sixteen — people became less supportive of Multiculturalism and more negatively ethnocentric. As they grew into 'early adulthood', their attitudes became more stable and less politically extreme. However, they also became less ethnocentric than they had been in early adolescence. Also, as they got older, the effect of education on ethnocentrism scores became increasingly pronounced, while educational differences were a factor of little significance among adolescents. There are a number of reasons why we might expect adolescents to be more ethnocentric.

Firstly, and most obviously, adolescence involves the development of a distinct personality profile. Soto et al. (2011) have shown that the personality traits of Agreeableness and Conscientiousness tend to increase with age with the exception of a dip during early adolescence when both of these traits go into reverse for a short period before continuing to increase in late adolescence. The possible reason for this, it might be speculated, is to aid a psychological break with the parents. Rekker et al. and Soto et al. use different terminology for the same time period, so the results replicate each other. But this raises the question of why this happens. The development of the late adolescent brain leads to experiencing certain negative feelings more strongly and it is this which may be the motor, partly, of increased ethnocentrism. For example, a number of studies have reported that both boys and girls appear to peak in terms of experiencing feelings of anxiety during late adolescence (see Arnett, 2007, p. 116). These tend to decrease thereafter.

Secondly, it is widely agreed that adolescence is a time of profound change. Not only does a person's body change but his brain changes. In mid-adolescence the temporal cortex, an area which processes music and language as well as social factors such as facial recognition and mood attribution, reaches its peak volume. The pre-frontal cortex, the seat of abstract and symbolic thought, also reaches its peak volume at this point. During adolescence the amygdala, a structure which encodes negative memories, gains peak volume as well. This causes adolescents to become withdrawn and anxious but better at being conditioned by negative stimuli. Adolescents also use the amygdala to a greater extent than adults who will, for example, use the frontal cortex (rational thought) to a greater extent in making evaluations. Adolescents display an elevated response to dopamine, which rewards us with pleasurable feelings for engaging in evolutionarily useful behaviour. For all these reasons, the adolescent is no longer a child but is not really fully an adult and he is left questioning who precisely he is. He may experiment with different forms of identity — seen in fleeting youthful engagement with political protest, the arts or religion — in order to eventually discover who he is. The benefits of the 'adolescent personality' to evolution are relatively clear. A longer adolescence allows for a period of learning which makes the organism better able to survive in a highly selective environment, as was our environment until the Industrial Revolution. By slowing down the organism's development and introducing a lengthy juvenile and adolescent period, the organism has a longer period in which to learn about its social and broader environment before it becomes sexually active and tries to reproduce. There may also be some benefit at the group level to the creativity unleashed by the personality-intelligence combination found in late adolescence as we have noted that genius — and original discovery — is associated with high intelligence and moderately high psychoticism, meaning that lesser creative achievement may be associated with the adolescent period. But, clearly, the downside to adolescence is experiencing certain negative feelings very strongly, such that one can be successfully conditioned against damaging courses of action (Alacorta, 2012). This would increase stress, which appears to be associated with ethnocentrism.

The experimentation aspect in adolescence may itself heighten stress. The adolescent will usually experience his first sexual relationship and the breakdown of this relationship, he may experiment with different social groups and find himself disillusioned and marginalized along the way, and he is likely to move out of his parents' home and begin to fend for himself, semi-independent of his family. In addition, he will have to make important and potentially irreversible decisions about the direction of his work life and his relationships. All of this will place the adolescent under a great deal of stress and it is likely no coincidence that religious conversion experiences, which have been shown to be underpinned significantly by stress, tend to occur, if they occur at all, during late adolescence (see Dutton, 2008; Conn, 1986). Of course, it would appear likely that this increased level of stress would potentially heighten feelings of ethnocentrism and, in this regard, it is noteworthy that many religious groups can be understood to be highly group-centric. They have strong group borders, a clear sense of differentiation between the in-group and the out-group, they cast the in-group as morally and spiritually superior to the out-group, and they have difficult tests of membership. Indeed, Dutton (2008), in analysis of fundamentalist Christian student groups, found that the more identity-challenging, and thus stressful, the university environment was the more fundamentalist the main evangelical student group tended to be.

A third possibility is that humans are evolved to be particularly ethnocentric at a particular age. This would potentially make sense in evolutionary terms. We have seen from computer modelling that a significant selection pressure in favour of ethnocentric behaviour is group conflict. In such conflicts, we would expect each group to oppose each other using the most physically able members of the group and these would usually be those of the age group that is now classed as late adolescent. This being the case, there would be an evolutionary benefit to this particular age-group being especially ethnocentric in their behaviour. At the individual level, being strongly ethnocentric at that age would allow you, if you survived, to prove your physical ability, rendering you sexually selected for. However, being similarly ethnocentric at an older age or at a younger age would involve taking a far greater risk which would be far more likely to limit your individual and family fertility. At the group level, the group which possessed the most ethnocentric late adolescents would be more likely to triumph in any group conflict. If the blip in negative ethnocentrism increasing in late adolescence were for evolutionary reasons, we would expect it to be more pronounced among males than females because it would be males who would be fighting on behalf of the tribe. This is precisely what Rekker et al's data showed. In addition, Van der Graaff et al. (2014) and others have found that there is a temporary dip in empathy during adolescence and that this is more pronounced among boys than girls. This is precisely what we would predict if the findings reflected an evolutionary strategy to deal with group conflict. It would benefit the boys, though not the girls, to be particularly aggressive at about this age as they would be the ones fighting the members of outgroups. Interestingly, Figueredo et al. (2011) found that males were more ethnocentric than females even when males' generally faster Life History was controlled for. This would imply that males are simply evolved to be more ethnocentric than females independent of the kind of personality or Life History strategy they have. Figueredo et al. (2011, p. 27) explain this in the same way that we have explained

Rekker et al's findings. They state: 'We attribute this additional effect of the traditional predominance of males as participants in intergroup warfare within the overwhelming majorities of ancestral as well as contemporary human societies. Male humans were typically the warriors and could therefore be expected to evolve more negative ethnocentrism as an adaptation to that historical role'.

The idea that age and sex differences in ethnocentrism can be reduced to group and individual selection would obviously be the least question-begging of the explanations we have advanced. Clearly, it is true that the stressful nature of adolescence may increase ethnocentrism but this raises the question of why ethnocentrism, at that time, is higher in males even when Life History strategy is controlled for. An evolutionary model answers all of these questions. The relationship between age, gender, and ethnocentrism, then, has important implications for understanding why some regions should be more ethnocentric than others when salient other factors are approximately controlled.

Firstly, if a society has a relatively large proportion of young people then we would expect it to be more ethnocentric than an older society. Accordingly, we would expect the Europe of a century ago to have been more ethnocentric than now not only because of lower genetic diversity (due to higher child mortality) and higher levels of stress, but also due to the fact that the average person would have been younger. In most Western European countries, the life expectancy is around eighty and the average person — the person of median age — is approximately forty years old, as of 2014. According to the *CIA World Fact Book* (2014), the median age is considerably lower in less developed countries. In Burundi, for example, it is just seventeen while in Niger it is fifteen. This factor alone would make these countries — and Western countries when they had similar conditions — far more ethnocentric.

Clearly, a second relevant factor is the gender balance. Boys are more negatively ethnocentric than girls firstly because they follow a faster Life History strategy and, secondly, seemingly for evolutionary reasons. Accordingly, a young population will also mean a larger number of young males and these will be highly negatively ethnocentric. But, clearly, any country which had significantly more young boys than young girls would be ethnocentric for that reason. According to *CIA World Fact Book* (2014), the populations in China and India, in particular, have considerably more males than females both among those under fifteen and those aged fifteen to sixty-five, probably due to the infanticide or selective abortion of girls, who are less culturally desirable than boys. To a lesser extent, this gender imbalance exists in Saudi Arabia and other countries in the Middle East and North Africa. We would expect this gender imbalance to have four obvious effects which might increase ethnocentrism either directly or indirectly.

1. The societies would be relatively negatively ethnocentric because there would be such a large percentage of men and particularly young men.

2. But, in addition, these societies would be home to a relatively large percentage of single men who would have little hope of having children. Indeed, in that the females would select in favour of high-status males (see Buss, 1989) they would also indirectly select in favour of K-strategy males and thus against the more ethnocentric males as these would tend to be faster Life History strategists. In any polygamous society, this effect would be even more pronounced because it would be even more difficult for a low-status male to have children. Furthermore, in a monogamous society where living standards are low and there is little, if any, social security for the impoverished, women would be more strongly motivated to sexually select in favour of social status and thus K-strategy and low-status young men would be left without the possibility of having children. As such, one way that these sexually rejected fast Life History strategists could realistically pass on their genes would be by adopting a strategy of inclusive fitness based

around the group. This being so, we would have a situation where the most negatively ethnocentric males would be motivated to be strongly positively ethnocentric in order to maximize their genetic fitness. So, we can start to understand why suicide bombing would be a prevalent strategy among Muslims in the Middle East and on the Sub-Continent.

3. Most crime is committed by young men, something especially true of violent crime. This is because young men are particularly high in testosterone which makes people aggressive and means that they have poor impulse control (Wilson & Herrnstein, 1985). As such, in a society with a large number of single young men there would be a great deal of violent crime, rendering the society very dangerous. We have already seen that an unstable environment increases ethnocentrism and so we would expect such societies to be high in ethnocentrism on this basis as well. The youth gangs that would consequently develop would also be expected to attempt to pass on their genes via gang rape so we would expect gang rape to be a particular issue in such societies, leading to prohibitions on the freedom of young women, who would need to avoid being targeted. In the case of gang rape, we would assume that the gang's most dominant male would rape the woman first with the remainder following in an approximate pecking order. Assuming the female became pregnant, in a society in which abortion was illegal or expensive or dangerous, the gang members would all have some chance of passing on their genes this way because the gang leader might not necessarily have the highest sperm count or the strongest semen.

4. We would expect these men to try to emigrate to another country—especially a wealthier one—where the female selection on the social status of the male might be accordingly lower and where they, therefore, might be more able to have children within marriage, perhaps bringing a cousin wife from their native country. In the West, they would be able adequately to live off unemployment

benefits or in a low-status profession. In addition, we would also expect these men to form gangs and engage in gang rape, especially, due to negative ethnocentrism, of native young girls, something which has been documented in the UK (see McLoughlin, 2016). However, it must be emphasized that a large body of research has shown that migration is predicted by intelligence (see Jensen, 1998). This being so, we would not expect that the extreme fast Life History strategists of such countries would emigrate to the West because they would lack the necessary organization, future orientation, industriousness and intelligence to be able to successfully make the journey and overcome its many attendant obstacles. Even so, we would expect the resultant immigrant population to be relatively ethnocentric.

Dutton et al. (2016a) tested this hypothesis by looking at median age and male to female ratio, both of which were taken from the *CIA World Factbook*. They found, with a sample of fifty-eight, that median age was significantly negatively associated with positive ethnocentrism ($r = -0.5$). That is to say, a younger median age means a more nationalistic country, as might be predicted by higher stress at a young age. The relationship with negative ethnocentrism was, however, non-significant. There was no significant relationship in terms of male to female ratio.

4. Pregnancy

Navarette et al. (2007) found that women in the first trimester of pregnancy displayed elevated levels of positive ethnocentrism; that is favouritism towards the in-group. They explained this finding in terms of vulnerability to infection being heightened during this period of the pregnancy. However, we would suggest that a simpler explanation is that the first trimester of the pregnancy is the most dangerous and stressful period of the pregnancy as it is when the baby is developing at a very basic level. The nature of the environment at this point during the pregnancy will have the greatest impact on whether there will be birth defects, and if the woman miscarries then it is most likely to happen at this stage. This information is now widely known, so we would expect this period to be especially stressful for the expectant mother, potentially evoking higher levels of ethnocentrism. In addition, even if such information were not known, we would predict that higher ethnocentrism among women during the first trimester would be beneficial because they would be exposed to fewer dangerous pathogens. As such, this would make staying with people you know a more attractive option in these circumstances, and the researchers used as their measure of ethnocentrism the relative attractiveness of an American over a foreign target. Further, it would be adaptive to strongly bond with sources of coalitional support during periods of vulnerability and this could be aided by finding them more than usually attractive.

This finding may have some small impact on the degree to which a society is ethnocentric. Until a few hundred years ago, women would have spent much of their child-bearing years pregnant due to the fact that child mortality rate was so high that only having high fertility could ensure that one had any surviving children at all, let alone grandchildren. As such, the women in such a society would be expected to more ethnocentric — quite apart from other factors — than women in societies that have lower levels of female fertility because a higher percentage of them would be pregnant at any given time. Unfortunately, I can find no data on the per cent of a country who are pregnant at any given time.

5. Ethnic Diversity

In defending the sociobiological understanding of ethnicity we have already explored, to some extent, the relationship between ethnic diversity and ethnocentrism. Drawing upon research by Vanhanen (2012) and Salter (2007) we have shown that when two ethnic groups are in conflict then we would expect an increase in both positive and negative ethnocentrism. However, it is important to distinguish this from the concept of 'ethnic diversity', wherein a community is composed of people of various different ethnicities that are not necessarily in a state of severe conflict. When this situation is achieved it has a clear effect on ethnocentric behaviour. If a multi-ethnic community is faced with a threat from outsiders it will tend to behave in a less ethnocentric way than will a mono-ethnic community.

Belgian sociologist Marc Hooghe and colleagues (Hooghe et al., 2009) note that a large body of research has found that there is a negative relationship between ethnic diversity and social cohesion, specifically trust. In multi-ethnic communities trust levels are reduced not just between ethnic minorities and ethnic majorities but actually between members of the ethnic majority group that live in the ethnically diverse community (e.g. Alesina & La Ferrera, 2002). It is unclear quite why trust is reduced even among the majority ethnic group. One possibility is that there is now the risk that any member of the majority ethnic group may defect and achieve status by creating a coalition with the ethnic minorities and this would not previously have been a feasible possibility. Another possible explanation is that members of the majority community see that other members of the community have, together, permitted the incursion of a different ethnic group into the community and, therefore, they cannot be trusted to defend it from outsiders. However, this research tends to use just one attitudinal aspect and, in each case, focus on one country, usually the USA. Hooghe et al. employed a variety of attitudinal aspects and examined twenty European countries. For example, with regard to the measure 'social cohesion' they used not just 'trust' but also 'ethnocentrism'.

The authors note that there are variations in the nature of the immigrants taken into different European countries. In some cases, they are linguistically, culturally and genetically closer to the native inhabitants than in other cases, so we would expect this to have some effect on the extent to which social cohesion might be damaged. Drawing upon data from OECD surveys, Hooghe et al. found that, within Europe, generalized trust is the highest in what they term the 'Scandinavian countries' of Sweden, Denmark, Norway, and Finland. In these countries, negative ethnocentrism (the authors use 'ethnocentrism' to mean this) is also relatively low. General trust levels are lowest in Portugal and Greece while negative ethnocentrism is highest in the former Communist countries of Eastern Europe. However, of all the countries examined, Greece had the lowest levels of generalized trust and the highest levels of negative ethnocentrism. Hooghe et al.'s findings on national level trust and ethnocentrism generally did not reach statistical significance with the exception of the inflow of foreign workers, which was shown to reduce generalized trust. Also, a large increase in asylum seekers was shown to increase ethnocentrism. Hooghe et al. conclude that their findings show that ethnic diversity does not reduce social cohesion but this appears to be a very odd conclusion since most of their findings, though they do not reach significance, are in the expected direction of ethnic diversity indeed reducing social cohesion; moreover, a number of these findings are statistically significant. This would potentially imply that further research, with larger samples, would place their findings in line with those of others.

More recent research, in the UK, has again replicated the finding that the higher a community's level of ethnic diversity is, the lower are the levels of generalized trust even within ethnic groups (Sturgis et al., 2011). The authors stress that the effect size is relatively small but, nevertheless, it is significant. British researcher James Laurence (2008) has also shown that community cohesion in the UK is reduced the more ethnically diverse the community is, implying that generalized trust is probably reduced as well. Hooghe et al.'s argument that the USA may be somehow exceptional in terms of its race relations can also be countered by research from Canada which has found that ethnic diversity strongly reduces general trust there. This is lessened, though not entirely neutralized, if 'contact' (such as sexual relationships) develop between the different ethnic groups (Stolle et al., 2008). Of course, this is not surprising because we have already discussed the way in which humans can create coalitions, and thus bonds, with members of different ethnic groups if these serve their own interests. Friendship can be seen as an example, to some extent, of overcoming the instinct to be only with those who are strongly genetically similar in order to create a useful coalition, though even this appears to involve a genetic dimension. Laurence (2013) finds that diversity undermines social capital at the neighbourhood level but does not reduce overall levels of individual engagement. This means that people stop participating in community activities and simply use that time to see family members and friends — in other words, people who are more genetically similar to them than the broader community of their own ethnicity would be. This finding, though not expanded on by Laurence, is interesting because it implies that living in an ethnically diverse area decreases an important aspect of ethnocentrism at the group level but may even increase it at a closer genetic level.

Although some of the findings show that this is only a weak predictor, the direction of the evidence is that generalized trust — even between those of the same ethnicity — is reduced in multi-ethnic societies. The result, according to some studies, is a reduction in civil society, which is predicated on trust. These findings have obvious implications for levels of positive ethnocentricity. A multi-ethnic society will be less likely than a mono-ethnic society to successfully defend itself against incursion from outsiders for three key interrelated reasons. Firstly, there will be lower levels of general trust; such individuals will be less willing to make sacrifices for the society because they will be less confident that others will do the same. Secondly, there will be lower levels of positive ethnocentrism — as manifested in acts of self-sacrifice predicated on trusting that the co-ethnic would do the same for them — even within ethnic groups in this society. As such, even the majority ethnic group will be relatively unwilling to engage in the ethnocentric behaviour that would be necessary to repel any invading force. Thirdly, as Hooghe et al. have shown, ethnic minorities will tend to support immigration. This is because displacing the majority population will be in their interests since it will reduce the influence of this population and potentially increase the influence of their minority group. So, we might expect certain minority groups to actively collaborate with an invading force, especially if they were more genetically similar to it than they were to the majority population.

Conversely, as we have already discussed in relation to Vanhanen's (2011) research, we would expect that a situation of specific ethnic conflict would increase levels of ethnocentrism. Living in a multicultural community would seem to reduce positive ethnocentrism and increase negative ethnocentrism because it reduces trust at all levels. However, if a society is effectively segregated along racial lines, with quite separate areas occupied by each race, then this would be a situation of ethnic conflict and we would expect heightened levels of ethnocentrism in both groups. Vanhanen argues that the closer in number to each other the two groups are, the more likely they are to mutually perceive each other as a threat, leading to heightened ethnocentrism on both sides of the ethnic divide. Or, to put it another way, the greater the percentage of the country's population that is one particular ethnic group, the less ethnically heterogeneous (EH) the country can be understood to be.

Based on this measure ethnic heterogeneity (EH), Vanhanen examined differences in the level of ethnic conflict (EC) based on a scale of (1) being low and (5) being high. Vanhanen's categories were: (1) Minor incidents at a local level, minor ethnic political parties or interest organization. (2) Significant local ethnic violence, significant ethnicity-based parties or interest groups, institutionalized ethnic discrimination. (3) Violent ethnic conflict, separatist strivings in parts of the country, important ethnic political parties and interest groups, serious discrimination against a subjugated ethnic group. (4) Civil war, ethnic rebellion, terrorism, separatist wars, ethnic political parties/interest groups dominate politics, large ethnic groups repressed, ethnic refugees. (5) Violent ethnic civil war dominates politics, ethnic cleansing genocide.

Drawing upon an analysis of 176 countries, Vanhanen found that there was a 0.66 correlation between the extent of ethnic conflict and the level of ethnic heterogeneity. This finding would be congruous with the view that where there is no clearly dominant ethnic group then every group — including the largest group — is under threat from every other group. This would appear to increase not just negative but also positive ethnocentrism, because Vanhanen's measure of 'Ethnic Conflict' includes behaviour which involves self-sacrifice on behalf of the ethnic group such as warfare, suicide bombing and general risky, law-breaking behaviour. On this basis, Vanhanen lists 176 countries and scores them in terms of Ethnic Conflict and Ethnic Heterogeneity. As discussed, the correlation was 0.66 and he provides explanations for the various outliers. So, we would predict that ethnic conflict within a country — and thus ethnocentrism within that country — will be higher the less dominant the largest ethnic group is. However, that very same internally ethnocentric country would have very low levels of trust as a nation and, as such, would have difficulty mobilizing against an invader in a positive way, such as where self-sacrifice was required for the country.

On the other hand, Vanhanen's research shows that there is a negative association between ethnic conflict and standard of living. So, based on 176 countries, EC correlates with democratization at −0.22, with Human Development Index 2010 at −0.39, and with PPP/ GNI per capita 2008 at −0.253. It makes sense that Ethnic Conflict would be associated with a reduced standard of living for a number of reasons. A high level of ethnic conflict would render the society dangerous and unstable and so discourage long-term projects, and this would be reflected in a lack of cooperation and trust in the society, which would essentially be embroiled in a war of varying degrees of intensity. However, for this reason we would expect that it would be extremely stressful to live in a highly ethnically heterogeneous society and in that ethnocentrism appears to be highly instinctive we would expect such stresses to increase both in-group (in terms of the ethnic group) ethnocentrism and out-group ethnocentrism, rendering such societies relatively hostile to foreigners.

As discussed, Dutton et al. (2016a) tested ethnic conflict and found that there was no significant relationship with ethnocentrism. There was also no significant relationship, at the country level, between ethnic heterogeneity and ethnocentrism. However, all of the relationships were positive and in the range of 0.3 to 0.8. So, with a larger N it may be that a significant relationship would reveal itself.

6. Intelligence and Education

Hooghe et al. (2009) speculate on why Greece is an outlier among Western European countries in terms of trust and negative ethnocentrism. One possibility is average IQ. Average IQ has been shown to be positively associated with trusting people (e.g. Hooghe et al., 2012) even when controlling for key variables such as education (Carl & Billari, 2014), and as we have discussed above, ethnocentrism is associated with a fast Life History strategy, an aspect of which is low intelligence at the group level. The relationship between intelligence and trust may result from the way in which less intelligent people will be less able to work out whether someone is trustworthy, meaning it would make more sense for them to trust nobody (Carl & Billari, 2014). In addition, in Western countries, voters for strongly ethnocentric parties have the lowest average IQ based on studies of large cohorts (e.g. Deary et al., 2008). Indeed, even in non-Western countries voters for 'far right' parties, which tend to be the most negatively ethnocentric, generally have the lowest average IQs, as has been shown in Brazil, for example (Rindermann et al., 2012). The average IQ of Greece, at around 92, is the lowest of the countries in the OECD survey drawn upon by Hooghe et al. (Lynn & Vanhanen, 2012) which may contribute to explaining the country's low score on trust and its high score on negative ethnocentrism.

Hodson and Busseri (2012) used a large UK sample (N 15,884) and found that childhood IQ was negatively associated with holding 'racist' attitudes as an adult, mainly due to the association between low IQ and extreme right-wing ideologies. This relationship was found even when controlling for socioeconomic status and education level. Drawing upon the US General Social Survey between 1972 and 2010 (N 44,873), Wodtke (2016) also found that racial prejudice was negatively associated with intelligence. However, this was a weak association, of around 0.2. Dhont and Hodson (2014) have produced a literature review showing that even when controlling for variables, such as education level, there is a weak negative correlation between cognitive ability—general intelligence as well as different forms of intelligence—and prejudice.

As such, it is reasonable to conclude that low intelligence is associated with relatively high levels of negative ethnocentrism, so this is a factor in negative ethnocentrism in African and Middle Eastern countries as well. It could be argued, as we have already discussed, that more intelligent people are better attuned to the dominant ideology of Multiculturalism in Western countries and, as long-term thinkers, can see the benefits of conforming to it. Moreover, as intelligence tends to predict cooperative behaviour they have a desire to conform to the dominant ideology and, as such, through effortful control persuade themselves that they are not negatively ethnocentric and nor are they even positively ethnocentric (see Woodley of Menie & Dunkel, 2015, and Dutton, 2013). The difficulty with this argument, in this instance, is the evidence that even in countries where Multiculturalism is not the dominant ideology, supporting the most highly ethnocentric parties is still associated with lowest intelligence, when we might expect this to be true of supporting the extreme left if this theory were accurate (see Dutton, 2014). As such, the simplest explanation for all of these findings is that we have an instinctive drive towards out-group prejudice. Intelligence permits us to suppress this for a number of reasons: it makes us curious about new things as it correlates with the Intellect facet of Openness-Intellect; the intelligent will be better able to evaluate whether or not to trust people, rendering the default option of distrust of all outsiders less adaptive; intelligent people are more empathetic and so less likely to simply dismiss people and their feelings, and they are less black and white in their thinking.

Moreover, American philosopher Nathan Cofnas (2016) has argued that 'evolutionary novelty' (or 'evolutionary mismatch') needs to be defined as 'deviations in the environment that render biological traits unable, or impaired in their ability, to produce their selected effects' (Cofnas, 2016, p. 507). If 'evolutionary novelty' is thus defined, argues Cofnas, then the ecology is changing and so is constantly 'evolutionarily novel' and intelligence will help one to respond to it, meaning part of intelligence will involve reacting to this novelty. Indeed, as our evolved instincts will increasingly be 'mismatched' with the environment, the ability to solve problems — the essence of intelligence — will involve being non-instinctive and attracted, therefore, to mismatches; to the evolutionary novel. When defined in this way, I and Dutch psychologist Dimitri Van der Linden (Dutton & Van der Linden, 2017) argue, it starts to make sense that intelligence predicts attraction to evolutionary novelty, as being attracted to evolutionary novelty means being attracted to that which is non-instinctive, and being non-instinctive assists in solving new problems. Dutton and Van der Linden note that intelligence is associated to a variety of non-instinctive preferences: not wanting children, being relatively nocturnal, experimenting with homosexuality, and not being religious (see also Kanazawa, 2012). It would follow that, all else being equal, intelligence would predict being attracted to the idea of having friends and sexual partners from a different race and thus seeming low in negative ethnocentrism. This being the case we might even expect inter-racial relationships to be socioeconomically curvilinear with the highly intelligent (and thus high status) pursuing them due to their attraction to the evolutionarily novel and those very low in status (extreme r-strategists) pursuing them due to their focus on physical markers of health and genetic variety. On this basis, then, we would expect societies with higher average intelligence to express lower levels of negative ethnocentrism and, due to the high levels of trust, higher levels of positive ethnocentrism. However, once these societies came into contact with foreigners we might expect these same characteristics to push them to extend the boundary of their in-group beyond the ethnic group.

There is fairly direct evidence with regard to negative ethnocentrism. It has indeed been found that having high social intelligence, which as we have discussed is partly a function of high general intelligence, is negatively associated with negative ethnocentrism (Dong & Collaco, 2009). Lynn and Vanhanen (2012) have actually proven a relationship between the extent to which a society has liberal values and its average intelligence. Using a sample of 127 countries, they find that the relationship between national IQ and liberalism is 0.51, it is 0.43 between postmodern values and national IQ, and 0.45 between modernist values and national IQ. In each case, these values include ideas of treating people equally and not being prejudiced. But there would also be an indirect reason for this association. Lynn and Vanhanen (2012) have shown that intelligence strongly predicts numerous measures of civilization such as education, literacy, per capita income, poverty, inequality, crime rate, political stability, political freedom, corruption, religiousness, access to health care, health, infant mortality, sanitation, and even happiness. In essence, living in a low-IQ, uneducated society can be understood as extremely stressful and, as such, we would expect people in such societies to be more prejudiced to outsiders.

A large body of evidence has also found that education, in Western countries, predicts lower levels of negative ethnocentrism. This has been found by Hooghe et al. (2009) and is implied in studies such as Deary et al. (2008) who found that the least intelligent in the 1970 UK cohort voted for the most ethnocentric political parties at the 2001 General Election. As such, we would predict that the more educated a country is the lower would be its levels of negative ethnocentrism. There are a number of interrelated reasons why we would expect this to be the case. Firstly, education level at both the individual and national level has been shown to be significantly explained by differences in intelligence. For example, school performance correlates with intelligence at 0.7 (Jensen, 1981) while there is a 0.6 correlation between national level of tertiary education and national IQ (Lynn & Vanhanen, 2012). We have seen that intelligence suppresses negative ethnocentrism so we would expect highly educated countries to be less ethnocentric. Secondly, the intelligence and education level of a society are associated with how developed it is and so how safe and stable it is to live in. As such, a more educated society would be less ethnocentric for that reason as well. Thirdly, national intelligence would be damaged by living in a society with low levels of education. As we have discussed, 20% intelligence is a matter of environmental variables such as a stimulating environment. A less literate society would be less intellectually stimulated, in small part leading to a lower IQ and thus higher levels of negative ethnocentrism. In addition, Lynn and Vanhanen (2012) have shown that all of the correlates of intelligence tend to be significantly associated at a national level. As such, an uneducated society would be likely to have poor living conditions, poor access to health, high levels of infectious disease and poor sanitation. These variables would have a negative impact on brain development and so a negative impact on the average IQ of the population. As such, a low level of societal education would be likely to indirectly push up out-group prejudice.

The studies on intelligence and ethnocentrism tell us little directly about the relationship between intelligence and positive ethnocentrism. However, this can be inferred via the extent to which members of an ethnic community are prepared to engage in acts of self-sacrifice on behalf of it. An example of this would be the degree to which a country is democratic. Vanhanen (2012) has shown that democratic systems are less likely in ethnically divided societies. This is because they involve many individuals making personal sacrifices on behalf of the group and having a high level of trust in the group, these being markers of positive ethnocentrism. Lynn and Vanhanen (2012) found that, drawing upon data from 188 countries, the correlation between democratization and national IQ was consistently in the region of 0.5. Any form of civic pride may be understood to be an aspect of positive ethnocentrism and Deary et al. (2008) found that intelligence predicted degree of civic participation, as exemplified in the propensity to turn up to vote. Clearly, therefore, there is only a moderate correlation between national IQ and democratization. One of the difficulties with this analysis is that it is a measure of trust in the nation state. As Vanhanen has observed, countries with low average intelligence as less likely to develop a successful nation state because they will be more likely to be heavily divided along the lines of tribe and clan.

Again, Dutton el. (2016a) tested the relationship. They drew upon the national intelligence data in Lynn & Vanhanen (2012). There was a significant negative association between national IQ and positive ethnocentrism ($r = -0.4$). In other words, the less intelligent a nation is, the more nationalistic it is. There was also negative association between negative ethnocentrism and IQ but it was non-significant. It may be that less intelligent nations are more instinctive — due both to low intelligence and greater stress — and, therefore, more positively ethnocentric.

7. Conclusion

In this chapter, we have found that poverty and infant mortality rate are positively associated with positive ethnocentrism while infant mortality rate is positively associated with negative ethnocentrism. Median age is negatively associated with positive ethnocentrism, meaning a young society is more nationalistic. The gender balance does not appear to make a difference. However, less intelligent societies are more ethnocentric in both senses.

CHAPTER TEN

Industrialization and the Decline of Ethnocentrism

1. Introduction

In this chapter we will look at industrialization and dysgenics. We will see that both of these processes have had a significant environmental and genetic impact on differences in levels of ethnocentrism between countries as they have developed since around 1800 due to their impact on the variables which are associated with ethnocentrism that we have already established. They help to explain the low ethnocentrism of the West, compared to developing countries.

2. General Effects of Industrialization: The Decline of Religion

We would expect industrialization to have a number of significant effects on the degree to which people were ethnocentric as well as one very specific effect.

In terms of general effects, we have already seen that stress is associated with heightened ethnocentrism and especially heightened negative ethnocentrism. However, in numerous ways industrialization would be expected to reduce levels of stress. Modernization has created conditions in 'modern' countries that heavily reduce stress. Since the nineteenth century, Western European people have had the causes of many of their fears effectively controlled. Europeans need no longer fear numerous formerly devastating diseases, nor need they fear famine, predators, lawlessness nor death in a whole host of accidents, and their material standard of living has undergone considerable improvement (see Clark, 2007). There is even a (relatively comfortable) safety net in welfare states, which almost all Western European countries have to varying degrees. For these reasons, we would expect people in more developed countries to generally experience low levels of stress and this would be expected to reduce the extent of their negative ethnocentrism.

This reduced level of stress would then have a number of effects which would further impact the level of ethnocentrism. Firstly, we have seen that religiousness is associated with stress and that those who are more stressed or more subject to the experience of stress are prone to be more religious. There is abundant evidence that the extent to which people believe in God has declined throughout the twentieth century (see Dutton, 2014) just as the stress model would predict and, just as it would predict, this decline has gone into reverse during periods of intense stress in the twentieth century, such as during World War II (see Bruce, 2002). As we have discussed already, religiousness can be understood as a means of making the group which adopts it more ethnocentric and thus better able to compete in the battle of group selection. Those who are religious are both more positively and more negatively ethnocentric. Seemingly because a moral God is watching over them, they behave in a more pro-social way. It is has also been shown that people who believe they are being watched will behave in a more pro-social way and even cues of being watched, such as picture of a face on the wall, increase pro-social behaviour (Bateson et al., 2006). This being the case, we might expect that declining religiousness would be paralleled by a decline in pro-social behaviour, including positive ethnocentrism. Religious people have a strong sense of group identity and we have already seen that having a strong sense of group identity is associated with negative ethnocentrism.

Accordingly, as religion declines we would expect that a smaller and smaller section of society would be members of what is, in broad terms, a highly ethnocentric group and, indeed, a group which often acts as proxy for genes. The religious group performs this function because the significantly heritable nature of religiousness of around 0.44 (see Dutton, 2014) means that religious people will tend to assortatively mate. As such, whatever some religions may profess about the equality of Man, 'religion' can be regarded as a kind of proxy for genetic differences and, as we have discussed, it may even be a more reliable proxy, in some instances, than supposed ethnicity based on physical appearance. These possibilities are evidenced by the clear association between religiousness and racial ethnocentrism: people who are more religious have been found to be more negatively ethnocentric (e.g. Shinert & Ford, 1958) and more nationalistic (Eisinga et al., 1990). This is to be expected if religiousness is a proxy for genetic interests. Moreover, though there are exceptions to this, most religions have historically sanctified the group — such as the tribe or nation — to which its members belong. Even though Christianity professes a universalist model in theory, the practice is very different. At times of war, the leaders of Christian nations may assert that 'God is on our side' and that the enemy, though supposedly Christian, are actually in league with the Devil. Thus, religiousness would be expected to increase ethnocentrism (positive and negative), while its decline would reduce ethnocentrism because God would no longer be there to demand selfless behaviour on behalf of his eternally important group. With the decline of religion, one's ethnic group would no longer be perceived as having any intrinsic — let alone eternal — importance. This would mean that there would be less of a motivation to fight for its preservation; in other words, less of a motivation to be ethnocentric.

3. Dysgenics

We have already noted evidence that certain genes appear to be connected to ethnocentrism as well as evidence from computer modelling that ethnocentrism is very likely to be selected for when two distinct ethnic groups come into conflict. The conditions followed in these computer models replicate — in a simplified form — the conditions operating under Natural Selection. Under these harsh conditions, the organism — and more broadly the ethnic group of which it is a part — will adapt physically and psychologically to its particular ecology. As we have already seen, this process leads to modal racial and ethnic differences in morphology and in psychological traits. Each generation, many offspring will be born with mutant genes. These will almost always be damaging, meaning that the offspring will almost always be less adapted to the environment because of them, something that will manifest itself in poorer health and general psychological deficiencies. A combination of natural and sexual selection will ensure that those who carry these mutant genes will either not breed at all — often because they will die in childhood — or will not be particularly fertile even if they do breed, having even less healthy offspring with an even higher mutational load. Accordingly, each generation, the brutal process of Natural Selection ensured the Darwinian 'Survival of the Fittest' and, until the Industrial Revolution, around 50% of those born across Europe would not reach adulthood. These unfortunate children would, in general, be those who had poor immune systems, meaning they were not strong enough to fight off childhood diseases, or those who carried mutant genes leading to assorted disorders. In addition, work by Clark (2007) has shown that pre-Industrial society also selected for intelligence insomuch as this predicted socioeconomic status and this in turn predicted completed fertility with the richer 50% of the population enjoying a 40% fertility advantage over the poorer 50%.

Richard Lynn (2011a) has documented the way in which the Industrial Revolution halted and then reversed this process of Natural Selection in a phenomenon known as 'Dysgenics'. The Industrial Revolution can be understood to have considerably weakened Natural Selection by, in numerous respects, reducing natural harshness. Its achievements have included inoculation against childhood diseases, ever-improving standards of medical science, hugely improved sanitation and living conditions for most people, considerably cheaper nutritious food, the ability of the same land area to support a much larger population due to mechanization and improvements in agriculture, the safety net of the welfare state, and even treatment to help those who are infertile have children. The consequence of this is that close to all children who are born will reach an age where they will be able to have children and if some dysgenic effect means that they cannot have them naturally then processes such as IVF can, in many cases, assist them. Though there is still some sexual and natural selection against those who have extremely poor genetic fitness, in general, most people who desire to have children are able to have them. At the dawn of the Industrial Revolution, in 1750, the British population was around 6 million. This was the country's carrying capacity at that time and famine was an on-going problem. Now it is around 65 million. Clearly, under conditions of pre-Industrial selection, the population would be around 6 million, meaning that over 90% of the current population would either be dead, or, in most cases, would never have been born, because child mortality would have been about 50% every generation all the way back to the Industrial Revolution.

Lynn (2011a) has shown that the modern British population can be understood as a genetically sick population which has been subject to many generations — around eight if we take thirty years to be a generation — of dysgenic fertility on health. This dysgenic effect is illustrated by roughly accurate predictions made in 1989 that in, in Western countries in the subsequent thirty years, there would a 26% increase in haemophilia, a 22% increase in Cystic Fibrosis, and a 300%

increase in Phenylketonuria, all of them genetic disorders with the latter appearing relatively frequently be mutation. In addition, Lynn has demonstrated that Industrialization has led to a dysgenic effect on intelligence. Currently, among females in Western societies and to a lesser extent among males, IQ is weakly negatively associated with fertility, at around −0.2 in the case of females. The most intelligent females have no children at all while the least intelligent, within the normal IQ range, have the highest fertility.

Lynn suggests a number of reasons for this pattern. Firstly, pre-industrial conditions selected the most strongly against the poor, with a poverty being predicted by relatively low intelligence. Industrialization — due to inoculations, generally improved conditions and a relatively lavish welfare state — would remove this obstacle to the fertility of the less intelligent. It would also remove the need for anybody to have large numbers of children as children generally could be essentially guaranteed to survive. As such, large families would be a function of impulsive sexual behaviour, which would be predicted by low intelligence. Secondly, contraception, once developed, would be more efficiently used and more likely to be used by the more intelligent. Thirdly, the emancipation of women would mean that the more intelligent women would become educated and delay motherhood. They would then have a small number of children and would be more likely to find that they had left motherhood too late and had become infertile. Consequently, we would expect intelligence to have decreased between 1900 and now.

British psychologist Michael Woodley and his team (2014) have shown that this indeed the case. Using reaction times as a proxy for intelligence as they robustly correlate, they show that reactions times lengthened appreciably in Western countries between 1900 and the year 2000. They estimated that average IQ in Western countries in this period had fallen by around fifteen points. Woodley et al. also argued that this was congruous with a reduction in the per capita number of highly significant inventions over this period and even with a decline in the ability to distinguish between colours, this also being a function of intelligence (Woodley of Menie et al., 2016). The extent of the decline is likely to reflect dysgenic fertility.[21]

Following this line of research, it would seem very probable that there were other psychological characteristics, beyond intelligence, which would cease to be selected for upon the collapse and reversal of Natural Selection. Indeed, it could be argued that any psychological characteristic which might be understood to be essential to the survival of an individual, or group, would be likely to decline in terms of the percentage of the population carrying the genes which underpin it, as genes which do not lead to it would no longer be selected out. Religiousness may be one such example. As we have discussed, religiousness would be useful in pre-history because it would reduce stress at the prospect of mortality or due to other existential problems, and it would increase pro-sociality (helping the individual and group to survive). This would also help the individual and group to survive, especially in periods of conflict. In addition, at the group level, it would provide a strong motivator for self-sacrifice and give the entire group a sense of eternal certainty. In terms of sexual selection,

---

21 As an aside, it should be noted that the Flynn Effect has been documented throughout the twentieth century. It refers to a secular rise in IQ scores of about three points per decade in Western countries up until about 1997, when the scores began to decline. However, it has been shown that the increase was on the parts of the IQ test that are the poorest measures of general intelligence and the most influenced by environment. By contrast, the decline has been on general intelligence, which is highly genetic. The 'rise', therefore, was not a genuine rise in intelligence, but a reflection of the imperfect nature of IQ tests. These tests measure general intelligence but also narrow intelligence abilities which are weakly correlated with general intelligence. Even though general intelligence was falling, industrialization had created a society which forced us to think in a more and more analytical, scientific way. This ability was pushed up so much that it manifested itself as a secular rise in IQ scores. However, it now appears to have reached its genotypic peak, meaning that the underling fall in intelligence is now revealing itself even on IQ tests (see Dutton & Charlton, 2015).

religiousness would be an important marker of a cooperative personality. The benefits to religiousness are evidenced in the way that in modern societies it is still positively associated with fertility and negatively associated with mental health problems (Rowthorn et al., 2011). 'Religiousness' is positively associated with fertility in a linear way, such that the more religious — and religiously observant — have the highest fertility and intended fertility while the non-religious have the lowest (e.g. Frejka & Westoff, 2006; Hayford & Morgan, 2008). It is also around 0.4 genetic.

It may even be that religiousness is part of a bundle of 'natural' inclinations and abilities and that all of these are not selected for so strongly once Natural Selection ceases. This would explain why religiousness is associated with such vital instincts as the desire to have children and also with the ability to have children. In other words, religiousness may evidence a lower impact from damaging mutant genes which move us away from the optimum level of adaptation to the pre-Industrial environment. Indeed, it is noted that older adults who frequently attend church have better immune systems than older adults who do not frequently attend church in the USA. It has been noted that there is no apparent environmental explanation for this finding, such as that the adults with better immune systems are physically more able to attend church or that the immune system is boosted by some psychological effect of attending church (Koenig et al., 1997). Thus, a possible explanation is that we are evolved to be religious over many generations and, accordingly, those who are religious simply have fewer mutant genes, something reflected in an optimally functioning nervous system. In this regard, Dutton et al. (2017) have argued that religiousness, which as noted is significantly genetic, was increasingly selected for in complex societies up until industrialization. Thus, with the degeneration of selection, they predicted that atheism would be associated with physical markers of genetic mutation, because physical and mental mutations tend to be comorbid and around 84% of the genome relates to the brain. Consistent with this, they showed that atheism, and generally not worshipping a god, is indeed associated with a variety of indicators of mutation: poor mental and physical health, left-handedness, autism, fluctuating asymmetry, and psycho-sexual problems. These are all signs of 'developmental instability' (the inability of an organism to produce a normal phenotype) and thus mutation. Their prevalence is increasing in Western countries and they are significantly genetic (Woodley of Menie et al., 2017). In that we are supposed to be right-handed, left-handedness reflects an asymmetrical brain and it is associated with many other signs of developmental instability, such as mental instability (Blanchard, 2008).

Prior to industrialization, children with mutant genes had poor physical health so they died young and didn't reproduce. They would also, disproportionately, have had poor mental health and been lacking in adaptive instincts, such as religious belief or ethnocentrism. With industrialization, they survived and procreated, leading to a rise in atheism and the correlation between atheism and markers of mutational load. So, research by Dutton and his team demonstrates that atheism is a sign of mutation. It deviates from our evolved instincts (which kept us from becoming extinct under conditions of selection) and, consistent with this, atheists are relatively lacking in the desire to have children, another basic instinct (see Rowthorn et al., 2011). Religiousness is associated with good physical and mental health *not* because religion causes people to be healthier but because health and religiousness both reflect low mutational load. Thus, the length of time which Europe has been subject to industrialization — which would increase mutational load — would also reduce its religiousness and so its levels of ethnocentrism. This is in line with the 'Social Epistasis' model (Woodley of Menie et al., 2017) which we will discuss below.

We have already noted the parallels between religiousness and ethnocentrism. Thus, it would seem quite possible that there would be genes associated with aspects of ethnocentrism and that these would be carried by a diminishing proportion of the population as

Natural Selection became weaker and weaker. Under conditions of Natural Selection, we would expect conflict between different groups for scarce resources. These would not just be between different ethnic groups, but between other genetic cleavages such as between different religious groups, different regional groups, and even between different clans. Those who behave — on average — in a more ethnocentric manner would be likely to survive this harsh group selection, causing genes which did not result in optimum, and relatively high, levels of ethnocentrism to be selected out as these carriers of these genes would be less successful at passing them on. With the rise of the Industrial Revolution, we would expect this process of group selection to weaken and the standards of living would significantly rise for all members of a given a society, meaning that conflict over resources would have less of an impact on group fertility. It would then follow that selection for ethnocentrism — or against low ethnocentrism — would lessen and the ethnocentric portion of the population would shrink in parallel with shrinking religiousness.

Dutton (2014, p. 248) has shown that religious belief has declined in industrialized countries throughout the twentieth century. For example, according to UK Gallup polls, belief in God was 78% in 1957 but 70% in 1993. Much of this may be a consequence of improved living conditions and reduced stress. But, as we noted above, even in modern Western societies, religiousness predicts the desire to have children as well as actually having higher fertility (e.g. Rowthorn et al. 2011). So, we would expect that the percentage of the population who believed in God would decrease due to the enormous stress-reduction brought about by the Industrial Revolution, something which would also be sufficient to overwhelm any potential boost to religious belief brought about by dysgenics on intelligence. Religiousness would also not be so strongly selected for because those who lacked genes for religiousness would be less stressed by their natural environment than in the past and, in some cases, could be cured by mind-altering drugs if their stress levels did become too high. So, religiousness would be selected for to a much lesser extent, and life would be less stressful, making people less religious. But this could only be maintained up to a point. Three factors would bring about its reversal:

1. The societal group who remained religious even in spite of the low levels of stress, what we might call the congenitally religious, would have higher fertility than the non-religious, because religiousness predicts the desire to have and ability to have children.
2. The less intelligent would have higher fertility than the more intelligent and intelligence is negatively associated with religiousness.
3. The maintenance of civilization, and thus low stress, is underpinned by a society's intelligence (Lynn & Vanhanen, 2012). Accordingly, we would expect religiousness to decline due to the Industrial Revolution but then eventually rise from the grave, a point that has been statistically demonstrated by American psychologist Lee Ellis and his colleagues (Ellis et al., 2017).

Another relevant factor may simply be genetic diversity. Due to the weakening of Natural Selection, it would follow that populations are going to be more genetically diverse than they were before. Following Genetic Similarity Theory, and our discussion of cousin marriage, we would expect this to reduce levels of ethnocentrism. Put simply, the populations are less 'families' than they once were. Immigration from other ethnicities would make this even more pronounced and would also reduce trust levels even among Europeans. Indeed, it could be argued that this process has happened before, though it did not progress as far. Meisenberg (2007) has observed that when civilizations become advanced the standard of living among the higher classes increases to such an extent that their stress levels drop to a point where they start questioning their religiosity. He claims that this is what happened towards the end of Roman Civilization, and it likely helps to explain the low levels of ethnocentrism observed at this point in Rome's history when foreigners were effectively permitted to take over the city.

It was also noted as Greek civilization went into decline, observes Meisenberg. In addition to the environmental influence, there is also a degree to which selection would have become relaxed compared to its previous intensity, leading to spiteful mutations, such as atheism or lack of religious belief.

4. Mutational Meltdown in Mouse Utopia

The earlier Industrialization arrived in a country, all else being equal, the less ethnocentric we would thus expect the country to be, at least during a particular period in its history. Indeed, with very little Natural Selection we would eventually expect a situation where the majority of the population were physically and mentally ill, substantially lacking in any of the instincts or abilities necessary to survive in the pre-Industrial environment. Overwhelmed by harmful mutations, the population would experience mutational meltdown and would simply collapse, which would eventually mean the recreation of conditions of Natural Selection. If a population which had, until more recently, been subject to Natural Selection began to compete with this sick population — before it collapsed — it would soon dominate it, not least due to it likely being more ethnocentric, more religious, fitter, and more fertile. The remnant dominated population would then be characterized, compared to the members who had not procreated, by lower intelligence and higher religiousness; these being the two factors that would predict fertility.

This collapse in the instincts which permit a group to survive has been documented in mice, though when drawing comparisons, it must be remembered that humans are not precisely the same as mice. American ethologist John Calhoun (1917–1995; Calhoun, 1973) performed a fascinating experiment on mice which he began in 1968 in a laboratory at the University of Maryland. In this laboratory he created the so-called 'Mouse Utopia'. This was a veritable heaven for mice in which there would be (1) no emigration by lower-status mice to suboptimal habitats as there would be abundant replica habitats and the utopia would be impossible to escape from; (2) no resource shortage or inclement weather; (3) no disease epidemics (this was ensured by taking extreme precautions to ensure that no epidemics could develop); and (4) no predators.

In July 1968, four pairs of house mice — each isolated for the preceding twenty-one days — were introduced into the sixteen-cell 'mouse universe'. After 104 days (Phase A) the first litter was born, resulting in social turmoil as the mice learned to live together. Following this establishment of territories by the eight colonists, the population rose exponentially, doubling around every fifty-five days until it reached 620. This marked the start of Phase B. At this point, population growth slowed until doubling occurred only every 145 days. Periodically, in Phase B, young born at this point would have their own young, contributing to the growth of population in which mice, unlike in the wild, were able to become elderly in significant numbers. By the end of Phase B, all the desirable space was filled with polygynous social groups controlled by dominant males. The more dominant the male was, the larger and more fertile his social group tended to be. There were fourteen social groups composed of 150 adults. Each group was composed of about ten adults, including a dominant male, associated males and females, and their offspring. There were 470 such offspring and they had all received good maternal care and early socialization. So, there were three times as many younger as older animals, a far greater ratio than would exist in the wild.

At day 315, Phase C began and population growth slowed markedly. Normally, more mice survive to maturity than can find social niches and so these lower-status mice will tend to emigrate in search of such a niche. As this was prevented, a large number of males — unable to successfully compete for a social niche — simply withdrew physically and psychologically from territorial males and ganged up together. They would occasionally fight each other over tiny issues, such as two males returning from drinking, but they would do little else. Low-status females would withdraw to high nesting boxes but were not aggressive towards each other. However, territorial males were constantly confronted with subordinate males trying to take over their territory and, as there were so many of them, the ability of territorial males to control their territory declined. This left nursing females exposed to nest invasion. The females would then take on the role of the absent male. They would become extremely aggressive and even generalize this aggression to their own young. Young mice would be ejected from the nest too young and abandoned by their mothers during transit to new nest sites. Conception declined while re-absorption of foetuses increased. This behaviour hugely increased mortality and evidenced a societal breakdown. Hereafter, Phase D — the death phase — began. Population increase ceased on day 560. After day 600, no mice survived past weaning. The last conception was documented on day 920. By 1st March 1972, the average age of the colony was 776 days, which was 200 days beyond the average age of mouse menopause. On 22nd June 1972, the population was just 122 — 22 male, 100 female — and by May 1973, 1720 days after colonization, all the mice were dead.

Calhoun argues that the high population density of the Mouse Utopia meant that mice started life without proper affective bonds with their mothers, could not develop proper bonds as adults due to the constant passage of other mice, and therefore failed to develop complex behaviours such as courtship and appropriate maternal behaviour. However, Calhoun's study of the mice in Phase C raises an intriguing issue in this regard. Of the females aged 334 days at autopsy, only 18% had ever conceived, whereas in the wild they would each have had five or more successfully reared litters by that age. The male equivalents of these barren females were known as 'the beautiful ones'. They never sexually approached females and nor did they ever fight other males. They simply ate, drank, and groomed each other. Almost all of the adult mice in phase D were these two types and so the colony died out.

The experiment is fascinating in terms of understanding the post-Industrial evolution of humans and a possible decline in ethnocentric behaviour. Woodley of Menie et al. (2017), in discussing this very experiment, has made two crucial points. Firstly, we would expect all mutations, both physical and mental, to be interrelated because they broadly reflect the same thing: developmental instability. Indeed, he shows that this is the case with facial asymmetry being weakly negatively associated with intelligence. Secondly, due to the complexity of the brain (84% of our genes are related to the brain), behaviour would be extremely sensitive to mutation accumulation. By extension, in social animals, where behaviour is anyway complex, even small accruals in mutations could lead to pathological forms of behaviour and the rapid breakdown of society. This may be what happened in the Calhoun experiment.

But, clearly, there are a number of factors that would slow down the decline in humans, though not, perhaps, in a particular ethnic group. If we assume that the mice are English people, not only would there be a small amount of emigration but the humans would have evolved to be more cooperative meaning that there would be lower levels of polygyny and a far smaller section of the society composed of 'gangs' of violent low-status males. This would mean that the threat which these gangs posed to the normal functioning of society would be reduced. But what could not be stopped would be mutational meltdown which is likely what can be seen in the rise of 'the beautiful ones' as well as in the rise in the females who have no interest in having children. Calhoun puts the pathological behaviour of 'the beautiful ones' solely down to the fact that they have not been properly reared as a consequence, ultimately, of over-population. However, this seems rather unlikely as sexuality in humans has been shown to be significantly heritable based on twin studies. For example, the available research on homosexuality indicates that it is significantly genetic: around 0.39 genetic in adult men and 0.19 genetic in adult women (Långström et al., 2010). In much the same way, the non-aggressive personalities of these mice are quite remarkable given that the heritability of personality has already been shown to be around 0.66 in humans (Lynn, 2011a). Similarly, the pathological behaviour of the females, as well as health problems like reabsorbing foetuses, would also be likely to be significantly genetic in origin. Furthermore, the Mouse Utopia did not reach anything like a level that could be said to be 'over-crowded' when the reduction in fertility began. This reduction happened after only a few generations; implying that some other factor must have been involved, such as weakened selection for healthy or psychologically normal mice.

In addition, it is unclear why overcrowding would lead to the complete extinction of the colony. If there was no genetic dimension involved in the collapse, we would expect the last mice to be born to have an instinct to breed and to do so. As such, although we should not play down the environmental impact on behaviour, it is probable that the collapse of Natural Selection significantly explains what happened in the Mouse Utopia. Put simply, there was no longer intense selection for dominant males or for highly maternal females. As such, the percentage of the population comprised of non-dominant males, and their degree of non-dominance, increased to a point where the entire male population were 'the beautiful ones'. In the same way, there was no longer selection for maternal females and so, eventually, all of the females were disinterested in motherhood. This was due to a combination of genetics (mice carrying genes which made them behave in this way) and environment (these mice undermining the structures through which non-mutant mice learnt adaptive behaviour).

Accordingly, we might expect a comparable pattern in humans after many generations in an environment marked by dysgenic fertility. We would expect behaviour patterns which had previously ensured the survival of the group — such as ethnocentrism and the consequent motivation to protect the group's genetic interests — to decline. This is clearly in evidence in Political Correctness, Multiculturalism and other movements, spear-headed by Europeans, which promote the interests of non-Europeans in Europe. To the extent that religion is a group-selected trait, it can also be seen in the rise of atheism which is itself damaging to the group's levels of ethnocentrism. We would also expect the simple desire to breed to decline as mutations accrued, something which Woodley of Menie et al. (2017) have noted. They refer to the rise in 'spiteful mutations' which cause people to act against their own genetic interests. And if these people influence society, they can persuade even non-carriers of these 'spiteful' genes to act in self-destructive ways and they can undermine structures — such as religion — which help to promote group interests. Woodley of Menie et al. call this 'social epistasis'. As a consequence, modern (liberal) religion and ideology — far from being an indirect means of genetic preservation — would in fact reflect a sick society's growing desire to destroy itself. An obvious example can be seen in the ideology of Multiculturalism and Political Correctness.

Nationalism is generally in the genetic interests of the group that advocates it. Marxism can assist in the pursuance of genetic interests in a number of ways. Clearly, it is in the interests of the working class who advocate it. But it can also be in the interests of certain members of the elite. By advocating Marxism, they can engage in competitive altruism, by seeming as though they deeply care about the poor. This attractive quality could help them to gain power and so aid the genetic interests of their family and their associates. They could become the new ruling class. If they were already part of the ruling class, and they destroyed much of this class in order to gain power, then this would potentially damage their genetic interests, but this would depend on the extent to which it benefitted their closer kin.

Multiculturalism takes this further. It is clearly in the genetic interests of ethnic minorities within a nation to espouse this as it will promote their own genetic interests. Indeed, in this regard, MacDonald (1998) has argued that Jewish people are very prominent among Multiculturalist, and generally anti-traditionalist, thinkers in Western countries. He further argues that these senior figures identified as Jews and regarded the movements in which they were involved as advancing Jewish interests. MacDonald's research in this area has been heavily criticized. But it is seemingly clear that cultural relativist anthropology was founded by American Franz Boas (1858–1942), which moved the subject away from evolutionary science and towards Leftist advocacy. Psychoanalysis, which does the same, was founded by Freud. Postmodernism is strongly associated with Jacques Derrida (1930–2004). Theodore Adorno (1903–1969) effectively argued that nationalism reflected a pathological 'authoritarian' personality. The most prominent critics of Sociobiology (and evidence for race differences in intelligence) have been Ashley Montagu (1905–1999), Stephen J. Gould (1941–2002) and Richard Lewontin, whom we met earlier. MacDonald observes that these researchers are all Jewish and identified as such, and he avers that analyses of their writings indicates that they realized that their research was advancing Jewish interests. However, one of the most prominent books to set out race differences in intelligence to a large audience was *The Bell Curve* by Richard Herrnstein (1930–1994; Herrnstein was Jewish) and Charles Murray (Herrnstein & Murray, 1994). So, clearly, not all scholars use their research in this way. MacDonald's idea is certainly interesting in terms of evolution and future research could look into this in a highly statistical manner.[22]

---

22 In scholarship on ethnicity, it may be noted that both Ernest Gellner and Eric Hobsbawm were Jewish. Both argued that European nationalism was an accident of historical circumstances and that there was nothing primordial or 'natural' about it. It could be argued that, in so doing, they were undermining European nationalism and thus promoting Jewish interests. However, I can find no evidence that Gellner, for example, consciously did this. He also turned his intellectual fire on other movements which he regarded as non-rational, such as psychoanalysis, which was founded by a Jewish person (see Gellner, 2008) and cultural anthropology, which was strongly influenced by Boas (Gellner, 1995). A detailed critique of MacDonald's model has been present by Cofnas (2018) in

But just as with Marxism, Multiculturalism can be used as a means of competing for moral status, so permitting — for example — a group that is not, or not quite, the elite to displace the elite, using ethnic minorities as part of a coalition force to help them do so. But Multiculturalism differs from Marxism because it inherently involves damaging the genetic interests of the entire native group (including those of the new elite), which is not necessarily the case with Marxism.[23] Those who advocate Multiculturalism seem to have lost an important instinct towards group — and thus genetic — preservation. Once a society, as a whole, espouses Multiculturalism as a dominant ideology then the society is acting against its own genetic interests and will ultimately destroy itself. Indeed, MacDonald (2004) has argued that anti-Semitism can be regarded as a European evolutionary strategy. In effect, it is an example of negative ethnocentrism and Multiculturalism acts to suppress all forms of native ethnocentrism.

Indeed, Multiculturalism will actively invite into Western countries — and promote the welfare of — members of ethnic groups from less industrialized countries. These countries will have been subject to dysgenics for fewer generations so this alone may mean they are more ethnocentric. In a sense, the mass-immigration inspired by Multiculturalism is akin to introducing wild animals into a zoo full of domesticated ones. Accordingly, the wild animals will simply outbreed and come to take over the Western country in question. It seems fairly clear that in the early 2000s this is precisely what is happening in Western countries (see Murray, 2017). The ideology of Multiculturalism allows its European advocates to attain socioeconomic status and so they advocate and enforce it; but they are also often able to insulate

---

which it is argued that Jews are significant in all intellectual movements except anti-Semitic ones due to their high intelligence.

23 Some pro-Multiculturalism or Marxist groups, it should be said, also draw upon aspects of nationalism, but this will usually involve a form of nationalism which is antithetical to a 'powerful' nation, such as Scottish nationalism and its desire to break away from the English (see Dutton, 2002).

themselves from many of its short-term negative effects such as inter-ethnic violence. The failure to consider the long-term implications of such an ideology, in terms of genetic interests, would seem to imply a low level of ethnocentrism. As we have discussed, this may be in part for environmental reasons. Even more extreme, in terms of the damage to genetic interests, than Multiculturalism, would be animal rights activism wherein the interests of the human species were subordinated to that of other species. In line with Woodley of Menie et al.'s (2017) model, we have already noted that atheism is associated with mutant genes, and Multiculturalism and Marxism tend to be atheistic. It is true that Marxism has many aspects of religiosity (see Dutton, 2014) but it does lack belief in god, in a way which is untrue, for example, of Buddhism because Buddha is either worshipped as a god or Buddhism is practiced alongside another religion (see Dutton et al., 2017).

Indeed, I have looked elsewhere (Dutton, 2018) at clear evidence that the belief in Multiculturalism is a sign, in part, of high mutational load. It has been found that Republican voters are more physically attractive than Democrat voters (Peterson & Palmer, 2017). Berggren et al. (2017) have found that in Europe, the USA and Australia, people rate 'right-wing' politicians as more physically attractive than 'left-wing' politicians. The authors provide an economic explanation: 'Politicians on the right look more beautiful in Europe, the United States and Australia. Our explanation is that beautiful people earn more, which makes them less inclined to support redistribution'. The problem with this argument is that there is far more to being a 'right-wing' politician than not supporting economic socialism. The current consensus in psychology is that two broad dimensions are necessary to describe sociopolitical attitudes (Duckitt et al. 2002). One of these is 'resistance to change' or 'traditionalism' and the other is 'anti-egalitarianism' or justification of inequality. Bergman et al.'s interpretation does not explain why good-looking politicians are more likely to be traditionalist.

An alternative explanation to Berggren et al.'s, which is far less question-begging, is that egalitarianism, the questioning of religious tradition and the promotion of Multiculturalism (that is modern Leftist ideas) would have likely been met with horror by populations that lived under the harsh conditions of Natural Selection. Populations which were so low in ethnocentrism to espouse Multiculturalism and reject religion would simply have died out. It therefore follows that the espousal of leftist dogmas would partly reflect mutant genes, just as the espousal of atheism does. This elevated mutational load, associated with Leftists, would be reflected in their bodies as well as their brains. Accordingly, we would expect them to have higher fluctuating asymmetry in face—reflecting mutation—and this is indeed the case.

It might be averred that this model is problematic because it would be likely that ethnocentrism was selected to an optimum level and thus mutation would cause deviation from this level in either direction, rendering mutational load also associated with extreme positive and negative ethnocentrism. But I do not see this as a problem. Dutton et al. (2017) have shown that under conditions of selection we evolved a very specific kind of religion: the collective worship of moral gods. They show that both atheism and religious deviations from this, such as belief in the paranormal, are associated with markers of mutation. There is a substantial degree to which 'religiousness' crosses over with being 'right-wing' in industrial societies. Indeed, the Right Wing Authoritarian Scale (RWA) and the Fundamentalism Scale have been shown to significantly correlate at 0.75 (Laythe et al., 2001), meaning they are strongly the same. Thus, it may be that the central factor is atheism. This may be underlie extreme Leftism, though future research would have to test this. Moreover, it may be that high mutational load would be associated with extreme *negative* ethnocentrism, but in that this is effectively a form of despising those who are genetically different from yourself it would ultimately lead to individuals who were anti-social malcontents, unlikely to pass on their genes. It is possible many 'Lone Wolf' nationalist terrorists, such as Thomas Mair who murdered the British MP Jo Cox during the 2016 European Union referendum campaign, are precisely such people (*BBC News,* 23rd November 2016). Positive ethnocentrism, as we have seen, is inherently adaptive.

However, there is a key difference between the Mouse Utopia and our own Human Zoo. Unlike in Mouse Utopia, among humans there would be no scientists to enforce the 'utopia'. Consequently, eventually average human intelligence would fall so low that the utopia could not be sustained. It would collapse back into pre-modern conditions of selection and in those conditions the genes that predicted health, intelligence, ethnocentrism and religiousness would likely be once again strongly selected for.

5. Conclusion

Reviewing the body of evidence, it seems probable that the early arrival of the Industrial Revolution in Europe, as a result of Europe's high level of genius, would appear to have significantly reduced the degree to which Europe is ethnocentric. Firstly, it reduced stress and mortality salience and so religiousness and, secondly, it would appear to have set off a process of dysgenics, meaning that ethnocentric and religious instincts would be less strongly selected for. However, we have noted that religiousness is still associated with fertility even in this context, though intelligence is negatively associated with fertility. Accordingly, we would expect civilization to effectively collapse. However, religious people of not especially high intelligence would be the survivors and these people would also, likely, be relatively ethnocentric.

CHAPTER ELEVEN

Why Did Different Ethnicities React Differently in 2015?

1. Introduction

Why is it that some countries or groups of countries appear to be more ethnocentric than other countries? Why has Europe's so-called 'refugee crisis' evoked such different responses in different nations and in different sub-groups within these nations? This study provides us with some fairly clear answers to these questions. As we have seen, positive and negative ethnocentrism do not inter-correlate, meaning they have substantially separate causes. Below we outline the key causes.

2. Positive Ethnocentrism

(A) RELIGIOUSNESS

Positive ethnocentrism is negatively associated with atheism. In other words, countries that don't believe in God are less likely to be positively ethnocentric. It may be that this is a reflection of national atheism levels and low positive ethnocentrism having a number of common causes. However, as we have discussed, it seems more likely that belief in God, and often the accordant belief that your people are blessed by God, augments positive ethnocentrism. It may also be that these countries have fewer spiteful mutant genes.

(B) LOW NATIONAL IQ

Low national IQ predicts high levels of positive ethnocentrism. On the one hand, it may be argued that low IQ makes us more instinctive and we are likely to have a group-selected instinct towards positive ethnocentrism. Kahneman (2011), for example, has argued that logical thinking is a form of effortful control that allows us to see the world objectively and move beyond our instincts. On the other hand, this may be a function of low-IQ societies being very stressful to live in, because they tend to be poor, unstable and corrupt (see Lynn & Vanhanen, 2012). As we have seen, stress induces positive ethnocentrism.

(C) POVERTY

The second of the two possibilities, above, is evidenced by the fact that poverty is significantly positively associated with positive ethnocentrism as it would likely make people stressed and instinctive. This is evidenced in data on GDP and per capita income.

(D) MORTALITY SALIENCE

This stressor also predicts positive ethnocentrism, as evidenced in the significant relationship between infant mortality rate and positive ethnocentrism.

(E) LOW MEDIAN AGE

In essence, young societies are more positively ethnocentric. Indeed, factor analysis by Dutton et al. (2016a) found that this was the biggest single predictor of national differences in positive ethnocentrism. This may be because a relatively young age, and a society having a relatively young age, is associated with a series of factors which would predict generalized ethnocentrism. A young median age would tend to imply a high birth-rate and a low life expectancy. These traits are associated with societies that have high levels of poverty, low levels of socioeconomic development and low average IQ. Certainly stress and mortality salience, as well as low IQ, have been shown to be associated with elevated levels of positive ethnocentrism at the individual level. In addition, poorer countries, and lower-IQ countries, tend to be more religious than wealthier countries, and religiousness has been shown to be associated with elevated levels of positive ethnocentrism. So, it may be that a cluster of factors that are associated with positive ethnocentrism are also associated with a country having a low median age, possibly explaining this result.

As discussed, cousin marriage was close to reaching significance as being positively associated and was significant in terms of a desire to fight for the country. This is likely because societies that practice cousin marriage lack sufficient trust to develop large states. Their states are tribally divided but they will defend themselves against the likely genetically more distant outsiders. As noted, this implies that a small gene pool would predict positive ethnocentrism. It may be that both cousin marriage and extreme religiousness relate to positive ethnocentrism because a common factor underpins them all, such as a specific position on the $r-K$ spectrum.

3. Negative Ethnocentrism

(A) FAST LIFE HISTORY STRATEGY

We found a number of gene forms and highly genetic characteristics which we associated with fast Life History. These, in turn, positively predicted high levels of negative ethnocentrism. Not only does this evidence the veracity of the sociobiological model of 'ethnicity' but it is an important conclusion in itself. Indeed, factor analysis by Dutton et al. (2016a) found that this was one of the single most important contributions to national differences in negative ethnocentrism.

(B) RELIGIOUSNESS

More religious countries were more negatively ethnocentric. This is understandable in terms of the foreigner being perceived as somehow less godly and also in terms of religiousness being associated with low levels of mutation.

(C) COUSIN MARRIAGE

Factor analysis also revealed that this had an important unique contribution to understanding national differences in negative ethnocentrism. As we have discussed, it can be seen as the product of a fast Life History, would reduce the gene-pool into distinct tribes, and would evidence low levels of trust. Accordingly, it would elevate negative ethnocentrism.

In addition, low intelligence seems to predict important aspects of negative ethnocentrism, as does stress. In addition to these we have observed the possible salience of specific gene variants and ethnic diversity.

4. Group Differences in Ethnocentrism

We have found there to be clear race differences in ethnocentrism. South Asians, Arabs and North Africans are more ethnocentric than Europeans. Though they lack pride in their often artificial nation states, they are strongly willing to fight for their communities. It would seem that the two interrelated reasons for this are cousin marriage and religiousness. These factors cause them to be both more positively and negatively ethnocentric than are Europeans. We have also observed that Sub-Saharan Africans are higher in negative ethnocentric behaviour than Europeans. Their high negative ethnocentrism would be predicted by a fast Life History Strategy. Any higher positive ethnocentrism — though we did not find this — would be predicted by a relative lack of societal development, meaning that they are canalized into small tribes of strongly interrelated people, rendering it in their genetic interests to act altruistically for the good of the tribe, at least in contrast to certain aggressors who are relatively genetically distant. We also noted that Northeast Asians are higher in both positive and negative ethnocentrism than Europeans. This would appear to be because the extreme harshness of the environment has rendered them much more strongly group selected.

Europeans, we have noted, seem to be uniquely low — in comparison to other races — in positive and negative ethnocentrism. A feasible reason for this is that they had traded a strategy based around ethnocentrism for a strategy based around producing genius. This has allowed them to be highly inventive and thus expand and dominate other peoples. As long as the benefits of this genius strategy have been strong enough to outweigh the negative impact of low ethnocentrism then this strategy has worked in terms of expansion. However, industrialization has meant that a number of factors have conspired to ensure that the European ethnocentrism is too low for the strategy to work any longer. The collapse of Natural Selection has led to greater genetic diversity, meaning that Europeans are less genetically interrelated than they used to be. Low Natural Selection, along with decreasing stress and mortality salience, has also led to the collapse of organized religion and rise of maladaptive ideologies which are actively against the genetic interests of Europeans. Greater ethnic diversity within European societies has led to reduced levels of trust. And to this, the relatively high intelligence of Europeans — combined with low levels of stress — makes them extremely low in evolved instincts.

If we return to the stark difference in how Eastern Europe reacted to the 'Great Migration', in comparison to Western Europe, we start to understand the difference. Eastern Europe has been industrialised for a smaller amount of time, meaning smaller gene pools, it is poorer, mortality salience is higher, it is a more stressful place to live, many parts of Eastern Europe are relatively religious or, at least, ideologically nationalistic as a reaction against Communism, and there are low levels of ethnic diversity. In addition, many Eastern European countries have never been expansionist. They have adopted a much more ethnocentric strategy based around Herder's ideal of the ethnic group and its bonds of blood. Eastern Europe is, in many ways, what Western Europe was before World War II, preserved under permafrost.

5. Conclusion

At the moment, this study is limited by the relatively small sample size pursued by the World Values Survey and the fact that alternative sources have not asked questions that can be understood in terms of national differences in ethnocentrism. However, we have surveyed the causes of individual level differences in ethnocentrism and found that many of these are still significant factors in terms of group level differences even in spite of the relatively small sample of countries.

It would appear that modern day Europe is extremely low in positive and negative ethnocentrism and we have set out the reasons why. In addition, Europe is increasingly allowing into its borders people who are extremely high in ethnocentrism as predicted by their high levels of religiousness, low median age, their practice of cousin marriage, low average intelligence, and (likely) relatively low mutational load. We have noted that the ethnocentric strategy will, eventually, tend to dominate all other strategies in the battle of group survival. Alternate strategies can also work, such as the development of large and highly inventive coalitions, but these cannot last if they promote ideologies which are actively to the detriment of their genetic interests, as is happening with Political Correctness, which actively promotes the effective destruction of European people. Accordingly, we can cautiously predict that, if there is no radical geopolitical change, the power of peoples who are relatively deficient in ethnocentrism, such as Europeans, will decline, while the influence of relatively ethnocentric peoples, such as the Northeast Asians and the Muslim world, will rise. But, as we have seen, evolution does not stop and, with the collapse of Europeans, they are likely to become more religious and more ethnocentric, as these are selected for under harsh conditions and are associated with the stress of harsh conditions.

Charles Darwin commented in 1871 in *The Descent of Man*: 'A tribe including many members who, from possessing a high degree of the spirit of patriotism, fidelity, obedience, courage, and sympathy, were always ready to aid one another, and to sacrifice themselves for the common good, would be victorious over most other tribes, and this would be natural selection'. This seems not only to be highly accurate but also highly relevant for European people today. They are low in ethnocentrism and, under certain conditions, this will lead to their being displaced by groups that are higher in ethnocentrism than they are. We are now living under these conditions. But it will be the collapse of their civilization and power that will likely lead, many years hence, to their becoming more ethnocentric once again.

References

Aboud, F. (1988). *Children and Prejudice*. London: Blackwell.

Adams, W. (1st January 2006). Mixed Race, Pretty Face? *Psychology Today*, https://www.psychologytoday.com/articles/200601/mixed-race-pretty-face.

Adler, C. & Jacobs, J. (1906). Consanguinity among Jews. *Jewish Encyclopedia*, http://www.jewishencyclopedia.com/articles/4611-consanguinity-among-jews.

Adorno, T.W., Frenkel-Brunswik, E. & Levinson, D. (1950). *The Authoritarian Personality*. New York: Harper.

Agroskin, D. & Jonas, E. (2013). Controlling Death by Defending Ingroups — Meditational Insights into Terror Management and Control Restoration. *Journal of Experimental Social Psychology*, 49: 1144–1158.

Akbar, J. (4th September 2015). Revealed: How the Five Wealthiest Gulf Nations Have so Far Refused to Take a Single Syrian Refugee. *Daily Mail*, http://www.dailymail.co.uk/news/article-3222405/How-six-wealthiest-Gulf-Nations-refused-single-Syrian-refugee.html.

Alacorta, C. (2012). Adolescence and Religion: An Evolutionary Perspective. In P. McNamara & W. Wildman, (Eds). *Science and the World's Religions, Volume 1: Origins and Destinies*. Santa Barbara, CA: ABC-Clio.

Alberts, S. (1999). Paternal Kin Discrimination In Wild Baboons. *Proceedings of the Royal Society of London*, B 266: 1501–1506.

Alesina, A. & La Ferrera, E. (2002). Who Trusts Others? *Journal of Public Economics*, 85: 207–234.

Allik, J. (2007). Geographical Distribution of Mental Abilities and Its Moral Consequence. *European Journal of Personality*, 21: 707–708.

Altemeyer, B. (2003). Why Do Religious Fundamentalists Tend to Be Prejudiced? *International Journal of the Psychology of Religion*, 13: 17–28.

Anderson, B. (1983). *Imagined Communities: Reflections of Nations and Nationalism*. London: Verso.

Anon. (1901). *Memorials of the Duttons of Dutton in Cheshire With Notes Respecting the Sherborne Branch of the Family.* London: Henry Sotheran & Co.

Appleyard, D. & Goldwin, C. (5th February 2016). Our Love Was Colour Blind ... But Our Families Weren't. *Daily Mail,* http://www.dailymail.co.uk/femail/article-2045815/Our-love-colour-blind--families-werent-Mixed-race-couples-generations-tell-stories.html.

Arden, R. & Adams, M. (2016). A General Intelligence Factor in Dogs. *Intelligence,* 55: 79–85.

Arnett, J. (2007). *International Encyclopaedia of Adolescence.* New York: Taylor & Francis.

Atzmon, G., Hao, L., Pe'er, I. et al. (2010). Abraham's Children in the Genome Era: Major Jewish Diaspora Populations Comprise Distinct Genetic Clusters with Shared Middle Eastern Ancestry. *American Journal of Human Genetics,* 86: 850–859.

Axelrod, R. & Hammond, R. (2003). The Evolution of Ethnocentric Behaviour. Midwest Political Science Convention, April 3–6, 2003, Chicago, IL. http://www-personal.umich.edu/~axe/research/AxHamm_Ethno.pdf.

Baker, J. (1974). *Race.* Oxford: Oxford University Press.

Baldick, C. & Bate, J. (2006). *The Oxford English Literary History: 1910–1940.* Oxford University Press.

Baldwin, D. (2010). *Robin Hood: The English Outlaw Unmasked.* Stroud: Amberley Publishing.

Bamshad, M., Kivisild, T. Watkins W. et al. (2001). Genetic Evidence on the Origins of Indian Caste Populations. *Genome Research,* 11: 994–1004.

Banton, M. (1998). *Racial Theories.* Cambridge: Cambridge University Press.

Barnett, S. M. & Williams, W. (2004). Review: *IQ and the Wealth of Nations. Contemporary Psychology,* 49: 389–396.

Barr, C. S., Schwandt, M. L., Lindell, S. G., Higley, J. D., Maestripieri, D., Suomi, S. J., & Hellig, M. (2008) Variation at the μ-Opioid Receptor Gene (OPRM1) Influences Attachment Behaviour in Infant Primates. *Proceedings of the National Academy of Sciences,* USA, 105: 5277–5281. https://doi.org/10.1073/pnas.0710225105.

Barrios, G. (1992). *New Perspectives in Psychology.* Quezon: Rex Printing Company.

Barth, F. (1969). *Ethnic Groups and Boundaries: The Social Organization of Cultural Difference.* Long Grove: Waveland.

Bateson, M., Nettle, D., & Roberts, G. (2006). Cues of Being Watched Enhance Cooperation in a Real World Setting. *Biology Letters,* 2: 412–414.

BBC News. (23rd November 2016). Thomas Mair: Extremist Loner who Targeted Jo Cox. http://www.bbc.com/news/uk-38071894.

BBC News. (22nd September 2015). Migrant Crisis: EU Ministers Approve Disputed Quota Plan. http://www.bbc.com/news/world-europe-34329825.

BBC News. (19th August 2015). Migrants Crisis: Slovakia 'Will Only Accept Christians'. http://www.bbc.com/news/world-europe-33986738.

Bede. (1890). *An Ecclesiastical History of the English People.* (Trans. T. Miller). London: English Text Society.

Benoist, A. de. (2004). *On Being a Pagan.* Atlanta, GA: Ultra.

Benson, P. (2002). *Ethnocentrism and the English Dictionary.* London: Routledge.

Berggren, N., Jordahl, H. & Poutvaara, P. (2017). The Right Look: Conservative Politicians Look Better and Voters Reward It. *Journal of Public Economics,* 146: 79–86.

Bergh, R. (2013). *Prejudiced Personalities Revisited: On the Nature of Generalized Prejudice.* PhD Thesis: Uppsala University.

Bernier, F. (1684). 'New division of earth by the different species or races that inhabit it'. (Trans. by T. Bendyphe in 'Memoirs Read Before the Anthropological Society of London', Vol. 1, 1863–1864, pp. 360–364).

Bittles, A. & Black, M. (2015). Consanguineous Marriage in Asia. Global Patterns and Tables of Consanguinity. http://www.consang.net/images/c/cb/Asia.pdf.

Bittles, A. & Black, M. (2010). Consanguinity, Human Evolution and Complex Diseases. *PNAS,* 107: 1779–1786.

Bittles, A. & Huissain, R. (2000). An Analysis of Consanguineous Marriage in the Muslim Population of India at Regional and State Levels. *Annals of Human Biology,* 27: 163–171.

Bizumic, B. (2017). *Ethnocentrism: Integrated Perspectives.* London: Routledge.

Bizumic, B. (2015). Ethnocentrism and Prejudice: History of the Concepts. *International Encyclopedia of Social and Behavioural Sciences.* Amsterdam: Elsevier.

Bizumic, B. (2014). Who Coined the Concept of Ethnocentrism? A Brief Report. *Journal of Social and Political Psychology,* 2: 3–10.

Bizumic, B. & Duckitt, J. (2012). What Is and Is Not Ethnocentrism? a Conceptual Analysis and Political Implications. *Political Psychology,* 33: 887–909.

Bizumic, B. & Duckitt, J. (2008). 'My Group Is Not Worthy of Me'. Narcissism and Ethnocentrism. *Political Psychology,* 29: 437–453.

Blaustein, A. R. & O'Hara, R. (1981). Genetic Control for Sibling Recognition? *Nature,* 290: 246–248.

Blanchard, R. (2008). Review and Theory of Handedness, Birth Order, and Homosexuality in Men. *Laterality*, 13: 51–70.

Blume, M. (2009). The Reproductive Benefits of Religious Affiliation. In E. Voland & W. Schiefenhövel (Eds). *The Biological Evolution of Religious Mind and Behavior*. New York: Springer.

Bodmer, W. F. & Cavalli-Sforza, L. L. (1976). *Genetics, Evolution and Man*. San Francisco: Freeman.

Boyd, W. (1950). *Genetics and the Races of Man: An Introduction to Modern Physical Anthropology*. New York: Little Brown & Co.Cohen, M. (2002). An Anthropologist Looks at 'Race' and IQ Testing. In Fish, J. (Ed.). *Race and Intelligence: Separating Science from Myth*. Mahwah, NJ: Lawrence Erlbaum. Graves, J. (2002). The Misuse of Life History Theory: J.P. Rushton and the Pseudoscience of Racial Hierarchy. In Fish, J. (Ed.). *Race and Intelligence*. Mahwah, NJ: Lawrence Erlbaum.

Boyer, P. (2001). *Religion Explained: The Human Instincts That Fashion Gods, Spirits and Ancestors*. London: William Heinemann.

Boztas, S. (5th February 2016). These are the Toughest Places for Asylum Seekers to Enter Europe. *Daily Telegraph*, http://www.telegraph.co.uk/news/worldnews/europe/12140900/These-are-the-toughest-places-for-asylum-seekers-to-enter-Europe.html.

Brewer, M. (1999). The Psychology of Prejudice: Ingroup Love and Outgroup Hate? *Journal of Social Issues*, 55: 429–444.

Broman, S., Brody, N., Nichols, P. et al. (1987). *Retardation in Young Children*. Hillsdale, NJ: Erlbaum.

Brownstein, R. & R. Rainey, R. (2004). Bush's Huge Victory in the Fast-Growing Areas beyond the Suburbs Alters the Political Map. *Los Angeles Times*, (22nd November): A1, A14–A15.

Bruce, S. (2002). *God is Dead: Secularization in the West*. Oxford: Blackwell.

Burrows, T. (6th September 2015). Benjamin Netanyahu Says Israel Has Treated 1,000 Wounded Syrians — But Refuses to Take in Refugees Because the Country Is 'Too Small'. *Daily Mail*, http://www.dailymail.co.uk/news/article-3224394/Israeli-Prime-Minister-rejected-calls-opposition-leaders-Syrian-refugees-saying-country-small.html.

Buss, D. (1989). *The Evolution of Desire: Strategies of Human Mating*. New York: Basic Books.

Caccone, A. & Powell, J. (1989). Evolutionary Divergence among Hominids. *Evolution*, 43: 925–942.

Calhoun, J. (1973). Death Squared: The Explosive Growth and Demise of a Mouse Population. *Proceedings of the Royal Society of Medicine*, 66: 80–88.

Carl, N. & Billari, F. (2014). Generalized Trust and Intelligence in the United States. *PLOS ONE*, https://doi.org/10.1371/journal.pone.0091786.

Carmi, S., Hui, K., Kochav, E. et al. (2014). Sequencing an Ashkenazi Reference Panel Supports Population-Targeted Personal Genomics and Illuminates Jewish and European Origins. *Nature Communications*, 5: 4835.

Castleden, R. (2003). *King Arthur: The Truth Behind the Legend*. London: Routledge.

Cavalli-Sforza, L. L., Menozzi, P., & Piazza, A. (1994). *The History and Geography of Human Genes*. Princeton, NJ: Princeton University Press.

Cavalli-Sforza, L. L. & Bodmer, W. (1971). *The Genetics of Human Populations*. San Francisco: Freeman.

Center for Jewish Genetics. (2015). https://www.jewishgenetics.org/familial-dysautonomia.

Chagnon, N. (2013). *Noble Savages: Life Amongst Two Dangerous Tribes—the Yanomamö and the Anthropologists*. New York: Simon & Schuster.

Chagnon, N. (1968). *Yanomamö: The Fierce People*. New York: Holt, Rinehart & Winston.

Chalmers, A. (1999). *What Is This Thing Called Science? An Assessment of the Nature and Status of Science and Its Methods*. St. Lucia: University of Queensland Press.

Charlton, B. (15th December 2015). Group Selection Does Not Require Competition between Groups. *Intelligence, Personality and Genius*, http://iqpersonalitygenius.blogspot.fi/2015/12/group-selection-does-not-require.html.

Cheon, B., Livingston, R., Hong, Y. & Chiao, J. (2014). Gene × Environment Interaction on Intergroup Bias: The Role of 5-HTTLPR and Perceived Outgroup Threat. *Social Cognitive and Affective Neuroscience*, 9: 1268–1275.

Chiao, J. & Blizinsky, K. (2010). Culture–Gene Coevolution of Individualism–Collectivism and the Serotonin Transporter Gene. *Proceedings of the Royal Society, B*. https://doi.org/10.1098/rspb.2009.1650.

Clark, E. & Hanisee, J. (1982). Intellectual and Adaptive Oerformance of Asian Children in Adoptive American Settings. *Developmental Psychology*, 18: 595–599.

Clark, G. (2014). *The Son Also Rises: Surnames and the History of Social Mobility*. Princeton: Princeton University Press.

Clark, G. (2007). *A Farewell to Alms: A Brief Economic History of the World*. Princeton: Princeton University Press.

Clark, V. & Tuffin, K. (2015). Choosing Housemates and Justifying Age, Gender and Ethnic Discrimination. *Australian Journal of Psychology*, 67: 20–28.

Cochran, G. & Harpending, H. (2009). *The 10,000 Year Explosion: How Civilization Accelerated Human Evolution*. New York: Basic Books.

Cochran, G., Hardy, J., & Harpending, H. (2006). Natural History of Ashkenazi Intelligence. *Journal of Biosocial Science*, 38: 659–693.

Cofnas, N. (2018). Judaism as a Group Evolutionary Strategy: A Critical Analysis of Kevin MacDonald's Theory. *Human Nature*, https://doi.org/10.1007/s12110-018-9310-x.

Cofnas, N. (2016). A Teleofunctional Account of Everyday Evolutionary Mismatch. *Biology and Philosophy*, 31: 507–525.

Cohen, T., Vardi-Saliternik, R. & Friedlander, Y. (2004). Consanguinity, Intracommunity and Intercommunity Marriages in a Population Sample of Israeli Jews. *Annals of Human Biology*, 31: 28–48.

Coid, J., Kahtan, N., Gault, S., & Jarman, B. (2000). Ethnic Differences in Admissions to Secure Forensic Psychiatry Services. *British Journal of Psychiatry*, 177: 241–247.

Coleman, J. (1997). Ancient Greek Ethnocentrism. In J. Coleman & C. Walz. (Eds.)., *Greeks and Barbarians: Essays on the Interactions between Greeks and Non-Greeks in Antiquity and the Consequences for Ethnocentrism*. Bethesda, MA: CDI Press.

Conn, W. (1986). *Christian Conversion: A Developmental Interpretation of Autonomy and Surrender*. New York: Paulist Press.

Connor, W. (1994). *Ethno-Nationalism: The Quest for Understanding*. Princeton: Princeton University Press.

Coon, C. S., Garn, S. M. & Birdsell, J. B. (1950). *Races: A Study of Race Formation in Man*. Springfield, Ill: Thomas.

Coren, S. (1994). *The Intelligence of Dogs: A Guide to the Thoughts, Emotions, and Inner Lives of Our Canine Companions*. New York: Bantam Books.

Cupucao, D. (2010). *Religion and Ethnocentrism: An Empirical-Theological Study*. Leiden: Brill.

Currie, T. & Mace, R. (2012). Analyses Do Not Support the Parasite-Stress Theory of Human Sociality. *Behavioral and Brain Sciences*, 35: 83–85.

Cvorovic, J. (2014). *The Roma: A Balkan Underclass*. London: Ulster Institute for Social Research.

D'Angelo, C. (14th March 2016). We Prayed for Paris but What about Turkey? *Huffington Post*, http://www.huffingtonpost.com/entry/pray-for-ankara_us_56e722c5e4b065e2e3d6f8b2.

Daniels, D. & Plomin, R. (1985). Differential Experience of Siblings in the Same Family. *Developmental Psychology*, 21: 747–760.

Dalrymple, W. (2004). *White Mughals: Love and Betrayal in Eighteenth Century India*. London: Penguin.

Darwin, C. (1871). *The Descent of Man, and Selection in Relation to Sex*. London: John Murray.

Darwin, C. (1859). *The Origin of Species By Means of Natural Selection: Or the Preservation of Favoured Races in the Struggle for Life*. London: John Murray.

Davies, B. (1978). The Moralistic Fallacy. *Nature*, 272: 390.

Dawkins, R. (1976). *The Selfish Gene*. Oxford: Oxford University Press.

De Dreu, C., Greer, L., van Kleef, G. et al. (2010). Oxytocin Promotes Human Ethnocentrism. *Proceedings of the National Academy of Sciences of the United States of America*, 108: 1262–1266.

De Oliveira, E., Carlson, T. & de Oliveira, S. (2009). Students' Attitudes Towards Foreign Born and Domestic Instructors. *Journal of Diversity in Higher Education*, 2: 113–125.

Deary, I., Batty, G.D. & Gales, C. (2008). Childhood Intelligence Predicts Voter Turnout, Voter Preferences and Political Involvement in Adulthood; The 1970 Cohort. *Intelligence*, 36: 548–555.

DeBruine, L. (2002). Facial Resemblance Enhances Trust. *Proceedings of the Royal Society of London*, B 269: 1307–1312.

Dhont, K. & Hodson, G. (2014). Does Low Cognitive Ability Predict Greater Prejudice? *Current Directions in Psychological Science*, 23: 454–459.

Dong, Q. & Collaco, C. (2009). Overcome Ethnocentrism and Increase Cultural Collaboration by Developing Social Intelligence. *Proceedings of the 2009 International Workshop on Intercultural Collaboration*, 215–219.

Duckitt, J. (2001). A Dual Process Cognitive-Motivational Theory of Ideology and Prejudice. In: Zanna, M.P. (Ed.). *Advances in Experimental Social Psychology*. San Diego: Academic Press.

Duckitt, J., Wagner, C., Du Plessis, I. & Birum, I. (2002). The Psychological Bases of Ideology and Prejudice: Testing a Dual Process Model. *Journal of Personality and Social Psychology*, 83: 75–93.

Dunkel, C. & Dutton, E. (2016). Religiosity as a Predictor of In-Group Favoritism within and between Religious Groups. *Personality and Individual Differences*, 98: 311–314.

Dunn, J. (6th February 2016). Iraqi Migrant Rapes a 10-Year-Old Boy at a Swimming Pool in Vienna and Tells Police It Was a 'Sexual Emergency' Because

He Hadn't Had Sex in Months. *Daily Mail,* http://www.dailymail.co.uk/news/article-3434708/Iraqi-migrant-raped-10-year-old-boy-swimming-pool-Vienna-told-police-sexual-emergency-hadn-t-sex-months.html.

Durrant, R. & Ellis, B. (2003). Evolutionary Psychology. In Gallagher, M. & Nelson, R. (Eds). *Handbook of Psychology: Volume I: Biological Psychology.* Hoboken: John Wiley & Sons.

Dutton, E. (2018). *How to Judge People By What They Look Like.* Amazon.com.

Dutton, E. (2014). *Religion and Intelligence: An Evolutionary Analysis.* London: Ulster Institute for Social Research.

Dutton, E. (2013). The Cultural Mediation Hypothesis: A Critical Examination. *Intelligence,* 41: 321–327.

Dutton, E. (2012). *Culture Shock and Multiculturalism: Reclaiming a Useful Model from the Religious Realm.* Newcastle: Cambridge Scholars Publishing.

Dutton, E. (2008). *Meeting Jesus at University: Rites of Passage and Student Evangelicals.* Aldershot: Ashgate.

Dutton, E. (2002). Nationalist Socialism? The Position of the Scottish Socialist Party in Contemporary Discourse on Scottish Nationalism. *Scotia: Interdisciplinary Journal of Scottish Studies,* 24.

Dutton, E., Madison, G. & Dunkel, C. (2017). The Mutant Says in His Heart, 'There Is No God': The Rejection of Collective Religiosity Centred Around the Worship of Moral Gods is Associated with High Mutational Load. *Evolutionary Psychological Science,* https://doi.org/10.1007/s40806-017-0133-5.

Dutton, E. & Madison, G. (2017). Execution, Violent Punishment and Selection for Religiousness in Medieval England. *Evolutionary Psychological Science,* https://doi.org/10.1007/s40806-017-0115-7.

Dutton, E. & Van der Linden, D. (2017). Why Is Intelligence Negatively Associated with Religiousness? *Evolutionary Psychological Science,* 3: 302–403.

Dutton, E. & Madison, G. (2016). Why Do Finnish Men Marry Thai Women But Finnish Women Marry British Men? Cross-National Marriages in a Modern, Industrialized Society Exhibit Sex-Dimorphic Sexual Selection According to Primordial Selection Pressures. *Evolutionary Psychological Science,* 3: 1–9.

Dutton, E., Madison, G. & Lynn, R. (2016a). Demographic, Economic, and Genetic Factors Related to National Differences in Ethnocentric Attitudes. *Personality and Individual Differences,* 101: 137–143.

Dutton, E., Van der Linden, D. & Lynn, R. (2016b). Population Differences in Androgen Levels: A Test of the Differential K Theory. *Personality and Individual Differences,* 90: 289–295.

Dutton, E. & Charlton, B. (2015). *The Genius Famine: Why We Need Geniuses, Why They're Dying Out, and Why We Must Rescue Them.* Buckingham: University of Buckingham Press.

Dutton, E. & Lynn, R. (2015). *Race and Sport: Evolution and Racial Differences in Sporting Ability.* London: Ulster Institute for Social Research.

Dutton, E. & Van der Linden, D. (2015). Who Are the 'Clever Sillies'? the Intelligence, Personality and Motives of Clever Silly Originators and Those Who Follow Them. *Intelligence,* 49: 57–65.

Dutton, E., te Nijenhuis, J. & Roivainen, E. (2014). Solving the Puzzle of Why Finns Have the Highest IQ, but One of the Lowest Number of Nobel Prizes in Europe. *Intelligence,* 46: 192–202.

Eap, S., DeGarmo, D., Kawakami, A. et al. (2008). Culture and Personality among European American and Asian American Men. *Journal of Cross-Cultural Psychology,* 39: 630–643.

Eisinga, R., Felling, A. & Peeters, J. (1990). Religious Belief, Church Involvement and Ethnocentrism in the Netherlands. *Journal for the Scientific Study of Religion,* 29: 54–75.

Ellis, F. (2004). *Political Correctness and the Theoretical Struggle: From Lenin and Mao to Marcuse and Foucault.* Auckland: Maxim Institute.

Ellis, L., Hoskin, A., Dutton, E. & Nyborg, H. (2017). The Future of Secularism: A Biologically Informed Theory Supplemented with Cross-Cultural Evidence. *Evolutionary Psychological Science,* https://doi.org/10.1007/s40806-017-0090-z.

Ervik, A. O. (2003). Review of IQ and the Wealth of Nations. *The Economic Journal,* 113: 406–408.

Evans-Pritchard, E. (1940). *The Nuer: A Description of the Modes of Livelihood and Political Institutions of a Nilotic People.* Oxford: Oxford University Press.

Eysenck, H.J. (1991). Introduction: Science and Racism. In Pearson, R. *Race, Intelligence and Bias in Academe.* Washington, DC: Scott Townsend Publishers.

Feist, G. (2007). *The Psychology of Science and the Origins of the Scientific Mind.* New Haven, CT: Yale University Press.

Feist, G. (1998). A Meta-Analysis of Personality in Scientific and Artistic Creativity. *Personality and Social Psychology Review,* 2: 290–309.

Figueredo, A.J., Gladden, P. & Black, C. (2012). Parasite Stress, Ethnocentrism, and Life History Strategy. *Brain and Behavioral Sciences,* 35: 87–88.

Figueredo, A.J., Andrzejczak, D., Jones, D., Smith-Castro, V. & Montero, E. (2011). Reproductive Strategy and Ethnic Conflict: Slow Life History as a Protective

Factor against Negative Ethnocentrism in Two Contemporary Societies. *Journal of Social, Evolutionary and Cultural Psychology*, 5: 14–31.

Fincher, C. & Thornhill, R. (2012). Parasite-Stress Promotes In-Group Assortative Sociality: The Cases of Strong Family Ties and Heightened Religiosity. *Behavioural and Brain Sciences*, 35: 61–79.

Freedman, R., Carter, M., Sbrocco, T. & Gray, J. (2004). Ethnic Differences in Preferences for Female Weight and Waist-To-Hip Ratio: A Comparison of African-American and White American College and Community Samples. *Eating Behaviours*. 191–198.

Frejka, T. & Westoff, C. (2006). Religion, Religiousness and Fertility in the U.S. and in Europe. Max Planck Institute for Demographic Research Working Paper.

Friedman, H. S., Tucker, J. Tomlinson-Keasey, C., Schwartz, J., Wingard, D. & Criqui, M. (1993). Does Childhood Personality Predict Longevity? *Journal of Personality and Social Psychology*, 65: 176–185.

Frydman, M., & Lynn, R. (1989). The Intelligence of Korean Children Adopted in Belgium. *Personality and Individual Differences*, 10: 1323–1326.

Gage, T. (2000). Variability of Gestational Age Distributions by Sex and Ethnicity: An Analysis Using Mixture Models. *American Journal of Human Biology*, 12: 181–191.

Gander, K. (13th September 2015). 'Today Refugees, Tomorrow Terrorists': Eastern Europeans Chant Anti-Islam Slogans in Demonstrations against Refugees. *Independent*, http://www.independent.co.uk/news/world/europe/refugees-crisis-pro-and-anti-refugee-protests-take-place-in-poland-in-pictures-10499352.html.

Ganley, C., Mingle, L. A., Ryan, A. M., Ryan, K., Vasilyeva, M., & Perry, M. (2013). An Examination of Stereotype Threat Effects on Girls' Mathematics Performance. *Developmental Psychology*. Advance online publication. https://doi.org/10.1037/a0031412.

Gellner, E. (2008). *The Psychoanalytic Movement: The Cunning of Unreason*. Oxford: Blackwell.

Gellner, E. (1995). *Anthropology and Politics: Revolutions in the Sacred Grove*. Hoboken: John Wiley & Sons.

Gellner, E. (1983). *Nations and Nationalism*. Ithaca: Cornell University Press.

Giddens, A. (1971). *Capitalism and Modern Social Theory: An Analysis of the Writings of Marx, Durkheim, and Max Weber*. Cambridge: Cambridge University Press.

Gobineau, A. de. (1915). *The Inequality of Human Races*. (Trans. A. Collins). London: William Heinemann.

Graburn, N. (2012). Severe Child Abuse among the Canadian Inuit. In Scheper-Hughes, N. (Ed.). *Child Survival: Anthropological Perspectives on the Treatment and Maltreatment of Children*. New York: Springer.

Grafen, A. (1990). Do Animals Really Recognize Kin? *Animal Behaviour*, 39: 42–54.

Grant, M. (1916). *The Passing of the Great Race: Or the Racial Basis of European History*. New York: Charles Scribner's Sons.

Greenberg, L. (1979). Genetic Component of Bee Odor in Kin Recognition. *Science*, 206: 1095–1097.

Greenwald, A.G. & Schuh, E.S. (1994). An Ethnic Bias in Scientific Citations. *European Journal of Social Psychology*, 24: 623–639.

Greitenmeyer, T. (2014). Playing Violent Video Games Increases Intergroup Bias. *Personal and Social Psychology Bulletin*, 40: 70–78.

Gumplowicz, L. (1879). *Das Recht der Nationalität und Sprachen in Oesterreich-Ungarn (The Right of Nationality and Languages in Austria-Hungary)*. Wagner'schen Universitäts-Buchhandlung, Innsbruck.

Guthrie, S. (2013). *Arab Women in the Middle Ages: Private Lives and Public Roles*. Suqi.

Hales, D. (2000). Cooperation without Space of Memory: Tags, Groups and the Prisoner's Dilemma. In S. Moss & P. Davidsson (Eds.), *Multi-Agent-Based Simulation, Lecture Notes in Artificial Intelligence* (pp. 157–166). Berlin: Springer.

Hamilton, W.D. (1964). The Genetical Evolution of Social Behavior. I and II. *Journal of Theoretical Biology*, 7: 1–52.

Hammond, R. & Axelrod, R. (2006). The Evolution of Ethnocentric Behaviour. *Journal of Conflict Resolution*, 50: 1–11.

Hampshire, K. & Smith, M. (2001). Consanguineous Marriage among the Fulani. *Human Biology*, 73: 597–603.

Hartshorn, M., Kaznatcheev, A. & Schultz, T. (2013). The Evolutionary Dominance of Ethnocentric Cooperation. *Journal of Artificial Societies and Social Simulation*, 16: 7.

Hauber, M.E. & Sherman, P.W. (2001). Self-Referent Phenotype Matching: Theoretical Considerations and Empirical Evidence. *Trends in Neuroscience*, 24: 609–616.

Huang B., Grant, B.F., Dawson, D.A. et al. (2006). Race-Ethnicity and the Prevalence and Co-Occurrence of Alcohol and Drug Use Disorders And Axis I and II Disorders: United States, 2001 to 2002. *Comprehensive Psychiatry*, 47: 252–257.

Hawkes, F. (2016). *The Perry Expeditions to Japan: 1852–1854*. Big Byte Books.

Hayford, S. & Morgan, S. (2008). Religiosity and Fertility in the United States: The Role of Fertility Intentions. *Social Forces,* 86: 1163–1188.

Healy, E. (2007). Ethnic Diversity and Social Cohesion in Melbourne. *People and Place,* 15: 49–64.

Hechter, M. (1975). *Internal Colonialism: The Celtic Fringe in British National Development.* New Brunswick: Transaction Publishers.

Helgason, A., Palsson, S., Gudbjartsson, D. et al. (2008). An Association between the Kinship and Fertility of Human Couples. *Science,* 319: 813–816.

Herder, J. G. von., (1795)., *Ideas Towards a Philosophy of the History of Mankind.,* Riga.

Herrnstein, R. & Murray, C. (1994). *The Bell Curve: Intelligence and Class Structure in American Life.* New York: Free Press.

Higham, J. P., Barr, C. S., Hoffman, C. L., Mandalaywala, T. M., Parker, K. J., & Maestripieri, D. (2011) μ-Opioid Receptor (OPRM1) Variation, Oxytocin Levels and Maternal Attachment in Free-Ranging Rhesus Macaques Macaca Mulatta. *Behavioural Neuroscience,* 125: 131–136. https://doi.org/10.1037/a0022695.

Hills, P., Francis, L. J., Argyle, M. & Jackson, C. (2004). Primary Personality Trait Correlates of Religious Practice and Orientation. *Personality and Individual Differences,* 36: 61–73.

Hirschfield, L. (1996). *Race in the Making: Cognition, Culture, and the Child's Construction of Human Kinds.* Cambridge, MA: MIT Press.

Hirszfeld, L. & Hirszfeld, H. (1919). Essai d'application des methods au probleme des races. *Anthropologie,* 29: 505–537.

Hobsbawm, E. (1990). *Nations and Nationalism Since 1780: Programme, Myth, Reality.* Cambridge: Cambridge University Press.

Hodson, G. & Busseri, M. (2012). Bright Minds and Dark Attitudes: Lower Cognitive Ability Predicts Greater Prejudice through Right-Wing Ideology and Low Intergroup Contact. *Psychological Science,* 23: 187–195.

Hodson, G., Hogg, S. & MacInnis, C. (2009). The Role of 'Dark Personalities' (Narcissism, Machiavellianism, Psychopathy), Big Five Personality Factors, and Ideology in Explaining Prejudice. *Journal of Research on Personality,* 43: 686–690.

Hoffman, P. (1994). The Science of Race. *Discover Magazine* (November).

Hooghe, M., Marien, S., & de Vroome, T. (2012). The Cognitive Basis of Trust: The Relation between Education, Cognitive Ability, and Generalized and Political Trust. *Intelligence,* 40: 604–613.

Hooghe, M., Reeskens, T., Stolle, D. & Trappers, A. (2009). Ethnic Diversity, Trust and Ethnocentrism and Europe: A Multilevel Analysis of 21 European Countries. *Comparative Political Studies*, 42: 198–223.

Hunt, E. (2011). *Human Intelligence*. Cambridge: Cambridge University Press.

Hunt, E. & Sternberg, R. J. (2006). Sorry, Wrong Numbers: An Analysis of a Study of a Correlation between Skin Color and IQ. *Intelligence*, 34: 131–139.

Hunt, T. (2003). *Defining John Bull: Political Caricature and National Identity in Late Georgian England*. Aldershot: Ashgate.

Imrie, S., Jadva, V., Fishel, S. & Golombok, S. (2018). Families Created by Egg Donation: Parent-Child Relationship Quality in Infancy. *Child Development*. https://doi.org/10.1111/cdev.13124.

Irwin, C.olin J. (1987). A Study in the Evolution of Ethnocentrism. In V. Reynolds, V. S. E. Falger & I. Vine (eds.), *The Sociobiology of Ethnocentrism: Evolutionary Dimensions of Xenophobia, Discrimination, Racism, and Nationalism*. London: Croom Helm.

Jacob, S., McLintock, M., Zelano, B. & Ober, C. (2002). Paternally Inherited HLA Alleles Are Associated with Women's Choice of Male Odor. *Nature Genetics*, 30: 175–179.

Jansson, F. (2013). Pitfalls in Spatial Modeling of Ethnocentrism: A Simulation Analysis of the Model of Hammond and Axelrod. *Journal of Artificial Societies and Social Simulation*, 16 (3) 2 http://jasss.soc.surrey.ac.uk/16/3/2.html.

Jayanetti, C. (17th April 2017). Yes, the Left Has a Racism Problem. *Politics.co.uk*, http://politics.co.uk/comment-analysis/2017/04/17/yes-the-left-has-a-racism-problem.

Jensen, A. R. (1998). *The g Factor: The Science of Mental Ability*. Westport, CT: Praeger.

Jensen, A. R. (1981). *Straight Talk About Mental Tests*. New York: Free Press.

Jensen, A. R. (1979). *Bias in Mental Testing*. New York: Free Press.

Johnson, J. (1798). *An Essay on the Principle of Population*. Printed for J. Johnson in St. Paul's Churchyard.

Joseph, J. (2006). *The Missing Gene: Psychiatry, Heredity, and the Fruitless Search for Genes*. New York: Algora Publishing.

Judd, C., Park, B., Ryan, C., Brauer, M. & Krauss, S. (1995). Stereotypes and Ethnocentrism: Diverging Inter-Ethnic Perceptions of African American and White American Youth. *Journal of Personality and Social Psychology*, 69: 460–481.

Kahneman, D. (2011). *Thinking, Fast and Slow*. New York, DC: Farrar, Straus and Giroux.

Kanazawa, S. (2012). *The Intelligence Paradox: Why the Intelligent Choice Isn't Always the Smart One.* Hoboken: John Wiley & Sons.

Kaszycka, K.A., & Strzalko, J. (2003). Race — Still an Issue for Physical Anthropology? Results of Polish Studies Seen in the Light of the U.S. Findings. *American Anthropologist,* 105: 114–122.

Kaufman, S., DeYoung, C., Reiss, D. & Gray, J. (2011). General Intelligence Predicts Reasoning Ability for Evolutionarily Familiar Content. *Intelligence,* 39: 311–322.

Kaznatcheev, A. (2010). *The Cognitive Cost of Ethnocentrism.* Paper presented at the Proceedings of the 32nd annual conference of the Cognitive Science Society, Austin, TX. Cited in Hartshorn et al. (2013).

Keith, A. (1922). The Dawn of National Life. Hammerton, J. (Ed.). *Peoples of All Nations.* London: Amalgamated Press.

Kinder, D. & Kam, C. (2010). *US Against Them: Ethnocentric Foundations of American Public Opinion.* Chicago: University of Chicago Press.

Kirkegaard, E. (5 May 2016). Who Prefers to Date People of Their Own Race? *Clear Language, Clear Mind,* http://emilkirkegaard.dk/en/?p=5952.

Koenig, H. (2012). Religion, Spirituality, and Health: The Research and Clinical Implications. *ISRN Psychiatry,* http://dx.doi.org/10.5402/2012/278730.

Koenig, H.B., McGue, M., Krueger, R.F. & Bouchard, T.J. (2005). Genetic and Environmental Influences on Religiousness: Findings for Retrospective and Current Religiousness Ratings. *Journal of Personality,* 73: 471–478.

Koenig, H., Cohen, H., George, L. et al. (1997). Attendance at Religious Services, Interleukin-6 and Other Biological Parameters of Immune Function in Older Adults. *International Journal of Psychiatry in Medicine,* 27: 233–250.

Kurzban, R., Tooby, J., & Cosmides, L. (2001). Can Race Be Erased? Coalitional Computation and Social Categorization. *Proceedings of the National Academy of Sciences,* 98: 15,387–15,392.

Kurzban, R. (16 November 2010). It's Only 'Good Science' If the Message Is Politically Correct. *Evolutionary Psychology,* http://www.epjournal.net/blog/2010/11/its-only-good-science-if-the-message-is-politically-correct/.

Laurence, J. (2013). Reconciling the Contact and Threat Hypotheses: Does Ethnic Diversity Strengthen or Weaken Community Inter-Ethnic Relations? *Ethnic and Racial Studies,* https://doi.org/10.1080/01419870.2013.788727.

Laurence, J. (2011). The Effect of Ethnic Diversity and Community Disadvantage on Social Cohesion: A Multi-Level Analysis of Social Capital and Interethnic Relations in UK Communities. *European Sociological Review,* 27.

Lavezzo, K. (Ed). (2004). *Imagining a Medieval English Nation.* Minneapolis: University of Minnesota Press.

Laythe, B., Finkel, D. & Kirkpatrick, L. (2001). Predicting Prejudice from Religious Fundamentalism and Right-Wing Authoritarianism: A Multiple Regression Analysis. *Journal for the Scientific Study of Religion*, 40: 1–10.

Långström N, Rahman, Q., Carlström, E. & Lichtenstein, P. (2010). Genetic and Environmental Effects on Same-Sex Sexual Behavior: A Population Study of Twins in Sweden. *Archives of Sexual Behavior,* 39: 75–80.

Levin, M. (2005). *Why Race Matters: Race Differences and What They Mean.* Oakton, VA: New Century Foundation.

LeVine, R.A. & Campbell, D.T. (1972). *Ethnocentrism: Theories of Conflict, Ethnic Attitudes, and Group Behavior.* Hoboken: John Wiley & Sons.

Lewis, G. & Bates, T. (2013). Common Genetic Influences Underpin Religiousness, Community Integration and Existential Uncertainty. *Journal of Research in Personality*, 47: 398–405.

Lewontin, R. (1978). Adaptation. *Scientific American*, 239: 212–230.

Li, W. & Lui, L. (1975). Ethnocentrism among American and Chinese Youth. *Journal of Social Psychology*, 95: 277–278.

Lieberman, L. & Reynolds, L. T. (1996). Race: The Deconstruction of a Scientific Concept. In L. T. Reynolds & L. Lieberman (Eds.). *Race and Other Misadventures: Essays in Honor of Ashley Montagu.* Dix Hills: General Hall.

Linnaeus, C. (1758). *Systema Naturae.* Stockholm: Salvius.

Littlefield, C. & Rushton, J.P. (1986). When a Child Dies: The Sociobiology of Bereavement. *Journal of Personality and Social Psychology,* 51: 797–802.

Livingstone, F.B. (1962). On the Non-Existence of the Human Races. *Current Anthropology,* 3: 279–281.

London Gazette. (19th April 2015). Second Supplement. War Office. https://www.thegazette.co.uk/London/issue/29135/supplement/3815.

Lownie, A. (2016). *Stalin's Englishman: The Lives of Guy Burgess.* London: Hodder & Stoughton.

Lumsden, C. & Wilson, E.O. (1981). *Genes, Mind, and Culture: the Co-evolutionary Process.* Cambridge, MA: Harvard University Press.

Lynn, R. (2011a). *Dysgenics: Genetic Deterioration in Modern Populations.* London: Ulster Institute for Social Research.

Lynn, R. (2011b). *The Chosen People: A Study of Jewish Intelligence and Achievement.* Augusta, GA: Washington Summit Publishers.

Lynn, R. (2006). *Race Differences in Intelligence: An Evolutionary Analysis*. Augusta, GA: Washington Summit Publishers.

Lynn R. & Vanhanen, T. (2012). *Intelligence: A Unifying Construct for the Social Sciences*. London: Ulster Institute for Social Research.

MacDonald, K. (2004). *Separation and its Discontents: Toward an Evolutionary Theory of Anti-Semitism*. New York: 1st Books.

MacDonald, K. (2002). *A People That Shall Dwell Alone: Judaism as a Group Evolutionary Strategy with Diaspora Peoples*. New York: Writers Club Press.

MacDonald, K. (1998). *The Culture of Critique: An Evolutionary Analysis of Jewish Involvement in Twentieth Century Political Movements*. Westport: Praeger.

Mackintosh, N. (2011). History of Theories and Measurement of Intelligence. In R. Sternberg & S. Kaufman. (Eds). *The Cambridge Handbook of Intelligence*. Cambridge: Cambridge University Press.

Mackintosh, N. (2002). Review: *Dysgenics: Genetic Deterioration in Modern Populations* by Richard Lynn. *Journal of Biosocial Science*, 34: 283-284.

Mackintosh, N.J. (1998). *IQ and Human Intelligence*. Oxford: Oxford University Press.

Martin, L. & Soldo, B. (1997). *Racial and Ethnic Differences in the Health of Older Americans*. Washington, DC: National Research Council.

Masters, W. & McMillan, M. (2004). Ethno-Linguistic Diversity, Government Expenditure, and Economic Growth across Countries. In F. Salter (Ed.). *Welfare, Ethnicity, and Altruism: New data and evolutionary theory*. London: Frank Cass.

Matthews, M. & Hamilton, B. (2016). Mean Age of Mothers on the Rise: United States, 2000-2014. *NCHS Data brief*, 232.

Maynard Smith, J. (1964). Group Selection and Kin Selection: A Rejoinder. *Nature*, 201: 1145-1147.

McAdams, D.P. & Pals, J.L. (2006). A New Big Five: Fundamental Principles for an Integrative Science of Personality. *American Psychologist*, 61: 204-217.

McCrae, R.R., Terracciano, A., & 79 members of the Personality Profiles of Cultures Project. (2005). Personality Profiles of Cultures: Aggregate Personality Traits. *Journal of Personality and Social Psychology*, 89: 407-425.

McLoughlin, P. (2016). *Easy Meat: Inside Britain's Grooming Gang Scandal*. Nashville: New English Review Press.

Mealey, L. (1985). The Relationship between Social and Biological Success: A Case Study of the Mormon Religious Hierarchy. *Ethology and Sociobiology*, 6: 249-257.

Meisenberg, G. (2015). Do We Have Valid Country-Level Measures of Personality? *Mankind Quarterly,* 55: 360–382.

Meisenberg, G. (2007). *In God's Image: The Natural History of Intelligence and Ethics.* Kibworth: Book Guild Publishing.

Messinger, G. (1992). *British Propaganda and the State in the First World War.* Manchester: Manchester University Press.

Milgram, S. (1974). *Obedience to Authority.* New York: Harper & Row.

Miller, G. (2000). *The Mating Mind: How Sexual Choice Shaped the Evolution of Human Nature.* New York: Anchor Books.

Minkov, M. & Bond, M. (2015). Genetic Polymorphisms Predict National Differences in Life History Strategy and Time Orientation. *Personality and Individual Differences,* 76: 204–215.

Minkov, M. (2014). The K Factor, Societal Hypometropia, and National Values: A Study of 71 Nations. *Personality and Individual Differences,* 66: 153–159.

Minkov, M., Blagoev, V. & Harris, M. (2014). Improving Research in the Emerging Field of Cross-Cultural Sociogenetics: The Case of Serotonin. *Cross Cultural Psychology,* https://doi.org/10.1177/0022022114563612.

Montagu, A. (1945). *Man's Most Dangerous Myth: The Fallacy of Race.* New York: Columbia University Press.

Murray, C. (2006). *Human Accomplishment: The Pursuit of Excellence in the Arts and Sciences, 800 BC to 1950.* New York: HarperCollins.

Murray, D. (2017). *The Strange Death of Europe.* London: Bloomsbury.

Murray, D., Schaller, M. & Suedfeld, D. (2013). Pathogens and Politics: Further Evidence That Parasite Prevalence Predicts Authoritarianism. *PLOS ONE.* http://journals.plos.org/plosone/article?id=10.1371/journal.pone.0062275.

Muthiah, S., MacLure, H. & O'Connor, R. (2014). *The Anglo-Indians: A 500 Year History.* New Delhi: Niyogi Books.

National Gaucher Federation. (2015). http://www.gaucherdisease.org/gaucher-disease-prevalence.php.

National Human Genome Research Institute. (2011). Learning About Tay-Sachs Disease. https://www.genome.gov/10001220.

Navarette, C., Fessler, D. & Eng, S. (2007). Elevated Ethnocentrism in the First Trimester of Pregnancy. *Evolution and Human Behaviour,* 28: 60–65.

Nechyba, T. (2004). Review of *IQ and the Wealth of Nations. Journal of Economic Literature,* 42: 220–221.

Nei, M., & Roychoudhury, A. K. (1993). Evolutionary Relationships of Human Populations on a Global Scale. *Molecular Biology and Evolution,* 10: 927–943.

Nelson, F. (3rd September 2015). Prepare Yourself: The Great Migration Will Be with Us for Decades. *Daily Telegraph.* https://www.telegraph.co.uk/news/uknews/immigration/11842760/Prepare-yourselves-The-Great-Migration-will-be-with-us-for-decades.html.

Nettle, D. (2007). *Personality: What Makes You the Way You Are.* Oxford: Oxford University Press.

Neuliep, J., Chaudoir, M., McCroskey, J. (2001). A Cross-Cultural Comparison of Ethnocentrism among Japanese and United States College Students. *Communication Research Reports,* 18: 137–146.

Norenzayan, A. & Shariff, A. (2008). The Origin and Evolution of Religious Pro-Sociality. *Science,* 322: 58–62.

Olff, M., Frijling, J., Kubzansky, L. et al. (2013). The Role of Oxytocin in Social Bonding, Stress Regulation and Mental Health: An Update on the Moderating Effects of Context and Interindividual Differences. *Psychoneuroendocrinology,* 38: 1883–1894.

Ontell, F., Ivanovic, M., Ablin, D. & Barlow, T. (1996). Bone Age in Children of Diverse Ethnicity. *American Journal of Roentgenology,* 167: 1395–1398.

Ostrer, H. (2001). A Genetic Profile of Contemporary Jewish Populations. *National Review of Genetics.* 2: 891–898.

Panayi, P. (1989). Anti-German Riots in London during the First World War. *German History,* 7: 184–203.

Peev, G. (31 December 2015). Don't Be Cold-Hearted to Our 1.1 Million Refugees: Merkel Begs Germans after Her Popularity Drops over Open Door Policy. *Daily Mail,* http://www.dailymail.co.uk/news/article-3380747/Don-t-cold-hearted-1-1million-refugees-Merkel-begs-Germans-popularity-drops-open-door-policy.html.

Penton-Voak, I.S., Perret, D. & Pierce, J.W. (1999). Computer Graphic Studies of the Role of Facial Similarity in Judgements of Attractiveness. *Current Psychology,* 18: 104–117.

Peterson, R. & Palmer, C. (2017). The Effects of Physical Attractiveness on Political Beliefs. *Politics and the Life Sciences,* 36: 3–16.

Phipps, C. & Rawlinson, K. (14th November 2015). Paris Attacks Kill More Than 120 People — as It Happened. *Guardian,* http://www.theguardian.com/world/live/2015/nov/13/shootings-reported-in-eastern-paris-live.

Piffer, D. (2016). Evidence for Recent Polygenic Selection on Educational Attainment Inferred from GWAS Hits. *Preprints,* https://doi.org/10.20944/preprints201611.0047.v1.

Pinker, S. (18th June 2012). The False Allure of Group Selection. *The Edge,* https://www.edge.org/conversation/the-false-allure-of-group-selection.

Pratto, F. & Glasford, D. (2008). Ethnocentrism and the Value of Human Life. *Journal of Personality and Social Psychology,* 95: 1411–1428.

Preston, D. & Preston, M. (2010). *A Teardrop on the Cheek of Time: The Story of the Taj Mahal.* New York: Random House.

Putnam, H. (1975). *Philosophical Papers I and II.* Cambridge: Cambridge University Press.

Putnam, R. (2000). *Bowling Alone: The Collapse and Revival of American Community.* New York: Simon & Schuster.

Putnam, R. (2007). E Pluribus Unum: Diversity and Community in the Twenty-First Century. The 2006 Johan Skytte Prize Lecture. *Scandinavian Political Studies,* 30: 137–174.

Rekker, R., Keijsers, L., Branjes, S. & Meeus, W. (2015). Political Attitudes in Adolescence and Emerging Adulthood: Developmental Changes in Mean Level, Polarization, Rank-Order Stability, and Correlates. *Journal of Adolescence,* 41: 136–147.

Reynolds, V., Falger, V. & Vine, I. (Eds). (1987). *The Sociobiology of Ethnocentrism: Evolutionary Dimensions of Xenophobia, Discrimination, Racism and Nationalism.* London: Croom-Helm.

Richards, V. (11th February 2016). Cologne Attacks: What Happened after 1,000 Women Were Sexually Assaulted? *Independent,* http://www.independent.co.uk/news/world/europe/cologne-attacks-what-happened-after-1000-women-were-sexually-assaulted-a6867071.html.

Riek, B.M., Mania, E.W. & Gaertner, S.L. (2006). Intergroup Threat and Outgroup Attitudes: A Meta-Analytic Review. *Personality and Social Psychology Review,* 10: 336–353.

Rindermann, H. (2007). The *g* Factor of International Cognitive Ability Comparisons: The Homogeneity of Results in PISA, PIRLS and IQ Tests Across Nations. *European Journal of Personality,* 21: 667–706.

Rindermann, H., Flores-Mendoza, C. & Woodley, M.A. (2012). Political Orientations, Intelligence and Education. *Intelligence,* 40: 217–225.

Rosenthal, F. (2014). *Man versus Society in Medieval Islam.* Leiden: Brill.

Rowe, D.C. & Osgood, D. (1984). Heredity and Sociological Theories of Delinquency: A Reconsideration. *American Sociological Review,* 49: 526–540.

Lightning Source UK Ltd.
Milton Keynes UK
UKHW030923080919
349328UK00003B/1001/P